CONFESSION OF A CATHOLIC

ALSO BY MICHAEL NOVAK

A New Generation: American and Catholic (1964)
The Open Church (1964)
Belief and Unbelief (1965)
A Time to Build (1967)
A Theology for Radical Politics (1969)
The Experience of Nothingness (1970)
Politics: Realism and Imagination (1971)
All the Catholic People (1971)
Ascent of the Mountain, Flight of the Dove (1971)
The Rise of the Unmeltable Ethnics (1972)
Choosing Our King (1974)
The Joy of Sports (1976)
The Guns of Lattimer (1978)
The Spirit of Democratic Capitalism (1982)

FICTION

The Tiber Was Silver (1961)
Naked I Leave (1970)

EDITED BY MICHAEL NOVAK

The Experience of Marriage (1964)
American Philosophy and the Future (1967)
Capitalism and Socialism: A Theological Inquiry (1979)
Democracy and Mediating Structures: A Theological Inquiry (1980)
The Corporation: A Theological Inquiry (with John W. Cooper, 1981)

CONFESSION

OF A

CATHOLIC

Michael Novak

1817

Harper & Row, Publishers, San Francisco

Cambridge, Hagerstown, New York, Philadelphia
London, Mexico City, São Paulo, Sydney

FIRST EDITION

Designer: Jim Mennick

Library of Congress Cataloging in Publication Data

Novak, Michael.
    CONFESSION OF A CATHOLIC.

    Bibliography: p. 219
    1. Catholic Church—Doctrinal and controversial works—Catholic authors. I. Title.
BX1751.2.N68   1983   230'.2   82–48426
ISBN 0-06-066319-7

83 84 85 86 87 10 9 8 7 6 5 4 3 2 1

Contents

Acknowledgments

A word processor is a marvelous instrument, but Gayle Yiotis, who runs ours, is even more marvelous. She outwitted machine and author many times.

My assistant and colleague Terry Hall helped me in countless ways to form judgments, search out sources, recall old books, recover particular passages—and meet a severe deadline.

Summer interns Vincent Fitzpatrick and Vivian Warner of the National Journalism Center and Daniel Kelly, fresh from Holy Cross College, helped enormously in tracking down useful quotes and challenging materials. Beginning work from the second draft, they made the third far richer.

My colleague Walter Berns helped with several critical passages. Among others who read all or part of one draft and raised important objections were David Burrell, C.S.C., James Schall, S.J., Jude Dougherty, Avery Dulles, S.J., John Langan, S.J., James Finn, Michael Scully, Charles Wood, David O'Brien, Philip Lawler and Neal Kozodoy. Each of them could write a more penetrating book. I learned from all.

My wife, Karen, was, as always, my toughest critic and best friend. She does not agree with everything in this book. Stubbornly, I persist.

Richard Novak is now seventeen years old, Tanya fifteen, and Jana ten. I hope they will pass this on to their children and grandchildren someday, for what I have here written was thus received. Immigrant parents once said to each child: "Keep the faith."

MICHAEL NOVAK

Washington, D.C.

The only possible excuse for this book is that it is an answer to a challenge . . . to a person only too ready to write books upon the feeblest provocation. . . . I have attempted in a vague and personal way, in a set of mental pictures rather than in a series of deductions, to state the philosophy in which I have come to believe. I will not call it my philosophy; for I did not make it. God and humanity made it; and it made me.

—G. K. CHESTERTON, *Orthodoxy*

Christian vitality is in every age very much less dependent on all that is discussed and done and picked to pieces on the world's stage than we are often led to believe. There is a life which is almost impossible to judge from the outside; and that life keeps itself going, passes itself on and renews itself under all the turmoil of politics, all the swirl of public opinion, the currents of ideas and the controversies, far removed from the scene of public debate, unsounded and untabulated.

—HENRI DE LUBAC, S.J.,
The Splendour of the Church

Learn to call sin sin, and do not call it liberation and progress, even if the whole of fashion and propaganda were contrary.

—POPE JOHN PAUL II,
L'Osservatore Romano, April 21, 1981

Introduction
Expelling the Smoke of Satan

Approaching his fiftieth year, a man may be excused the impulse to confess. Indeed, if it is his vocation to be a writer and a lecturer, his readers will from time to time ask him point-blank what he believes.

There is in my case an additional motive. For some years now I have been engaged in trying to write a theology of American culture. I have tried to understand the symbolic texture of daily religious life in America in such worldly matters as ethnicity; the rituals of the uniquely American sports, baseball, basketball, and football; the presidency; the labor unions; and the original political economy *(novus ordo seclorum)* it is the privilege of Americans to inherit. These studies involved broad reading, experiment, and adventure. The past fifteen years have not been idly spent.

For over a decade, although I wrote from time to time in Catholic and other religious publications, it was somewhat less frequently than earlier and more often on secular than on ecclesiastical matters. This was the division of labor that Vatican II seemed to have recommended: laymen and laywomen, in particular, ought to be concerned with the theology of the world.

As the 1980s approached, I became more and more alarmed by tides washing backward into the churches, just as they were being skeptically questioned in the newly self-critical secular intellectual community: radical feminism, gay liberation, utopian socialism, and geopolitical neutralism. Such ideas were suffering withering critique from those called by their suddenly defensive targets "neoconservatives," but who called themselves "neoliberals" or simply "realists." Yet in the Church, without such critique, what Cardinal Ratzinger has called a "decade of theological decadence" was wreaking its havoc. The main point of Catholicism—some were now saying—is community, the political and social liberation of the oppressed, identification with the poor, the triumph of revolution. Having rejected such uncritical slogans on secular grounds, I am not about to identify them with what I value most, next to conscience itself: my Catholic faith.

Pope Paul VI was crowned pope on June 29, 1963, during the Second Vatican Council, amidst the splendid pomp and vivid color of Rome. Nine years later he described the air within the Catholic Church in terms so shocking that they have been widely neglected since, having been dismissed even then by expert Catholic writers as the vision of a man losing his grip, too anxious, sour, or overwhelmed. Pope Paul VI preached these words on June 29, 1972:

Satan's smoke has made its way into the temple of God through some crack. . . . Doubt has entered our consciences, and it entered through windows that ought be open to the Light. . . . People thought that after the Council a day of sunshine would come for the history of the Church. There came, on the contrary, a day of clouds, storm, darkness, search, uncertainty. . . . There has been the intervention of a hostile power. His name is the Devil. . . . We believe in something preternatural that has come into the world for the very purpose of disturbing and stifling the fruits of the Ecumenical Council.[1]

Where those of us who promoted the changes wrought by the Second Vatican Council spoke only of the Holy Spirit, fresh air, and progress, the Pope spoke of suffocation, exhaust fumes, the Evil Spirit. Suppose that the Pope was more correct than we. If the invisible, odorless gas of Satan resides now in the air we take into our lungs even in church, how can we breathe free?

The struggle starts in the hearts of each of us. What do we believe? By what spirit do we live? In the long run, are the causes we now promote likely to prove as creative as we hope—or more destructive than we now see?

As I approach the age of fifty and look ahead either to death at any moment chosen by God or to a body of work yet to be accomplished (as much as the Lord wills), I believe I ought to clear my own decks. I want an account of my faith, written in the presence of God, which can be sized up by myself and others. A public person owes his readers as much. Saying the Creed with him in church every Sunday, they have a right to ask, what does this man actually believe? Look at him: philosopher, theologian, writer here and there. He should make clear what these ancient words of the Creed, which he said throughout his childhood, youth, and young adulthood, mean to him now.

Such an account should not be an academic treatise, nor should it describe, in Cardinal Newman's phrase, mere "notional assents." It should describe a particular man's real assents, that is, record the present level of his year-by-year appropriation of the faith. How much of the Creed does this man make his own? How much of it is real for him? In autumn 1982, *The Wanderer* carried a front-page, inch-high headline: MICHAEL NOVAK AND THE CATHOLIC CHURCH, and asked me to account for my faith.[2] It had not occurred to me to ask the writers of *The Wanderer* to do the same, but one imagines that each such account would be different from the others. Here is mine.

For ninety-two generations Christians have attempted to be faithful to the vision of reality communicated to them by God through Judaism, through Jesus Christ, and through the Holy Spirit at work among his people. Some fifteen generations after the death of Christ the Nicene Creed (like its earlier variants such as the Apostles' Creed) set forth, in a few crystalline lines, a vision Christians have continued to call to mind ever since, at every solemn celebration of the Eucharist and on many other occasions. This Creed is perhaps one of the most powerful short formulations in all of human history. It has transformed the world.

This is a Creed many often say together, in unison, the same words voiced by all. Yet each Christian meditates upon it from the viewpoint of a different experience. Under conditions of plague or extended prosperity, cruel oppression or gentle liberty, war or peace, each generation understands its phrases a little differently. For the words of the Creed are not merely words; they shape the way lives are lived. By those who live differently, their meaning is grasped differently. In saying the Creed, all are one, yet each is different. The same Creed is assented to by all, yet each believer utters a different Creed.

How there can be such unity in such diversity is best expressed by Cardinal Newman's distinction between *notional* and *real* assent. Abstractly, theologically, under the pressure of historical events and intellectual turmoil, the official meaning of each word, phrase, and proposition can be, and usually has been, carefully defined. The Catholic Church is not careless about words or their meanings. It has not been afraid to decide *yes* or *no* concerning rival interpretations. It has had a passion for intellectual precision. This passion is a source of vital life for a community that extends through centuries of history.[3]

On the other hand, no one can fairly believe that full Christian faith is manifested simply in the recitation of the proper words or even in the correct conceptual understanding of those words. These are important to the Catholic Church, but not sufficient. From notional assent, for which much study is required, each Christian must proceed to real assent: each must come to live the words, appropriate them, absorb them inwardly, until the correct words in the correct meaning give rise to the sort of understanding that results from experiencing their power and their truth in daily living.

This book, this confession, is the record of one such pattern of real assents. It is not written for theologians, but for ordinary believers, including those not Christian. It is not written in the notional mode, as a theological reflection aiming at conceptual precision. It is written in the experiential mode, reflecting one Christian's unique way of appropriating the Creed common to all. I have tried to keep my eyes upon what the Creed actually means to me as I live my life.

The focus of such a confession is on the faith confessed; it is not an autobiography. It is personal only insofar as the Creed can only be appropriated by individual persons in personal ways. Words of the Creed as ink marks on paper are unintelligible to the illiterate, but even when spoken, forming decipherable words and grammatical sequences, they are only as intelligible as each hearer makes them. And after each has grasped their grammar, each must further ask: how do these words alter my life? In this respect, according to an ancient proverb, the Creed is shallow enough for an ant to wade across and deep enough to drown an elephant. The fifty million Catholics of the United States confess fifty million different appropriations of the common faith, yet the Creed is the spine of the narrative each life tells. It is "confessed," that is, lived, not merely recited. Naturally, each life falls short.

Over time, people usually grow in understanding. Thus reflections on the Creed by the same person at different times ought to reveal at least in some ways quite different appropriations. Fundamentals may remain the same, as the identity of the person does, yet their lived meaning ought to have gained by experience. Unavoidably, then, a confession of faith is affected by the experience of living. It is a telling of a story up to a time; it is a story necessarily incomplete and told indirectly. While "Mind the teller, not the tale" would be poor advice, since this tale is not about the teller, at least a little about the teller is laid bare. The power of the Creed looms above him as a judgment.

If I were addressing these words directly to the Lord, as St. Augustine did in his *Confessions,* I would have much to say that I will keep private here. Were these words to be copied by hand and read by a self-selecting few, perhaps a more personal tone might be appropriate. A book aimed at immediate multiplication, however, deserves more reserve. The life of a Christian is lived in constant inner conversation with God, in terms so intimate, personal, and of such full and complete access to autobiographical detail that no other person, coming somehow upon their record, could ever be sure of understanding the tale fairly. God alone judges each of us; we cannot judge even ourselves. A Christian aware of this constant act of confession before a God who knows and understands everything—who wills it all (as a whole), and loves it all—is painfully aware of how poor all human judgment is. Not even the best of friends, not even the closest of spouses, is to the soul as God is.

Augustine permitted us to look in upon his soul's dialogue with God as I would not have the temerity to do. God knows all well enough. The faith of Christians is given for sinners, the mediocre, and the petty above all.

God well knows the misery of an inner life conducted in many sorrows and unhappy ways, in many struggles and contests, and how often the one who lives it has desired to be quit of it, willed death, willed that this life would speedily be over. One encounters many unexpected cruelties in life. Even if one has loved life and done one's best, still, seized by memories of certain deeds, thoughts, habits, and exchanges, one is much humiliated. In the end, all will be known. We shall each see each other as we are.

I have long wished to be as limpid in my approach to God (and others) as a trout stream in northern Iowa, each rounded rock shining through the flowing waters. From his mercy there is nothing to fear. Christian faith addresses this very disposition. We are what we are. God sees us as we are. Christ came for us. His lowliness as man mirrors ours. His rising again makes us, despite ourselves, God's.

Life is too short to live for less than truth. We begin in darkness enough and yet even our enemies, even when they muddy us unfairly —"Some dirt sticks longer than other dirt," Cardinal Newman writes, "but no dirt is immortal"[4]—do not entirely block the light. Writers are blessed with active enemies, often enough from all sides, a circumstance that has inspired the naming of St. Sebastian, pierced with arrows from many directions, as the patron saint of their profession. Writers have many persons telling them in public what to do and where to go, explaining to them their motives and more than guessing at their state of soul. Foes do not, oddly, share one's own self-love.

This book, then, is primarily a confession of faith. It is about the Catholic faith, nourished over ninety-two generations now by the Catholic people, as it is appropriated by one man almost half a world away from Jerusalem and Rome, in the year of Our Lord 1983.

Reflecting on the Catholic people around the world today, in the onset of my own middle age, I am obliged to rethink. As long as I can remember, I have felt special concern for the Catholic people of my time and place. For twelve years I studied diligently and with full heart for the Catholic priesthood. In the end, it seemed to me that I must think and write and act as a layman, eventually the father of a family, in the plain and ordinary role of the common believer. After considerable turmoil, yet in peace, I obeyed unmistakable signs. It seems to me that I did not so much "break" with my vocation as continue to follow it, in whatever places it has led.

At the time of the Second Vatican Council, I was privileged to be able to be present in Rome for the preparations in 1961, the second session in 1963, and part of the third session in 1964. As far back in life as memory travels, I have wanted to see a renewal of the church in our era, an *aggiornamento*, an "opening of the windows" of the church. Most of my first book, *A New Generation: American and Catholic*, was written before the Second Vatican Council had been summoned. The next one, *The Open Church*, contains my report on that Council up to its halfway point; it catches, I think, the essence of the Council's spirit.

In taking pen to paper a decade and a half later, I cannot help marveling at how much has been accomplished. The world—and the church—looks far different now in 1983 from its reality in 1965. Far more clearly, now, ours is one world. We saw it from the cameras on the moon in 1969, a blue-green ball in space, as perhaps our ancestors once imagined God saw it "from above." We saw all of it together, one planet, one human race, as far as we know alone in infinite space.

Meanwhile, since 1945, virtually every part of the world has experienced lower infant mortality, greater longevity, increased population, growing opportunities for literacy and education, unprecedented economic growth—and a vital awakening. Great misery and poverty remain, but these are no longer thought to be inevitable, as if the world were meant to be forever a "vale of tears." Now we see that poverty and misery *can* be lifted from the peoples on this earth. And if they can be, they *must* be. We have discovered a new moral obligation.

Today the church in Latin America is self-conscious and alert as never before. The church in Africa, amid persecution, is growing more rapidly than elsewhere. Asia, too, is awakening from a long slumber and some think the nations of southeastern Asia will be among the wealthiest per capita by the end of this century. For two generations Catholics everywhere said three Hail Marys at the end of every Mass for "the conversion of Russia" (how and when did the practice end?), and in Russia great souls like Solzhenitsyn and Sakharov have become the spiritual giants of our time. As for the church in the United States, before 1965 it was still looked down upon by the bureaucrats of the Roman curia as a child among the nations. Since then it has clearly become the church's eldest daughter, her chief financial support, a welcome source of much of her worldwide expertise and energy. It is a new world we face, and a new church.

Yet not all is well. The Second Vatican Council, while effecting some of the good that the progressives hoped of it, was also in some measure a loss for the Catholic Church (and for the world)—the very loss that some conservatives feared. No doubt the Holy Spirit acted. No doubt the Council was necessary. No doubt much new and fruitful life has been engendered. Still, through the little window that good Pope John XXIII opened "to let fresh air into the church" spirits other than the Holy Spirit blew in like a tornado and, like a tornado, wreaked destruction. The discernment of spirits is now necessary for survival. If one examines the "signs of the times," all are by no means positive.

Thousands of priests abandoned their ministry—as it were, three full divisions fled from the pope. One hundred thousand nuns left their communities. But statistics are not the heart of the matter.[5] The very meaning of Catholicism as a coherent people with a coherent vision has been threatened. What the barbarian invasions, centuries of primitive village life, medieval plagues and disease, wars, revolutions, heresies and schisms had failed to do, the Second Vatican Council succeeded in doing. It set in motion both positive forces and forces that squandered the inheritance of the church. It set aside many proven methods and traditions. It fostered some experiments that have worked and some that decidedly have not.

The Second Vatican Council was the first council to occur in an age of universal communication. The actual treatises it developed and voted on (quite conservative documents, after all) were only one part of its outcome. The other and more immediately potent outcome was the impression it created, the symbolic force it unleashed, through media of communication beyond its power to direct. Relatively few persons have read and studied its carefully drawn documents. Some of those who have—in study groups, in colleges and universities—have done so under the guidance of interpreters who stressed what was traditional in the documents and continuous with the past. But most seem to have done so under interpreters who stressed what was "new," treated the Council as a "breakthrough," made it seem to be a "liberation."

An "open church" is a marvelous thing, as is an "open society." But the church is not, and cannot be, like any other "open society." It is not formed by a social contract among individuals. It is formed by a covenant whose origin is God. It is formed by the brave upright yielding of obedience to God on the part of free men and free women. It is formed by freedom—and also by obedience. Obedience formed unfreely is not worthy of the God of the free conscience. But the free conscience not yielding obedience to God has broken contact with transcendence.

In celebrating an open church in my own report on the Council, I should have stated more clearly that "letting fresh air into the church" might not result in a room swept clean and well-aired, a room from which evil and ambiguity would easily be banished. As the jesters of the fountains bubbling everywhere in Rome know, clean well-lighted places attract seven demons worse than the first.[6]

Since the sweet, fresh days of the Council in Rome during 1962–1965, I have seen many individual lives ravaged by novel interpretations in faith and morals. The church has known much human frailty. The church is above all a church of sinners; sinners are at the heart of the church. But the new libertinism seems less the result of human frailty than of the ideology of "openness" and "liberation." Say anything. Do anything. You will find activist priests to lend you their collars. Perhaps the worst of this has passed. Experience has been cruel to innocence.

The postconciliar church is not even less clerical than it used to be. The new clerics include politics in their vocation, serve as foreign minister or minister of culture, sprinkle blood, lead demonstrations, and in general expand the mission of the clergy until it threatens to dominate every aspect of the social order. With all good intentions, the Catholic bishops of the United States develop their own foreign policy, even nuclear strategy. Simultaneously, many of the same clergy are drawn to collectivist visions of political economy; poverty is a "social sin." More and more, clerics define worldly issues and oblige laymen and laywomen to react. Insofar as "Peace and Justice" (but not Liberty) is statist, it speaks with the voice of Esau the sweet words of Jacob, disguising a hoarse ecclesiastical authoritarianism behind soft words of peace.

Monsignor Ronald Knox once wrote a brilliant book about the perennial temptation of the Christian church, because of its perfectionist strain, to give way to enthusiasm.[7] Like a moth toward flame, it is perennially drawn toward an overestimation of the power of the spirit. A church "not of this world" easily becomes utopian, and such an eventuality is usually manifested through rage against limitations, rage against the human body, rage against conditions of sin and injustice. One reads often today of Christians whose typical style is rage. After a meeting, for example, one woman writes that she closeted herself in a room and "screamed at God for creating a world in which men worked to deny women equality. I told him if I could get my hands on him, I'd kill him. As I screamed at God in that room . . . the only frustration I felt was that I didn't have the vocabulary I needed for this confrontation." Then she felt spiritual peace.[8]

Spiritual peace that comes through rage depends upon exhaustion. Spiritual peace that comes through humble submission to reality is quite different from a commitment not to be reconciled. And rage is neither the wisest nor the only engine of human advancement. When wisdom is present, sweetness flows within the breast, a quiet gratitude for the world as it is—this good world with its openness and possibility, its channeling and concentration, its kind tutoring through limits and adversity.

Christianity is a religion of wisdom, not rage; of realism, not perfectionism; of combat with the world, the flesh, and the devil, not appeasement. It brings not a peace that comes through understanding, but a peace that surpasses it. This is not the peace that follows rage, but the peace that sees through it. "Not as the world gives do I give peace."

Noting many possible differences in approach, I have begun to read the Creed with more reflectiveness and to try to clarify what I do actually believe. This confession represents the brief account I have given to myself. I am not where I was a decade ago, just as then I was beyond where I had been a decade before that. Such a record necessarily mirrors a pilgrim's progress.

"When I was fifteen," Cardinal Newman wrote in his *Apologia,* "a great change of thought occurred in me. I fell under the influences of a definite Creed, and received into my intellect impressions of dogma, which, through God's mercy, have never been effaced or obscured."[9] These words apply in my own case, from the first awakenings of reason at my parents' knees. Over the years, I have not much altered the fundamentals of my religious faith (although I hope pain has driven me deeper in understanding).

But I *have* changed not so much the substance as the direction of my views on political economy. Some who used to be my colleagues have, I think, changed more than I. Some were once, like me, moderate realists, liberal Catholics, but have since moved steadily in a radical socialist direction. I once also moved in that direction. *A Theology for Radical Politics,* reviewed in *Commonweal* as much too moderate to be genuinely of the Left, was the high point of that development.[10] Bitter experience caused me to back away and to search elsewhere.

Most of my many and vocal critics do not fault me for theological deviation; they fault me for breaking ranks on politics. At the latter post the flames are hottest. About theological principles latitudinarianism is the vogue. Among traditionalists, standards are reversed. Some care not whether you question, probe, explore, create—their litmus test is heartfelt verbal repetition. Of his accuser Mr. Kingsley, Cardinal Newman writes: "He appears to be so constituted as to have no notion of what goes on in minds very different from his own, and moreover to be stone-blind to his ignorance. . . . Had he been a man of large or cautious mind, he would not have taken it for granted that cultivation must lead one to see things precisely as he sees them himself."[11]

Today it seems difficult for those on the extreme religious Right to comprehend that there are serious Catholics who disagree with their vision of the Faith. It seems difficult for persons on the extreme religious Left to comprehend that there are serious persons who disagree with their views on political economy. Sheer goodness, both seem certain, is on their side. Instinctively, both hold that whoever disagrees with them has evil intentions and flawed character. I would be happy to learn from critics errors of fact or logic in my arguments. About my poor character, God knows far more than they.

For good and sound reasons, I have tried to resist in this book the impulse of autobiography. I first wrote, then set aside, nearly one hundred pages explaining how, on various matters, I have changed my mind since 1965. Very few of those changes are theological in nature or related to the Creed; most have to do with judgments about politics and economics. Such a discussion belongs in another book; still, I ought perhaps briefly to summarize its substance. Three experiences especially affected me.

First was the experience of student radicalism at the State University of New York at Old Westbury (1968–1972), which showed me conclusively some of the pathologies to which the Left is prey, and taught me that not only the Right has tyrannical and duplicitous tendencies. Second was the contemplation of genocide in Cambodia, the miseries of the "boat people" from Vietnam, and the accounts of life today in South Vietnam. These showed me that in my antiwar writings I had been mistaken about the North Vietnamese, the Viet Cong, and the moral meaning of the war in Vietnam. Third was a series of experiences during the congressional and presidential campaigns of 1970, 1972, and 1976. As I began to study questions of race, class, and ethnicity in greater detail, as I began to study the new growth and configuration of the Soviet military, and as I began to study questions of political economy, I was forced to see that many of my earlier prejudices and inclinations were out of touch with reality. Consistency had to give way to greater realism.

All these movements of thought led me to be as critical of the Left —that is, first of all, of myself—as I had earlier been of the Right. For anyone faithful to the relentless drive to raise questions, such an outcome should have come as no surprise. I wish I could say I had been knocked suddenly from a horse. Instead, my growing sense of unease and untruth was slow and cumulative. It was built up by a mass of detail.

Suffice it to say that I remain a Democrat, and that my preferred self-designation is "neoliberal"—a liberal who has, to borrow Irving Kristol's phrase, been mugged by reality and is now critical of the Left as well as the Right. For me, this designation means that I am critical of classical liberalism and the libertarians while valuing a liberal polity and a capitalist economy, under the judgment of Jewish and Christian values. Analogously, Daniel Bell once described himself as a conservative in culture, a liberal in politics, and a socialist in economics. (I do not share Professor Bell's socialism, and do not think even he can sustain it, except in some moral sense.) All this, in any case, is a matter for a book more on political economy than on faith, and more on the social ethics of the Catholic tradition than on the Creed itself.

Still, it has some relevance. Magazines I used to write often for—*Commonweal, The National Catholic Reporter, Christianity and Crisis*—I no longer feel quite at home in, although generous editors still occasionally open their pages to me. A drift to the Left, both in theology and in politics, has taken these magazines out of the orbit of what used to be called liberal Catholicism or biblical realism. That drift now seems to me in need of friendly but sustained critique. Others who think the same have joined me in founding *Catholicism in Crisis*.[12]

Thus I conclude these reflections on the Creed with a brief description of the current situation, as I see it, of the Catholic Church after Vatican II. This section will seem polemical to some. I have not tried to render a balanced portrait, but rather to diagnose starkly what seems to me to be going wrong. My motive for including this section is to make connection with the hopes I expressed nineteen years ago in *The Open Church*. For it was with growing concern that I first began to ask myself what being a Catholic means to me now, in my forty-ninth year. I do not ask my readers to agree with me in this section, only to focus their own critical eyes on our present circumstances. In the opening reflections on the Creed, our common faith may be more in evidence.

Part I, then, the longest and most important part, is a confession of faith: a reflection upon the Creed line by line. My aim throughout has been to let the Creed stand out. In that respect, this brief work is my *Orthodoxy*, not quite my *Apologia Pro Vita Sua*. Part II considers the state of the church since Vatican II.

Part I

CONFESSION OF FAITH: REFLECTIONS ON THE NICENE CREED

CREATOR, beyond any words of ours to describe!

Most gloriously You have disposed all parts of the whole universe. You are the true source of light and wisdom, You are their first and final cause.

Pour out now, I beg You, a ray of Your clear light upon my murky understanding, and take from me my doubly dark inheritance of sin and ignorance. You who inspire the speech of little children, guide and teach my tongue now, and let the grace of Your blessing flow upon my lips. Grant me a sharp discernment, a strong memory, a methodical approach to study, a willing and able docility; let me be precise in interpretation and felicitous in choice of words.

Instruct my beginning, direct my progress, and bring my work to its proper finish: You, who are true God and true Man, living and reigning forever!

—THOMAS AQUINAS

1. The Living Creeds

From the beginning, even in the New Testament, Christian preachers have used short formulae to indicate the difference that being a Christian makes. This difference consists of two parts: *seeing* the world differently and *acting* differently. And the reason for this important difference is a staggering one: it is that *God* has come to live within human beings. So Christianity is not to be understood as a new complex of human sentiments. It is rooted in a new *doctrine*, a new teaching, about *God's* action within humans. Since the source of spiritual power within Christianity is from God, keeping this doctrine straight is essential to Christianity's survival. To make Christianity a contrivance of human sentiment, habit, and preference, even a temporarily attractive one, is to eviscerate it. For this reason, Christianity, more than most world religions, devotes tremendous energy to clarity about its doctrine.

In the early generations of the church, creeds were used at adult baptisms to supply short and clear summaries of the essential commitments a convert was making. Records of these formulae from different places and times have been preserved. Amid many variations in word, phrase, and emphasis, the underlying unity on essentials is striking. When Christian faith collided with or seemed dangerously like the teachings of other religious bodies or philosophical teachings, Christian pastors stressed some formulae more than others or made some aspects more explicit while others continued to be taken for granted. Gradually, over time, certain of these creeds came into common usage over entire regions or even over the whole church. Much depended upon the intellectual dangers of time and place. Great struggles occurred over particular phrases.

Down through the generations two of these creeds have passed into common usage: the Apostles' Creed and the Nicene Creed. The Apostles' Creed is today taught to youngsters in their preparations for receiving the sacraments of reconciliation (penance) and the Eucharist. I always remember it for the mysterious phrase that Jesus, after his death, "descended into hell." That phrase has always seemed to me brave, comforting, and especially suited to this century.

The Nicene Creed—in a fuller version than the exact Greek text of Nicaea (A.D. 325)—has been in use at the celebration of the Eucharist for centuries. Until 1968, throughout the Western world, this creed was recited in Latin—with its beautifully chiseled and exact phrases, given clear intellectual context by centuries of disputation and precise commentary. More recently, the Nicene Creed has been recited in vernacular languages. A commission of English-speaking experts prepared an official English text in 1972; it is reprinted below with the other texts.

I do not like this new English text. It is vague at some places where bitterly fought theological struggles achieved superior clarity; it omits some important words; and it lacks poetic power. Its tone, by comparison with others, seems patronizing. Much more classic is the Latin text, sturdy and vigorous. I reprint it with the affection born of frequent use and long meditation. These are the words that sing in my ear with Gregorian chant. These are the words redolent with continuity and a certain universality of time and place. These are the words Augustine and Aquinas spoke, and St. Teresa and St. John, and many of our ancestors. One cherishes their very accent, the rise and fall of every syllable.

For completeness' sake, I also reprint a plain English translation, from my old Benziger Brothers missal of 1949, edited by Father F. X. Lasance. It follows the Latin faithfully and with simple elegance.

While presenting the text of the 1972 English version (since this is the one most English-speaking Catholics, alas, now encounter), I have chosen for my own reflections in subsequent chapters a more literary translation prepared just before the Second Vatican Council from a missal of exquisite scholarship produced by the Mame publishing company in Paris. The English edition was published by Helicon Press in Baltimore, now defunct. This version of the Creed, which I also include below, was poetically translated by a team of English priests and laymen. It has been for many years my favorite.

Christianity is most of all a life. While its power comes from God, through distinctive and precise teaching, this life cannot be wholly caught by any one set of words. Care about words is exceedingly important, for Christian life does not originate in human experience but in the Word of God. The words of the Creed are vessels, conduits, instruments—poor things—and yet they are our links to God. In this they mirror the use by God of Scripture itself. One might wish that God spoke directly to every human heart (and so He does), in such a way that the community of believers needed no poor formulae to keep its contact pure. But God chose to respect the limitations of human flesh, human intellect, and human social life. The manner in which He first revealed Himself is suited to our weakness. All sorts of ambiguities, doubts, and arguments, therefore, cloud our access to Him. Orthodoxy —straight teaching—is difficult to maintain. A pure stream of understanding, from God to us, must be fought for by every generation. Good Christians often disagree. New perplexities constantly arise. The room for error is great. The task of faithful understanding is arduous. It is no wonder that G. K. Chesterton found the struggle for orthodoxy an adventure, a romance. It is.

For it is no difficult trick to keep up with the spirit of one's age, to stay abreast, to become sophisticated and adept in the best convictions of one's period. But to see *through* those and to discern *in* them what is consistent with God's word and what is not is extremely difficult. One can err by too much caution and resistance on one side or by too much enthusiasm for the latest wisdom of the age on the other.

Being orthodox is neither a matter of rote nor a matter of holding enlightened opinions. It is a matter of living so as to see with God's eyes, as best a human can struggle to do. In this sense, it is a matter of orthopraxis—straight practice—as well as a matter of orthodoxy. For the heart and will always lead the intellect. That is why a heart that is humble is always a prerequisite for true belief, a heart that wills to do, not its own will, but God's. Our hearts are besieged, however, by errant loves as picnickers are besieged by gnats. Our attention wanders. We need the correction of one another. In the Catholic scheme of things we need the correction, above all, of those charged within our midst to preserve the essentials pure: the bishops and, among them, Peter. The bishops sometimes fail, as in the age of Arius. They also need the correction of the faithful. Somehow, through it all, God's grace brings us through, when we have struggled as best we can to be faithful. On Him we rely. In moments of great confusion, we rally to Peter—not because of Peter but because of God—and await the judgment of history and the judgment of God Himself.

The Creed of Nicaea is divided into four main parts, one for each of the Three Persons of the Holy Trinity and one for a brief conspectus of beliefs about this world and the next. The Creed dwells for some length on God the Father Almighty. It continues at still greater length on the nature and the historical life of God the Son. It is rather brief, although penetrating, about the Holy Spirit. Its last affirmations are succinct and enumerative, but much to the point. They dwell on the church, the remission of sins, and the resurrection of the flesh.

I reflect on each of these, line by line. But, first, the texts.

THE APOSTLES' CREED[1]

I believe in God, the Father almighty,
　Creator of heaven and earth;
　and in Jesus Christ, His only Son, our Lord:
　　who was conceived by the Holy Spirit,
　　born of the Virgin Mary,
　　suffered under Pontius Pilate,
　　was crucified, died, and was buried.
He descended into hell;
　the third day He arose again from the dead.
He ascended into heaven and sits at the right hand of God,
　the Father almighty; from thence He shall come to judge
　the living and the dead.
I believe in the Holy Spirit,
　the holy Catholic Church,

the communion of saints,
the forgiveness of sins,
the resurrection of the body,
and life everlasting. Amen.

THE LATIN NICENE CREED[2]

Credo in unum Deum,
Patrem omnipotentem, factorem caeli et terrae,
visibilium omnium et invisibilium.

Et in unum Dominum Iesum Christum,
Filium Dei unigenitum,
et ex Patre natum ante omnia saecula.
Deum de Deo, lumen de lumine, Deum verum de Deo vero,
genitum, non factum, consubstantialem Patri:
per quem omnia facta sunt.
Qui propter nos homines et propter nostram salutem
descendit de caelis.
Et incarnatus est de Spiritu Sancto
ex Maria Virgine, et homo factus est.
Crucifixus etiam pro nobis sub Pontio Pilato;
passus et sepultus est,
et resurrexit tertia die, secundum Scripturas,
et ascendit in caelum, sedet ad dexteram Patris.
Et iterum venturus est cum gloria,
iudicare vivos et mortuos,
cuius regni non erit finis.

Et in Spiritum Sanctum, Dominum et vivificantem:
qui ex Patre Filioque procedit.
Qui cum Patre et Filio simul adoratur et conglorificatur:
qui locutus est per prophetas.
Et unam, sanctam, catholicam et apostolicam Ecclesiam.

Confiteor unum baptisma in remissionem peccatorum.
Et exspecto resurrectionem mortuorum,
et vitam venturi saeculi. Amen.

THE BENZIGER TRANSLATION[3]

I believe in one God,
  the Father almighty,
  maker of heaven and earth,
  and of all things visible and invisible.
And in one Lord Jesus Christ,
  the only-begotten Son of God.
  born of the Father before all ages;
  God of God, Light of Light,
  true God of true God;
  begotten not made; consubstantial with the Father
  by Whom all things were made.
  Who for us men, and for our salvation
    came down from heaven.
  And was incarnate by the Holy Ghost
    of the Virgin Mary: and was made man.
  He was crucified also for us,
    suffered under Pontius Pilate, and was buried.
  And the third day He rose again
    according to the Scriptures,
    And ascended into heaven.
    He sitteth at the right hand of the Father:
  and He shall come again with glory,
    to judge the living and the dead:
  and His kingdom shall have no end.
And in the Holy Ghost, the Lord and Giver of life,
  Who proceedeth from the Father and the Son,
  Who, together with the Father and the Son, is
    adored and glorified:
  Who spoke by the Prophets.
And one, holy, catholic and apostolic Church.
I confess one baptism for the remission of sins.
And I expect the resurrection of the dead,
  and the life of the world to come. Amen.

THE HELICON/MAME TRANSLATION[4]

I believe in one God,
   the Almighty Father, maker of heaven and earth and of all things,
   visible and invisible.
And in one Lord Jesus Christ, the only-begotten Son of God,
Born of the Father before time was:
God born from God, Light born from Light,
   True God born from True God;
Begotten, but not made, of one essence with the Father;
   And through Him all things were made.
For us men and for our salvation He came down from Heaven.
He was incarnate by the Holy Spirit from the Virgin Mary, and was
   made Man.
Then, for our sake, He was crucified under Pontius Pilate:
He underwent His passion, and was buried.
On the third day He rose from the dead,
   as the Scriptures had foretold.
And He went up into heaven, where He sits at the right hand of the
   Father.
He will come again in glory to judge the living and the dead, and His
   kingdom will never end.
And I believe in the Holy Spirit, Lord and Life-Giver, who proceeds
   from the Father and the Son;
Equally with the Father and the Son he is worshipped and glorified;
   and he has spoken through the prophets.
I believe in one, holy, catholic and apostolic Church.
I affirm one baptism for the remission of sins.
And I look for the resurrection of the dead   .
   and the life of the world to come. Amen.

THE CONTEMPORARY ENGLISH TRANSLATION(1972)[5]

We believe in one God,
   the Father, the Almighty,
   maker of heaven and earth,

of all that is seen and unseen.
We believe in one Lord, Jesus Christ,
   the only Son of God,
   eternally begotten of the Father,
   God from God, Light from Light,
   true God from true God,
   begotten, not made, one in Being with the Father.
   Through him all things were made.
For us men and for our salvation
   he came down from heaven:
by the power of the Holy Spirit
   he was born of the Virgin Mary, and became man.
For our sake he was crucified under Pontius Pilate;
   he suffered, died, and was buried.
   On the third day he rose again
      in fulfillment of the Scriptures;
   he ascended into heaven
      and is seated at the right hand of the Father.
He will come again in glory to judge the living and the
   dead, and his kingdom will have no end.
We believe in the Holy Spirit, the Lord, the giver of life,
   who proceeds from the Father and the Son.
With the Father and the Son he is worshiped and glorified.
   He has spoken through the Prophets.
We believe in one holy catholic and apostolic Church.
We acknowledge one baptism for the forgiveness of sins.
We look for the resurrection of the dead,
   and the life of the world to come. Amen.

2. God the Father

I believe in one God,
the Almighty Father, maker of heaven and earth and of all
things, visible and invisible.

It is pointless to write about Catholicism without writing first about God. And that means to write about experience, of a sort.

It is difficult to describe the beauties of northern Iowa, where I write part of this, but it is not difficult here to feel close to God. One feels the implacable urge of the soil to burst into life. In every unattended cranny of the lawn thick weeds leap to knee height and dandelions are gigantic. Where the mower cannot reach, tall silver grass dwarfs two-foot pines along the drive.

The summer skies of Iowa glisten with paleness I have never seen elsewhere, lighter than a robin's egg, glowing silver through (I imagine) ozone. The thick clouds are not at all like Eastern clouds; often they are briskly blown by winds up high when no breeze stirs the August heat below. Immense sky commands nine-tenths of visual space. It frightens one accustomed to trees and monuments and concrete buildings blocking out the light. One feels unable to escape the gaze of God. A man stands up almost into Him.

Early in the morning, and in the evening as the sun sinks, the air lacks noonday tension, the buzz of baked blades of grass and maddened insects. In the morning every leaf seems fluid, moistened, soft, which by the afternoon is crisp, and in the evening loosens once again.

My favorite hours are spent out on the golf course. Unlike my son's grace, no part of my swing is natural. I play entirely with irons. A straight arc from a wood is beyond my skill. Like a baseball hitter I pull the woods, each great sweeping curve, into fairways to the left—or right. The pleasure of walking satisfies me. Every day new grass is mown. Every day the breeze blows in across the lake, cars roar and rattle down the sand-gravel road raising clouds of dust. The Cresco course is built around a cloud-reflecting lake. The saddle of an abandoned railroad mound divides holes four and five and serves as a hilltop tee for starting down the latter. For all nine holes one climbs, descends, shoots across ravines or even, for the bold, across a corner of the lake.

I try to play when others do not play: on the wet morning grass, in the hottest heat of noon, as the last one out at sunset. The colors of the maples, lake, and sky change through the day. The eye discerns dozens of shades of green, each in varying depths of shadow. The light falls so brilliantly at noon it hurts the eyes. Simply to avoid the glare, one watches foot follow plodding foot upon the dry and beaten grass.

For a certain type of human, and I am one, nature overpowers one with thoughts of God—not exactly thoughts, a full and resonant presence. This is a gift, I think. I do not *reason* from creatures to the Creator. Things do not seem like things to me. They seem like signs, presences, messages, and invitations; they seem personal. My heart opens. They fill it—not they themselves, but He who holds them out of nothingness, makes them to stand out.

I practice, sometimes, being an atheist, and I can do it. There have been times when God has long been absent from me and my heart dry and distant. Then things do appear like alien things, objects, fluids, grotesque impediments. Then everything seems loathsome, as in the early world of Jean-Paul Sartre (although I felt such things before I read him).[1] Of tricks of perception there are many, so I like to remind myself of darkness. The situation of the atheist seems safer to me, for if there is a God (I write this not in doubt) He cannot be a creature of my moods and sensibility. If God is, He is, regardless of my attunement. So it is actually more secure, as St. John of the Cross writes, to walk in emptiness, without security, and to believe without the feelings of belief, by the mind and will alone—or, better, by a quiet point below the busyness of mind and will, in darkness.[2]

I do not much trust (or like) people who are blissfully aware of God. Such moments in myself have not served me well. Those whom He loves God makes to suffer, runs a proverb utterly true. One cannot believe the demands God can make until He makes them. Then blissful certainty is thin and useless stuff, almost (but who can judge?) revolting. The merely blissful do not know, one wishes to say; they haven't begun to know.

So when we say, "We believe in God," it is not a feeling we are trying to articulate. We see nothing physical an atheist can't see. The darkness is identically the same. Except that, true enough, there is an inner movement, an inclination far deeper than emotion or sensibility, mind or will that pushes us forward like the growingness of things. It feels more like the action of another than like our own, yet it is perfectly our own, appropriate, and fitting. It feels like our true self. It has no eyes, is dark, obscure, but steady and propelling. I would write that faith is a force in us, but there is no coercion in it, no overpowering of the reason, no silencer of questions. It is, instead, like the force of questioning itself, it keeps coming, never satisfied, directing fresh attention, inquiring further. My mentor, Bernard Lonergan, calls it the drive to question. An ancient name for it is wonder. It is an instinct of the spirit deeper than any other instinct, the source of all our restlessness, the seed of our transcendence. Nothing satisfies us. Name something, achieve it, and it pales. There are always further questions. Faith comes like an arrow placed into this bow, shot toward a target the eyes can never reach.

"We believe in God," says the new translation of the Creed. The Latin text was better: *Credo in unum Deum, "I* believe in one God." One God and one I. It is from the depths of me, in solitariness, and not from the lockstep of some communal enthusiasm that I believe. In fact, one of the elementary tests of belief comes in isolation from all one's family, friends, supports. Faith strikes us most deeply when we are alone, not only alone but isolated from assistance. Then faith, so to speak, grows to adulthood in us; it stands alone. "If anyone comes to me and does not hate his own father and mother and wife and children and brothers and sisters, yes, and even his own life, he cannot be my disciple" (Luke 14:26). *Credo:* I like the Latin better. It speaks a truth missing in the recent stress upon community. Yet "we" is also correct.

"I Believe in God the Father." Down through the centuries, for

ninety-two generations, these words of the Nicene Creed have resounded against the ceilings of rooms in which the Eucharist has been celebrated. So even when the first word was "I," a community gave it voice.

"We," a people. Individual faith does not thrive in solitary conscience but among a people—among Peter and Paul, Barnabas, Margaret-Mary, Therese, Brendan Behan, Charles de Gaulle, a multitude of saints and sinners. Saints and sinners: not two categories but one. For the saints are also sinners who allow God's grace and mercy to show translucently.

The Catholic "we" transcends any parish community pronouncing the words in unison on Sunday, transcends each generation, transcends every era and all civilizations. It is also an institutional "we." The Nicene Creed was formally drawn up in committee and voted upon in a council of representatives of regional churches, with and under the legate of the Bishop of Rome. It represents a community; also an institution.

A community has organized itself institutionally, across the centuries, to formulate its faith exactly in ever new words and concepts, in order to have it faithfully heard, meditated upon, and by individuals accepted or rejected. Thus, in part it is a community that believes. Still, each person comes to believe in God deep in the silence of the soul. Autonomous individuals must one by one incarnate the faith. Each must learn the words grammatically. Far more difficult, each must absorb their meaning into attitudes, behaviors, actions: each must be shaped by their power. To be born a Catholic is to receive Catholicism as the story of one's life. But to profess Catholicism as one's own, in later consciousness, is to begin to *tell* one's story as a Catholic. Such stories are full of conflict, hazard, struggle, defeat. The variety is beautiful.

Humans are made in the image of God and the human vocation is to allow that image to unfold, as a seed of corn, pressed into warm earth, snaps its shell and sends life up. An infinity of human stories is required to mirror everything that God is.

To "believe *in*" is to live in a certain way; it is not merely to recite words. To "believe *in*" is not to "believe *that.*" To believe *that* God exists is not enough. To begin, mostly in silence, to converse with Him is to be aware of His presence, to know His attention to all things inside oneself and outside, to movements of emotion and thought, to events, to other persons, to the sunsets and the storms, to the cobalt sky and to the waterbugs skitting across the surface of the pond, in good times and in bad. To hear a good sermon is to feel God speaking in one's heart, as to hear a bad one is (however mildly) to suffer with Him on the cross.

I have seen in the eyes of atheists the difficulty they feel in trying to be sympathetic to what the believer means by "the presence of God." The sense of a world without God is not only different from the sense of His presence; it leaves one unable to imagine the latter. The believer feels equally helpless in speaking about it. How does one explain what it is like? It is not like seeing or hearing. No one sees God. Voices are not to be trusted. Feelings are deceptive. Images fall short. Concepts cannot contain God. What is it, then, this presence of God? In some sense, that presence is offered to every man and woman who lives. It takes root in odd ways, in unpredictable patterns. It is always there to be called upon, like the sun even when it is hidden above thick clouds which drift in various layers and at various speeds across a leaden sky. Daily familiar access to God's presence, however, seems in practice to be as much a gift as a resonant voice, a clear mind, a glorious laugh. Unlike other gifts, however, it is a gift toward which all are called, a gift within the reach of all. It is something of a mystery, the most puzzling fact about humans, that all do not accept this gift. What could possibly be threatening about it?

A Jesuit writer has recently described the God found in one part of the work of St. Thomas Aquinas: God the supreme being, pure act, infinite, eternal, unchanging, unaffected by the world. "He remains supremely happy whether we love Him or not. Whatever happens in our world literally makes not the slightest difference to his divine happiness."[3] This is not, the Jesuit thinks, the God of love depicted in the New Testament. He sees in the vision of Aquinas "the way to modern atheism. Many atheists think that if this is the only God there is, then it would be better to live without Him and to try to create a purely natural humanism." The writer rejects this God, in favor of a knowledge of God strictly dependent on what he learns through God's Son, the Christ: the God of Abraham, Isaac, and Jacob revealed in Jesus.

Yet surely there are more keys to modern atheism than those found in the thirteenth century. The Nicene Creed is at least as premodern as is the opening exposition of the *Summa Theologica*. The revelation of Jesus Christ is no less difficult for atheists. It, too, is full of ambiguities, contradictions, and incoherences. Indeed, some of us find necessary nourishment in thinkers like Aquinas. His words, in particular, speak to my mind and heart as do those of few others; his concepts and methods open the New Testament to me as those of few others do. I have read the *Summa* cover-to-cover three times and meditated on many sections, a passage at a time, for hours. No writer's mind has ever been so full of light: Angelic Doctor is an apt name for him.

Isn't it odd that Aquinas did not feel the conflict between his philosophical concepts and those of the New Testament in the way that the aforementioned Jesuit Father O'Donnell does? I do not find Father O'Donnell's commentaries on the New Testament superior on the essential points to those of Aquinas. Yet Aquinas pushes his mind beyond the colorful language of everyday use in order to construct a careful system of definitions and relations. He does so in order to throw marvelous light into shadowed corners and neglected chasms. He deals with perplexities that trouble the questioning intellect.

One of the greatest losses resulting from Vatican II is the abortion of the great Thomistic revival that had been in flower since 1878. Three generations of scholars had recovered brilliant treasures of the church and restored them for potent daily use. By the next generation these were arrogantly cast aside. The revival of Scripture studies, which has been offered as a replacement for the Thomistic revival, has in practice bred a legion of fundamentalists, simplifiers, and equivocators. (At the other extreme, it has also bred a certain number of dry and cynical rationalists.) Unless approached systematically, reflectively, and critically, Scripture alone can be made to yield themes of any sort, to serve any purpose. I have seldom met a pious fraud who could not cite Scripture to support his case. Scripture is the lifeblood of the church, but only systematic reflection on it builds the arteries and veins that bring that blood where it must go, in proper force and order. The church needs systematic theology for honesty's sake, for vigor, for life. There is a commonsense way of thinking about God, a way as close as possible to our own bodies and to our own familiar modes of perception. To think of God as "Love" strikes chords that are silent, at least at first, if one thinks of God as "Pure Act." (What *is* "Pure Act" anyway? A definition alone will scarcely help; one must begin to learn a novel way of conceiving of reality, of placing things in relation. Effort is required beyond the perceptions of common sense.) To think of God as being deeply affected by our behavior, angry at times, jealous, compassionate, forgiving, is far more consoling than to think of God as the unchanged Supreme Being and Unmoved Mover of the universe. It is touching to imagine a God as passional as ourselves. But these are, of course, mere images. For if we imagine that God has no body like ours, lacks our nervous system and glands, it becomes difficult to hold that He is "affected" in the way we are by anything at all. The consoling language of common sense breaks down as soon as it is examined critically.

There are here two quite different tasks for the Christian intellect. The first is to focus the inquiring mind on the question, How should I live? For this task, the language of human emotion and affection, human passion and struggle, human desperation and relief is both appropriate and necessary. Jesus spoke such a language far more often than he spoke the language of philosophers. For all Christians most of the time, and even perhaps for most Christians all of the time, this is the intellectual task that counts. First things first.

But there is a second task—not only to act as a Christian, but to understand. What do words about God mean? How do they cohere? In what sense are they nonsense and in what sense true? For this second task, the language of common sense—of the human body, passions, imagination, and daily commerce—will not suffice. That way lies fundamentalism.

Although I have eagerly read hundreds of books on the question of God, I have never found a writer whose views on these matters are so subtle, so limpid, so full of power as those of Aquinas. Much analysis of his work, whether by disciples or by opponents or by the merely curious, is useless for understanding him. In my experience, one must read Aquinas as one reads Scripture, in long contemplation, slowly, absorbing his point of view, trying to understand why he brings up the questions he does, and why he employs each specific word or distinction he chooses. One must try to go behind the screen of words to the active, searching mind that hit upon them. And one must meditate upon the Scripture he was himself contemplating as he wrote.

I do not mean to argue that all intellectually curious Christians ought to master St. Thomas, that St. Thomas is the only and sole master, that all creative systematic reflection ended with him, or that the best strategic intellectual move of the present generation would be to reinstitute the Thomistic revival and once again make Aquinas the doctor *primus inter pares* of the seminaries and universities. Here I content myself with a lesser observation. In the absence of Aquinas, the partisans of Scripture studies alone—the foes of systematic theology—have already run into insuperable questions of coherence, definition, consistency, and system. Inevitably, they will soon choose a philosophical master. The Germans and Swiss and Dutch are likely to do so first. It is probable that their choice, at first informal and implicit, later enthusiastic and detailed, will fall upon Heidegger and, above all, Hegel. Archbishop Helder Camara has recommended that Marx replace Aquinas. Such choices will lead to intellectual disaster.

To argue this warning in detail would take me too far afield at present. But there are signs that the disaster has already begun. Hegel is the master par excellence of a statist philosophy. Hegel will feed enthusiasm for strong central governmental authority. Hegel is an idealist, a writer about spirit, and so at first these political implications will be hidden from view. Metaphysically, Hegel will lead the mind away from biblical realism and toward gnosticism in every sphere. Sexual differentiation will, on Hegelian grounds, mean little. So will the incarnation of God in Jesus. We will each become part of the spirit of God manifested in the great collective spirit of the unfolding ages. This is a potent vision, with powerful mass appeal. But it is not, I think, the Christian spirit.

A small directional error at departure results in errors of immense distances as an ocean is crossed. Christian intellect will necessarily take up its speculative task. It will inevitably choose a philosophical master. It is one thing to recommend, in such a case, that pluralism ought to reign; of course, it should. It is another claim that which choices of master are made is a matter of indifference.

Having experimented broadly, having tested many systems for myself, I find no master closer to common sense, more imbued with fundamental realism, more illuminating in complexities and subtleties, more frequently compelling, more advanced than others on specific issues of importance than Aquinas. If each of us must make a choice, that is mine.

To believe in God the Father who is to be darkly conceived, as Aquinas perceives Him, is to begin with concrete things like a grain of sand, a steak, a cigar, a glass of stout, a human father. It is to be struck by the fact that such things *exist,* stand forth out of nothingness, are singular, individual, real. One forgets, for a moment, the *kinds* of things they are, their essences, their definitions. One is struck by singulars: by their stark existence in the light of day, in a moment of time. The trees Aquinas noticed breathing in the brilliant air under Italian sunlight in Orvieto have long since vanished. They did exist and now do not. He caught them in a rare and fleeting moment. That precious moment of existence enraptured him. He encountered it in each lily of the field, each person, each moment of time.

To exist, in his way of thinking, was to come into *act. Acts* pass. The word *act,* of course, is related to action; it points, so to speak, to a gerund: waving, seeing, growing, being. It is the gerundive nature of the universe, its history-in-being, that fascinated Aquinas. Thus, a threefold movement from *potency* to *act* to *passing out of existence* became central to the way Aquinas thought about each concrete thing or person he encountered in his life.

To "believe in God the Father Almighty, Creator of heaven and earth, and of all things visible and invisible," was for him to concentrate on the divine gerund, the divine actor, the divine exister, from whose existing all things exist. God is the energy that through the green grass shoots. To contemplate a grain of sand in the crease of one's palm is to catch a sidelong glance at the power of existing for a time in something that did not always exist and will not forever continue to exist. Its existing forces the mind toward every other existing thing and toward the act that raised all things from nothingness.

To think of God as the force, the power, the drive that energizes the transient existingness of things, that orders them in all their contingencies and schemes of probabilities, in their emergence and relations and passing away, is not so far as one might at first think from thinking of God as the Creator of heaven and earth.

To recognize, moreover, that such a God has, strictly, no need of creation, but created out of goodness and love and generosity, is to arrive not so wide of the mark of recognizing the God of Abraham, Isaac, and Jacob. To see that we humans are not only puny things, as well our anxieties instruct us, but less than good, attentive, and grateful persons, is not so far from the mark either. Coming to think of God through the signs abounding in His creation, one may only marvel the more when one discovers, through "Jesus Christ, His only son, begotten not made, born of the Father before all ages," that God so loved creation that He sent this only Son into it, to be crucified, die, and be buried. That, in principle, God could have been totally unaffected by the world but out of compassion allowed Himself to be so affected stuns the imagination as a merely anthropomorphic conception of God does not.

Far from diminishing the force of the New Testament, the way Aquinas thinks of creation sets that Testament in a context that inspires silent amazement.

It is exceedingly difficult, following the direction of Aquinas, not to feel such surges of love toward the God of whom he writes—and to recognize in such surges God's own proper life itself—as overcome the breast with sweetness.

What unity one feels, not only with Aquinas, but also with those others whose company he keeps alive—Gregory and Augustine, Matthew and Mark, Aristotle and Plato. Creator of all things, visible and invisible.

Then there is the troubling phrase, troubling at least for feminists: "God the Father." Indisputably, the God of Abraham, Isaac, and Jacob, the God of common sense and human metaphor, is a patriarchal

God. In the speculative view of Aquinas, of course, to rise above anthropomorphism is to enter the realm of critical intellect, to press the mind's light beyond the limits of the human body and the human imagination. God the Father Almighty, Creator of heaven and earth, is not a male in the way some humans are males. God is not embodied. The God who is Pure Act is neither masculine nor feminine. He is masculine in the Nicene Creed, however. The Nicene Creed does not speak of believing in God the Mother Almighty nor of her only Daughter. It might well have. For many persons in many other civilizations, the spontaneous way of thinking of God is to imagine an oceanic presence mothering us all. Nonetheless, neither Judaism nor Christianity, faced with the task of choosing metaphors from human experience, preferentially chose feminine metaphors.[4] The predominantly masculine choice is unmistakable. God is the Father, Jesus is the Son, and Jesus himself, gentle as a woman and in many ways closer to women than to men in his life, taught us to address God, not as "Our Mother who art in heaven," but as "Our Father."

Why?

I find it difficult to be persuaded that the answer lies in God's adaptation to human cultural conditions. The God of Judaism and Christianity did not in other matters hesitate to scandalize and shock the cultural presuppositions of His people. If God could choose to create the world as He wished, surely He could have chosen to reveal Himself as He wished to be revealed. God did not reveal Himself as She.

Why?

For myself, images of God as feminine have always been attractive: to think of wisdom as feminine; to speak, after Boethius, of Lady Philosophy; to admire the spirit of contemplation more than the active intellect; to learn the virtues of meekness, gentleness, humility, patience, and abandonment; to follow the model of the first of all Christians, Mary, in such an archetypal act of consent as, "Be it done to me according to Thy word"—these are qualities essential to the development of the male spirit. They lie behind the ideal of the gentleman. They suggest a difference between *animus* and *anima*.[5] To tutor the male spirit in *anima* is not the way of kingly or warrior cultures. Yet it is the way of a Christian culture, which slowly transformed the knightly culture of feudal, medieval Europe. Rude warriors, whose law was the survival of the stronger, were instructed that their perfection entailed learning *caritas, courtesy,* and *compassion*—the three C's of knightly instruction. A knight might be, in battle, ferocious in appearance, in heart, in deed; but he must also be gentle. The feminine spirit is essential to the creation of the gentleman. It is indispensable to Christian civilization.

Let us go back a little. We are meditating on God the Creator and God the Father. Let us try to imagine our way into God's place before (so to speak) creation had occurred. In creating all things, God could have given them any shape He chose. Knowing that He would reveal Himself to His creatures, He would design everything accordingly. In this respect, the differentiation of the sexes is one of the ways by which —in calling Himself Father—He revealed Himself. Clearly, God is not carnal, not sexed, neither male nor female. Yet the differentiation of human sexes was used by Him—"Father," not "Mother"; "Son," not "Daughter"—to suggest something about His own nature. What?

Sexual differentiation is somehow central both to the world as God created it and to the revealed nature of God. For some, feminism means that there is no significant difference between male and female; that both are persons; that "having a penis" is of no decisive spiritual importance. Some believe, therefore, that we must choose between the Christian Creed and feminism, that we cannot hold both.

For myself, it is a form of gnosticism to hold that human beings are primarily persons, to choose a language stripped of sexual differentiation, to speak, for example, of "chairpersons," and to refuse to see the enormous significance the Creator has imparted to being man and to being woman. In nature and in culture, these differences are plain. One might choose to resist them and to diminish them by every summonable energy. One might choose to make a new creation different from the one we have inherited. To what purpose? With what likely result?

Many women today report being offended and enraged by the sexist language, sexist structures, and sexist symbols of the Christian church. Being so offended and so enraged are learned, not natural, responses.

The symbol of God as Father is not necessarily related to any other aspect of feminism. We need not get into long controversies over the ordination of women, or whether "oppression" fairly designates the power of men relative to that of women, or any other theoretical issues. Every human being has a human father, and if *that* relationship is no obstacle to feminism, the fact that the Christian God calls Himself "Father" but not "Mother" should be no obstacle. Still, what does that selection of symbol mean?

One might begin by listing all the human experiences in which mothers and fathers differ. It would be wise to concentrate on matters accessible to simple people in all cultures, since biblical symbols address all humans everywhere. In their bodies and their minds, in affect and in sensibility, there may be differences worth noticing between being a mother and being a father. In some human situations, fathers commonly have superior power; in others, mothers. In sexual love, the experience of each is quite different, as is the experience of childbirth. Even the relation of a father to his sons and daughters seems, classically, to be different from that of a mother to her sons and daughters. The long eons during which fathers were hunters and warriors have, perhaps, left psychic marks. Glands of aggression may also be different. Attitudes toward peace and war may diverge. In any case, a complete profile of differences that persons commonly experience as mother or as father might serve to shed light on the symbol.

I see no reason, either in the abstract or based upon my own experience with women, why God might not have revealed Himself as Mother. The two most saintly Christians I have ever encountered are Dorothy Day and Mother Teresa; in spiritual power, I have met no one their superior. Not only does one often see strong women in politics and war (from Golda Meir, Indira Gandhi, Margaret Thatcher, and Jeane Kirkpatrick to Elizabeth of Hungary and Mary Queen of Scots and most of the reigning monarchs of Europe during several centuries), but one finds them everywhere in daily life—in one's own family and among one's teachers and friends. The capacities of women to extend human achievement are not in doubt. These are not mysterious matters. When a man long loves a woman it is her achievements that he loves; it is these that he admires in his wife, mother, daughters, and associates. Wisdom, courage, insight, endurance, decisiveness, competencies—these are the rocks and jewels of daily life. Men would not find it difficult to worship a God symbolized as Female, Mother, Lover, Woman.

There are, without question, many such elements already symbolized in the Christian God. In Latin and in Greek, many of the favorite names of God are inflected with feminine endings—words like wisdom and grace, power and tranquility. The symbols of the Holy Spirit often suggest the brooding, oceanic presence of the mother. The high role given to Mary the Mother of Jesus imports much of the same imagery into the religious sensibility of the Catholic tradition.

Nonetheless, the Creed says starkly "God the Father," as did Jesus in all his ascriptions of sexual imagery to God. Is there not something to learn from this? Indeed, I think it would be difficult, even for the most determined feminist, to think of the Christian God in a sustained way under symbols of the female and the mother. For a time, from certain angles, to capture certain lights, probably everyone does so. Why we cannot do so more thoroughly remains elusive. Much of the secret, I believe, lies in the fact that our sense of maleness and femaleness is largely inarticulate; it includes a far larger body of memory and experience than we can easily make conscious. The symbol "Father" makes the networks of the mind reverberate quite differently than the symbol "Mother." So many psalms, so many rituals, so many stories reinforce those reverberations. Overturning them would, truly, be as profound as starting a new religion. Its creed would have to be quite different.

Yet the One who calls Himself Father is also the Creator. It is not likely that in creating woman and in setting forth a relation of daughter to Father, He intended to harm either men or women. The love a Father feels for a daughter need fear no rival. The contemporary passion for interchangeability may affect our judgment, however. It seems to me that the Creed—and the symbol, God the Father—will outlive this contemporary passion.

To believe in God the Father is to believe that God calls females and males equally into his own life. It does not entail believing that there is no significant difference between mother and father or that to observe such differences is to be regarded as "sexist." God created them male and female and saw that they were good.

In an ideal world, would it be better if roles and possibilities were interchanged as thoroughly as possible, so that differences between male and female might be as far as possible abolished? One might try to create such a world, as an experiment, to see. Yet already one sees many signs that radical feminism has been much modified during the past fifteen years. Evidence continues to roll in of indisputable physical differences, hormonal differences, psychological differences, cognitive differences, differences with respect to biological "clocks," emotional differences, differences in life experience.

Individuals have only one short life. Today, as always, they must experiment, reflect, choose. Every choice has its price. In believing as I do in this matter, I may be wrong. In philosophy and theology, every thinker sometimes errs, and in many cases errors are ironically more illuminating, by a kind of refraction, than verities. In this respect, the sustained inquiry that constitutes philosophy and theology is not like inquiry in the sciences. Reflections from new angles of vision and from new lines of argument often shed sudden light upon sides of reality never seen before. For this reason, I have found my own faith much illuminated by the work of many to whose conclusions I cannot assent. I have not only special affection for but a profound sense of gratitude to feminist colleagues like Carol Christ, once a student of mine, for stubbornly honest, brave, and illuminating work.[6]

Human life is a journey through time. That journey ends for each and for all, and each must choose while consciousness lasts which story to tell. All such stories are precious. Even those who explore unmarked territory and find it, in the end, inhabitable are benefactors of the others. Henry Adams wrote a century ago of the role that Christianity played in the feminization of Europe, under the symbol of the Virgin, and of the secular masculinization of the West, under the symbol of the Dynamo.[7] Some feminists today, ironically, reject the Virgin and idealize the Dynamo. Perhaps this is because the Dynamo altered the daily conditions of the life of millions of women. It opened a window of opportunity for womankind. It is quite remarkable to see so many brave women become explorers, pioneers, adventurers.

Sons do not approach their earthly fathers as daughters do. Would it be surprising to find that the inner life of females is, on the whole, different from the inner life of males and that, in particular, their paths to God are fraught with different dangers?[8] It seems likely that we shall learn more and more in coming years about significant differences between the ways in which women journey toward God the Father and the ways in which men do so. We are likely to discover that women adventurers, pioneers, and explorers of our own generation have become locked in new and exceptionally rich and complex struggles with God.

God the Father is a combatant. He appears to love with a special love those who wrestle against Him. Job, too, cursed Him. As some women learn a certain self-assertiveness (there are many valiant women who have known it from birth, as any son, husband, and father intimately knows) and learn to practice the moves of *machismo,* some may end up not only with the psychological perplexities long encountered by daughters with their fathers but by those also long encountered by sons. Men, too, who are now being tutored by feminists (as well as by Jesus) to be meek and mild, gentle and peaceable, are likely to face a new stormy period with the Father Almighty and Lord of History. A revolt among men is surely brewing.

To believe in God the Father is not to seek peace. It is to enter into turbulent inner war. The peace that this God gives not only surpasses understanding but, altogether too often, attainment. To believe in Him is to accept the peace that comes through combat, the light that comes through harsh purgation.

In his lucid, poetic, and profound commentary on St. John of the Cross, the doctoral thesis he completed in 1948 just after his experiences in World War II, Karol Wojtyla, later to become Pope John Paul II, concludes his research with a passage from St. Thomas Aquinas. In approaching God, human understanding must undergo a sustained purgation. Much that hinders and distorts must be purged away. The way of this purgation is through darkness, suffering, night, and nothingness. Here male and female undergo purgation alike, as did St. Teresa of Avila and St. John of the Cross, companions in many trials and struggles during turbulent years. In prescient synthesis of their later teaching, Aquinas wrote:

There are two kinds of purity. The first is a dispositive purity that prepares for the vision of God, and this consists in the purgation of the affections from all inordinate attachments. This purity of heart is attained by means of virtues and gifts that pertain to the affective powers.

The second kind of purity of heart is quasi-perfect in relation to the vision of God. It is a purity of the mind purged of all phantasms and errors, so that the propositions concerning God are not received by means of corporeal images nor heretical distortions. This purity is effected by the gift of understanding.

Similarly, the vision of God is twofold. One is perfect vision whereby the divine essence is seen; the other is imperfect, whereby although we do not see what God is, we see what he is not. And the more perfectly we know God in this life, the more we realize that he exceeds anything that the human intellect can comprehend.

Both of these kinds of vision pertain to the gift of understanding; the first to the gift of understanding in its plenitude, as it will be in glory, and the other to the inchoate gift of understanding as it is experienced in this life.[9]

These words are valid and illuminating. They warn those who say they believe in God that they will bring much darkness and distress down upon themselves. For God makes Himself known only through the painful purification of the understanding. "If you would advance to Light, you must go by way of Darkness. If you would attain All, you must go by way of Nothing" (St. John of the Cross).

3. God the Son: True God

And in one Lord Jesus Christ, the only-begotten Son of God,
Born of the Father before time was:
God born from God, Light born from Light,
  True God born from True God;
Begotten, but not made, of one essence with the Father;
  And through Him all things were made.

If it is amazing enough that in our misery there is a God who knows our hearts, it is far more amazing and far more difficult to believe that this God became man—and that, if he did become man, he did so in the person of Jesus Christ of Nazareth. There are many other ways in which one might imagine God revealing Himself. If the God of justice and love is to appear in history, why did He appear in the guise of one who failed, who was crucified, and who died?

Nonetheless, the Christian believes that God did humble Himself in becoming a man, and in particular in becoming such a man as Jesus Christ. If the mind is in awe of God, in and of Himself, it is even more in awe of a God who would share human life as He shared it. Augustine recounts in his *Confessions* how for a long time he refused to believe in such a God:

I judged that such a nature as his could never be born of the Virgin Mary, without becoming intermingled in the flesh. How such a thing as I had figured out for myself could be thus intermingled and yet undefiled I could not see. So I feared to believe that he was born in the flesh, lest I be forced to believe him defiled by the flesh. Now will your spiritual ones gently and lovingly smile at me if they should read these confessions of mine. But such was I at that time.[1]

Furthermore, Jesus Christ not only shows us what God is like, He also reveals something about the structure of human life itself. He suffered His passion, was crucified, and died. The forces of evil and oppression were stronger than He. The liberation He came to bring does not liberate us from the structures of oppression, from evil forces of this world, or from the Prince of Lies. Romano Guardini writes in *The Lord:*

Why did Jesus come? To add a new, higher value to those already existent? To reveal a new truth over and above existing truth, or a nobler nobility, or a new and juster order of human society? No, he came to bring home the terrible fact that everything, great and small, noble and mean, the whole with all its parts—from the corporal to the spiritual, from the sexual to the highest creative urge of genius . . . has fallen away from God. Christ did not come to renew this part or that, or to disclose greater human possibilities, but to open man's eyes to what the world and human life as an entity really is; to give him a point of departure from which he can begin all over with his scale of values and with himself. Jesus does not uncover hidden creative powers in man; he refers him to God, center and source of all power.[2]

Like Poland during more than one thousand years under invading forces of the East and of the West, from the South and from the North, so every Christian must be struck with the power of evil in this world. God Himself would not remove such evil from the life of His Son. If He would not spare His Son, why would He more gently favor us?

The great heresy of our own time would deny this lesson of our faith. It holds that evil in this world is caused by "sinful structures." The utopian side of this belief is that there are sinless structures, and that our salvation in this world comes through these. But this is false faith. There are no sinless structures. Among political economies, for example, there are only more or less free, more or less productive, more or less just; the decisive question is always *compared to what?* Our salvation does not come from any imaginable social technique, social arrangement, or social engineering. Our salvation comes through Jesus, and Jesus suffered, died, and was buried. He was not liberated from sinful structures. Neither shall we be.

In this sense, Christianity is a realistic faith. All who accept this Creed accept the full weight of the flesh, the world, and the forces of evil. These will never disappear in history. We do not, and we cannot, look for such liberation within history. To do so would be to ask more for ourselves than Jesus received. To believe in Jesus Christ is to reject every false utopia, for Jesus came into this real world, He suffered within this real world, and He died at the hands of this real world.

This is not to say that a Christian may not believe in progress, and even in social revolution. It is to say that there is a difference between utopian revolution and realistic revolution. There have been many revolutions in history, but not all of them have improved the actual lot and daily liberties of their citizens. Hannah Arendt wrote wisely of these matters in *On Revolution*. [3] Utopian revolutionaries believe that evil comes from social structures and that when these are overturned, paradise will follow. By contrast, realistic revolutionaries recognize that evil flows from the human heart, that there are no sinless structures, and that, even in working for a revolution, they must give highest priority in thought and action to the checks and balances that will be put in place *after* the revolution. Utopian revolutionaries believe that revolution brings salvation. Realistic revolutionaries recognize that salvation comes not from this world or its structures, but only by faith and in eternity, not here. What Christians must be prepared to face under any possible social order is a struggle in the depths of their souls and in the institutions of this world. No possible stage of worldly liberty or affluence brings salvation. At every stage of human development, however privileged, there continue both the struggle of the soul between evil and good, between grace and self-destruction, and the combat of institutions.

These preliminaries being said, let us go back a little. Jesus is the stumbling block, not so much for the nonbeliever as for the believer. There is a tendency in Christian thought, a tendency that presses upward in every generation, to wipe away this stumbling block. Of course, the assault is seldom made directly. Although Jesus is not removed from the Christian faith, he is spiritualized. As St. Augustine notes, a false mediator is always put in place of the true. [4] Webs of evil are mentally brushed away, and the tangles of history are disregarded.

In contemplating the mistake made by traditionalists at the time of the Second Vatican Council, I fell back upon a single phrase to describe their theological attitude, a phrase that later caught on and came to be used by many other writers: nonhistorical orthodoxy.[5] This phrase had the merit of conceding to the traditionalists their fundamental desire to be faithful, while at the same time highlighting the otherworldly manner in which they had come to think of truth as eternal and unchanging. They had forgotten something important about incarnation. The world in which their theology moved was simpler than the actual world of history. It was a world of thesis, in which real events appeared only as hypothesis.

What the incarnation of Jesus Christ means, however, is that this world is a world of fact. It is a world of event. It is a world, not of geometry, but of stories. Contingency looms large in it. Events occur. And these mere happenings, not at all necessary or essential, but merely matters of fact, have become the axial points on which history turns.

The birth of Jesus Christ did not flow from necessity; it was, rather, a freely given invention of God's love. In Jesus, God manifests Himself not as logical essence, but as contingent fact. Jesus came as a man from a far country, a country that (from our point in time) would certainly rank among the least developed nations, poor, barren, without natural resources, with extremely high rates of illiteracy, infant mortality, and famine. According to eyewitnesses, Jesus Himself was an attractive figure, but virtually no one would on first sight have imagined that He could be God. In Him, God did not reveal Himself with the blinding light of the divine essence manifesting itself. He revealed Himself as a contingent fact, a human person living a human life for a brief time at a precise and relatively confined location in space. Jesus never ventured physically outside a circle of approximately one hundred miles. Most of what lay within that circle was desert.

G. K. Chesterton once described Jesus not as He appears to a believer, but as He appears to anybody, as He appeared to Chesterton himself when he was an agnostic. A critic had said that what we see in Jesus is a recognizable Jew of the first century, with the traceable limitations of such a man, to which Chesterton replied:

Now this is exactly what we do not see. If we must put the thing profanely and without sympathy, what we see is this: an extraordinary being who would certainly have seemed as mad in one century as another, who makes a vague and vast claim to divinity, who constantly contradicts himself, who imposes impossible commands, who where he seems wrong to us would certainly have seemed quite as wrong to anybody else, who where he seems right to us is often in tune with matters not ancient but modern, such, for instance, as the adoration of children. For some of his utterances men might fairly call him a maniac; for others, men long centuries afterwards might justly call him a prophet. But what nobody can possibly call him is a Galilean of the time of Tiberius. That was not how he appeared to his own family who tried to lock him up as a lunatic. That is not how he appeared to his own nation, who lynched him, still shuddering at his earth-shaking blasphemies.[6]

But the heretical spirit is alive in every century. What, then, is our own prevailing heretical tendency? The phrase which most exactly commends itself to me is "nonhistorical neodoxy." Father Donald Keefe of Marquette has remarked that some theologians who have followed Vatican II are equally as nonhistorical as those who went before, although in a different way.[7] For some of the newer activists, it is as if the world somehow started fresh just yesterday, or in any case about 1965. They have broken with the long, complex, historical traditions of the church. They have been so eager to "update" the teachings of the church, and not only to read but to devour "the signs of the times," that they have lost their moorings in Newman, Bellarmine, Aquinas, Augustine, and the rest. No, nowadays they take their purest signals from Jürgen Habermas, Herbert Marcuse, and recent sociology. They are not so eager to be faithful to the past as to the new and up-to-date: *neodoxy.*

This tendency was already apparent at the Second Vatican Council, but many of us failed to see how deep and pervasive the new appetite had grown to be. I interpreted the spirit of novelty about Vatican II as a spirit of creativity. I did not notice the rise of nonhistorical neodoxy. But I should have.

In the declaration on the church and the modern world, for example, in the passages on peace and war, a few dreadful simplifications occur. One reads in these passages intimations of a world entirely reasonable and without sin: a world without war.[8] This is not Christian experience. This is not the experience of Jesus Christ. The scriptural texts that ground the vision of peace (Micah, Isaiah) record an ancient, but never yet fulfilled, dream. We must, nonetheless, plod along within history itself, in this poor world as it is, as did Micah, Isaiah, and Christ.

"One Lord." The "liberation" brought by Karl Marx has never yet, in any nation, resulted in political or civil liberation, nor has it resulted in liberation of the human spirit. Marxist thought is attractive to many Christians, for it does speak about "liberation from oppression" and it does purport to be an "option for the poor." Yet it defines poverty in terms of money income, the ownership of property, and social class. It consists in a materialistic interpretation of poverty grafted onto a materialistic metaphysics. Some hope to avoid the materialistic metaphysics, while holding on to the materialistic analysis of social structures. This is an advance, but it does not go far enough.[9]

Even Marx held that the poor working classes, even in their unions, could not be the vanguard of the revolution. They would have to be led by those—necessarily from the educated bourgeoisie—who possessed true revolutionary consciousness. Marx held that even this consciousness is materialistic at its base. But there is no reason why others cannot notice that "consciousness," especially "true consciousness," is a rather more spiritual reality than Marx sometimes seemed to allow. (Marxist scholars debate whether Marx was *really* materialistic in his views or humanistic.) Whether metaphysically Marx really intended to exclude spirit and liberty from reality or not, his analysis of social structures is plainly materialist. The triumphant revolution of which he is the herald is a revolution in physical power and material ownership and social management. In these things he places domination.

Our Lord Jesus Christ has a very different view of poverty. Empty souls may characterize some persons of great material wealth. Those poor in the things of this world may be rich in God's eyes. Commenting on the Psalms, St. Augustine observed among those to whom he preached:

It is not a matter of income, but of desire. . . . Look at the rich man standing beside you: perhaps he has a lot of money on him, but no avarice in him; while you, who have no money, have a lot of avarice.[10]

For a Christian, "poverty of spirit" is a good. Such poverty is found in a heart given solely to God, a heart without attachment to the things of this world. In this sense, Christianity always has "an option for the poor." Yet insofar as the poor are moved by hatred, envy, and violence, by a desire for and in the spirit of the things of this world, their witness is not Christian. It is not the state of one's bank account—nonexistent or large—that commends one to the Gospels. In this sense, the option of Christianity is not bound to one social class or another. What our Lord Jesus seeks is the whole heart, mind, and soul of those who love Him. In every social and political location, men and women are called to do His work. In the sense that the rich and powerful have more resources, more is demanded of them. In the sense that the poor suffer more and have fewer resources, their situation cries out for greater material assistance and more immediate attention.

To serve the poor is, in a special way, to serve God. The Christian attitude toward the poor is quite different from that of the Marxist or the liberal humanist, however, for what the Marxist sees in the poor is a steppingstone to power, and what the liberal humanist sees is an object of compassion. For the Christian, the poor are remarkable since, in serving them, one serves Christ. The use of the poor as an ideological weapon is regarded by the Christian as a temptation, not as an ideal. It is entirely compatible with Christianity, however, even inspired by it, that one should labor to construct a political economy that respects the dignity and liberty of the poor while diminishing everywhere the ravages of material want.

As on poverty, so also on liberty, the gospel of Jesus is different from that of Marx. Liberty of conscience is of the essence. But such liberty also implies full freedom of association. Spiritual liberty also implies political and economic liberty. Concerning systems of political economy, Christians may have many diverse points of view. No system in history has been, is, or will be without sin. None will ever represent the full City of God.

Our Lord Jesus does not instruct us to place our faith in the structures of Caesar or in the structures of Marx, nor even in the structures of Jefferson. We may, indeed, prefer Jefferson to Caesar and Marx, and even hold that a society constructed as Jefferson would construct it is more compatible with the sinful yet graced nature of human beings as Jesus saw them than are the societies constructed by all the Caesars and Marxs of this world. Still, Jesus, not Jefferson, is the one Lord. The Kingdom of this Lord is "not of this world." But it is, quite plainly, *in* this world and within each one of us, at work in institutions as yeast in dough.

"The only-begotten Son of God." Our Lord Jesus is not, alas, the only-begotten Daughter of God. Surely, God, being history's Lord, could have chosen to enter history *either* as a daughter *or* as a son. He could even have entered history as *neither,* in the form of a pure spirit or, in modern terminology, a pure *person,* neither male nor female. The presence of angels—spiritual persons who act with insight, decision, love, that is, with all those activities we properly associate with personhood—was well known in the ancient world. Angels are unique and individual, subjects of insight and will, bearers of a proper name: Michael, Gabriel, Lucifer, Beelzebub, Raphael, and so on. In the biblical narrative, God often did enter history through the nunciature of angels. He could have chosen the form of an angel for His appearance as the Messiah. In that case, however, He would not have appeared in history as a human being, but as an emissary superior to human beings. He wished to assume the lowliest form. He came as a Son. He wished to be seen with the eyes, heard by the ear, touched by the hand. He came as one sex, not the other.

Nonetheless, conjoined with "Son of God," the emphasis of "only-begotten" falls not upon the entry of the Son into history, a free decision of God, but rather on the eternal generation of the Son from the Father. This is a generation not of choice but of necessity, rooted in the nature of God. No analogy for God's inner life is satisfactory, of course, some only less and some more so. Yet it is instructive that even for eternal generation the analogy of Son to Father is used, and that the analogy of Mother to Daughter will not work. So constrained, the Creed chooses the one analogy, not the other. Whether it is a question of the incarnation of the Son *in history*, or of the *eternal* generation of the Son from the Father, in both cases the masculine imagery is present.

These reflections do not entirely satisfy me. In trying to trace the ways of God, the mind falters. Nonetheless, the Creed asserts the one analogy, not the other, in a way that seems proper and just, unforced and natural. To think of these images as "patriarchal" rather than "matriarchal," however, seems to go too far. It is not *rule* by the father that is in question. It is, rather, the eternal generation of the Second Person by the First, both remaining One.

"Born of the Father before time was." Born of the Father, not the Mother. An odd choice of symbols. As in the brooding presence of the Godhead, images of femininity might have been equally effective and rather more touching to most humans. It is a universal human experience that during the first years of life one's mother is the source of nourishment and love, touch and kisses, fondling and constant presence. After many months of being carried, the child comes forth from the mother's womb and suckles at the mother's breast. A child's consciousness of its father is, in important human ways, secondary and learned later. For most of the peoples of history, the father is for the infant a more remote figure.

"Before time was," nevertheless, we are led to imagine not the Mother but the Father. And we are instructed to imagine the relation of God the Son to God the Father not at all as the relation of a child to a mother but, rather, as a son to a father. God is generated from God—in some obscure mystery of language—not as a child is generated from a mother but as a child is generated from a father. What can this mean?

Meditating on mysteries clearly intended not to reveal their secrets unequivocally, I have come to think as follows. In human birth, the identity of the mother is beyond dispute. From a certain womb the child clearly comes. But who is the father? That origin is rather less certain. The direct assertion of paternity is, in this sense, clarifying. Yet there is more to it than that. In the generation of a child, the mother receives and nourishes the seed over many months; the implanter of the seed acts more directly, more remotely, and in a limited way. The act of conception is more hidden, far more difficult to date and to define, than the act of implantation. To think of God as Father, however improper if taken literally, is to imagine agency of a sort different from that implied in thinking of God as Mother. To think of God as Son is to propose a quite different religion from one that, however noble, would think of God as Daughter.

Here C. S. Lewis makes an important point. Rationality seems to be on the side of those who think sex makes little difference with respect to God (or human acts). Clearly, females are as intelligent, capable, virtuous, and graced as males. Clearly, too, women can represent the human community as well as men can. Women are also, in holiness and piety, as "God-like" as men. Then Lewis turns the point around. Of course, a good woman may be like God; but can one say that God is like a good woman? Can one pray to "Our mother which art in heaven," or consider the Second Person of the Trinity as "the only-begotten Daughter of God," or think of the church as the bridegroom and Christ as the bride? "Now it is surely the case," Lewis writes, "that if all these supposals were ever carried into effect we should be embarked on a different religion." He continues:

Goddesses have, of course, been worshipped: many religions have had priestesses. But they are religions quite different in character from Christianity. . . . Christians think that God Himself has taught us how to speak of Him. To say that it does not matter is to say either that all the masculine imagery is not inspired, is merely human in origin, or else that, though inspired, it is quite arbitrary and unessential. And this is surely intolerable: or, if tolerable, it is an argument not in favour of Christian priestesses but against Christianity. It is also surely based on a shallow view of imagery. . . . a child who has been taught to pray to a Mother in Heaven would have a religious life radically different from that of a Christian child. And as image and apprehension are in an organic unity, so, for a Christian, are human body and human soul. . . . One of the ends for which sex was created was to symbolize to us the hidden things of God. One of the functions of human marriage is to express the nature of the union between Christ and the Church. We have no authority to take the living and semitive figures which God has painted on the canvas of our nature and shift them about. . . .[11]

When we think carefully about the time "before time was," before there were human beings—mothers, fathers, children—we realize that God is neither Father nor Mother. God is not sexed. God is not embodied as humans are. Our human metaphors fail to describe God's essence, God's substance, God's way of being. Whether I am male or female, God's way of being is far different from my way of being. He does not have a body like mine. Nor does He have the relation to other males or females of the sort that I, being male, have. God is neither daughter nor son, mother nor father, as we are.

Augustine chooses, therefore, a less physical symbol to express the generation of one from the other than the physical symbol of fatherhood and sonhood. He chooses the generation of the *verbum* (the word, the concept) from the act of insight. Augustine draws here upon a common human experience. Sometimes we see the point of a story, problem, joke, or sequence of events and exclaim, in a burst of insight, "I have it!" Then, with all eyes turned to us, we sometimes labor to bring forth in telling words what we have seen. In this sense there is a distinction between the burst of light, as it were, in which we first grasp the relevant connections, and the fully formed *verbum,* perfectly expressing that insight. Without the *verbum,* the insight cannot be stated. Without the insight, the *verbum* either does not come or seems wooden, by rote, unconvincing. One gives birth to the other. Every teacher learns that it is not enough to give one's students the *verbum* to memorize; the art of teaching consists in leading students to the point at which the living insight flashes for them, too, so that the paternity of *verbum* comes within their possession. In this relation of concepts to living intelligence Augustine saw a metaphor for generation that expresses, although from afar, how God the Father is related to God the Son, the Word spoken in history. The Word reveals its origin. The human encountering the Word grasps it as his or her own only in being received into the living insight from which the Word is begotten: by dwelling in God.

The Word has been spoken in history in the life and death of Jesus Christ. Yet to grasp this Word, one must grasp—more exactly, be grasped by—the light whence the Word springs. This Word grasped in history was begotten before history, "before time was."

"God born from God, Light born from Light." There is a distinction to be observed between the Word spoken in history and its Speaker, but the Creed insists upon their unity. The Word spoken speaks of God, speaks God, is God—God born from God. The Light grasped in the Word is the Light that gives it birth—Light born from Light. So as not to be in the least ambiguous, the Creed further insists: *"True God born from True God."* We are warned clearly not to imagine that Jesus, our one Lord, is a creature of God, a representative of God, a messenger from God, a symbol for God. He is true God.

These are, intellectually, almost insuperable words. They break the mind. Jesus of Nazareth is Lord God of all. God. The mind reels as if under the impact of fireworks in the night: noise, thunder, blinding flash, cascading sparks. A man who is God—the same God who is "maker of heaven and earth and of all things, visible and invisible." How could God continue to have made Himself so vulnerable, so difficult to accept? And if He did so enter history, why not with greater effect? Why in such an easily dismissed way? Is Jesus clearly so much better than Socrates, or Goethe, or Camus, or any others among the human beings we honor as the best of our race? It seems untoward that God should disguise Himself in so humble a form. The Creed, in any case, insists upon not being misunderstood.

"Begotten, not made, of one essence with the Father." The Lord Jesus is not manufactured, created, made, but begotten, spoken by, generated from, fully expressive of, of one substance with the Father.

There it is, again, *Father.* A symbol of generativity is required. Somehow, not only in biblical times but in our own time, the symbol *Mother* will not do. In the eyes of God, no question, males and females are equally dear, equally responsible for their own destiny. Yet, symbolically embodied as males and females, as mothers or fathers, sons or daughters, they do not have an identical relationship to generation. The *verbum* does not proceed from an insight as a child from a womb. An "only-begotten Daughter of the Mother" would not as exactly express the relation of the Word to the Almighty. We speak of the *verbum* as a concept; one conceives ideas. What implants the ideas is the active insight. The receivers of the Word—"Be it done to me according to Thy word"—are perfectly parallel to the Woman. The generator of the Word is perfectly symbolized in the image of the Father. The relation of the Light to the Word, Light born from Light, is tightly expressed in observing this difference between the sexes. Light begotten from Light is more like a child begotten by a Father than like a child conceived by a Mother. By insisting upon *Son* rather than Daughter, furthermore, as the symbol of the only-begotten, the Creed stresses a closer identity between the begetter and the begotten. Such reflections reinforce in one's mind the incarnational nature of Christianity. Christianity respects the limits, the differences, the concrete particulars of this world. It does not spiritualize our bodies away. It finds in their differences links to the nature of God.

"And through Him all things were made." Things are particular. They are made this way, although they might not have been. The world of possibles is quite different from the world of actual things. Actual things are delicious in their *thisness.* The quality of the light and the air of Palo Alto, where I once lived, is not that of Bayville, or Syracuse, or Washington, and the trees in our yard in each place were utterly distinctive. Each of our three children is so different from the other two. Each *thing* and *person* is, or seems to be, without a double, is itself. Yet all things were made *through Him.* In some way, each reveals Him. Each is a word spoken by Him. Each is a revelation of Him. Holding a snowflake in one's hand or a twig or a shell swept up on the beach, one is holding an image of Him. Our minds are constantly driven toward Him. Each moment is alive with Him. Respect for the contrariness, diversity, inimitability of things is a condition for learning of His infinity. All things made bear the pattern of Him through whom they await us along our path. "The world is charged with the grandeur of God" (Gerard Manley Hopkins).

In order to find God, therefore, it is not wise to reduce particular things to kinds, types, essences—to look, as it were, for invisible centers that reveal sameness. It is not correct to spiritualize things, looking beyond what the hand touches, the eyes observe, the nose smells. It is far wiser to study their contrarieties, their differences, their uniqueness, their *thisness.* Each thing is, as it were, a word uttered by the Word, an echo, a timbre, an accent of His. Each reveals whence it springs. Each may be loved as a gift. (My pen, this paper, this smooth-flowing black ink.)

The human person, of course, is even more distinctive than a thing. For each person is not only unique as each tree or puppy or rock is distinctive. Each is also an originating source of insight and choice. Each is not only a word spoken but a speaker. Each person is the teller of a tale, the liver of a life: a tale told not by an idiot but by a person able to imagine and choose, *an inventor.* A tale told also by *a discoverer.* [12]

For, in part, the secret of life is to discover who one is, to explore the particularities that the Word made uniquely in this self, and to utter it back fully in the universal chorus. In part, each of us discovering our uniqueness, we are also called to improvise and to invent, to use our liberty to its fullest to find unexpected resources in ourselves, not to hide from insecurities and to bury our talents safely, but to be a new voice, in this way imitating the Creator, uttering His word.

Our sexual differences, for example, do provide us with different human materials. It is correct, in one way, to see each of us as persons, as distinct from things. No person is an object. In another way, though, it is wrong to imagine ourselves as "persons"; that is, as if we were unsexed. We are embodied persons. To be a male is a different vocation from the vocation of being a female. To have, each of us, exactly the hands, knees, hair, teeth, build we do have is also to be differently called. Our individual anatomy *is* part of our destiny. What we create of it, discover in it, and invent from it is our story.

One of the most impressive differences between being male and being female is a different relation to time. For a man, the generation of a child may occur in virtually any decade of his adult life. For a woman, the "biological clock" is far more constrained. The rhythm of fecundity within each month is also different for each sex. The ancient metaphor that women are closer to "nature" and men closer to "history," and that men *in this respect* have the larger liberty, is founded in reality. The narrative of the life of the female and that of the male is, accordingly, different. To see in this difference the will of God, to cherish it, and to draw out from it its possibilities is part of the prayer of Mary: "Be it done to me according to Thy word" and of the prayer of Jesus: "Thy will, not mine, be done." This prayer unites the sexes, while respecting their differences.

The story of God become man is, like ours, equally a matter of particulars, a destiny, *this* and not *that*. A human story cannot be the story of every possibility. It is a record of choices. A choice of *this* forecloses a choice of *that*. The use of liberty requires the surrender of liberty. It requires one step at a time, one decision at a time. It proceeds by way of a choice, a freely chosen (or at least freely accepted) definition. Little children given full liberty to play immediately define limits. The carpet becomes an island, the woodwork a sea. "You be the teacher, I'll be the pupil." "Pretend this is the edge of the street." We like to think that liberty looks to the infinite, the blue sky of the undefined, for we would like to be angels. It is harder to learn that liberty means the execution of choices, and that every choice excludes possibilities. We mourn lost possibilities; the taste of what might have been is always near our dreams. But we are humans, in flesh and in time, and in each staccato second we choose against many other possibilities to do what we now do. Thus, liberty is exercised by definition.

So it was also with God become human. A choice had to be made: In the form of a woman or in the form of a man?

Jesus came as a man. Suppose he had come as a woman. The same words said by a woman and by a man often have quite different symbolic meanings, depending in part on the social context, but also depending in part upon the differences implicit in maleness and femaleness with respect to fundamental aspects of human life. The male brings forth from himself no new infant, nor does he suckle a child; nor, in making love, are his actions and attitudes, reflexes, and nerves those of a woman.

There is tremendous variety between persons of each sex, between social customs, and between historical eras. Yet Christianity did not come at the same time to all nations. The Slavic nations received Sts. Cyril and Methodius only in the tenth century A.D., Ireland St. Patrick in about the fourth century, Japan St. Francis Xavier in the sixteenth. The historical record is finite, the range of historical circumstances quite large. Consider feminism in this light. Under what circumstances would God have made a clearer revelation of His being had He come as a woman? In some cultures of the world, deities have often been imagined as females. In some religions, priestesses have played central roles. In many cultures and epochs, including our own, empresses and queens have exercised preeminent power. For the God of Christianity to have come in the form of a woman does not seem, on the face of it, to have been impossible for God.

If we further suppose that God would, in either case, have chosen to make the same revelation through roughly the same sequence of deeds and words, would the choice of incarnation as a woman have made any difference?

In certain respects, indeed, the impact of the man-God Jesus upon history has in fact been to feminize Christian cultures, to soften the impulses of warriors and barbarian tribes, to make gentleness, obedience, meekness, and patience paramount civilizing ideals, to create, or at least to nourish, the ideal of the gentle man. Jesus the Christ was manly. Yet it cannot be denied that images of an "effeminate" Jesus are not entirely false to the historical record. Jesus was not warlike, nor did he celebrate the martial virtues, nor praise the lordly virtues. He systematically rebuked the prevailing ways of power and authority. He emphasized an important sort of inwardness: "The kingdom of God is within you."

Whether in Galilee or in Egypt, in Greece or in Rome, among the Franks or the Angles and Saxons, the Huns or the Slavs, the ideal type of manly behavior was that of the hunter and the warrior, the brigand or the knight, the soldier or the legionnaire. Hardly a man in Europe was not, at some time, called into military service. The world for most of its recorded history has been constantly warlike. Every city and town was walled for defense; the countryside belonged to marauding bands. Physical strength was for every settlement a first line of defense.

In such a world, I think, a Daughter of God coming as the Son of God came, speaking of gentleness and humility, would have conveyed a message quite different from that of Jesus. The transvaluation of all values would have been less complete. For women in childbirth and nurture have necessities of peace which the men who protected them could recognize as wholly natural while not being quite their own. The appeal for peace by a Daughter of God would have lacked the voice of contradiction so striking in Jesus. Her voice would have been the voice of nature and nurture, not the voice of contradiction. A woman of peace is not so shocking as a man of peace.

The appeal of Mary, the Mother of Jesus, for the knights of medieval Europe bears out my point. The Queen of Peace, the Madonna, offered Christian Europe a natural, culturally grounded way of expressing the message of Jesus. Behind Mary, however, stood the more severe *Pantocrator*, Lord of All Things, whose law she expressed in such accessible terms. Her motherly humanity touched all. She held the Judge in her lap; but she was not the Judge.

The Christian God is, in a sense, a motherly God. He reveals Himself in Jesus as compassionate and kind, meek and humble, self-effacing, the opposite of domineering. Yet this God is also Judge, impartial, damning some and electing others, at a distance from his children no mother assumes.

4. God the Son: Incarnate

For us men and for our salvation He came down from heaven.
He was incarnate by the Holy Spirit from the Virgin Mary, and
was made Man.
Then, for our sake, He was crucified under Pontius Pilate: He
underwent His passion, and was buried.
On the third day He rose from the dead, as the Scriptures had
foretold.
And He went up into heaven, where He sits at the right hand
of the Father.
He will come again in glory to judge the living and the dead,
and His kingdom will never end.

"For us men and for our salvation He came down from heaven." For
us "humans," but perhaps especially for us "men." Given the actual
ways of the historical world, the salvation brought by Jesus does not,
in fact, bear equally upon men and women. Christianity is rather more
culturally natural to women, less fully contradicts the lessons a woman
learns from nature, and more directly contradicts the laws of a man's
nature and culture. True enough, Christianity treats women and men
equally as hearers and doers of the Word. Each is called to take up a
cross, to do difficult and decisive deeds, and to build up the kingdom.
Women hear a challenge as profound as that heard by men. A radical
equality is manifest. Nonetheless, nature and culture alike teach
women lessons that, applied to males, more sharply contradict the laws
of history. The fate of civilization in Christian lands has long depended
more decisively upon changes made in the ways of men than upon
changes made in the ways of women. For knights and warlords, for
rowdy archers and charioteers, the learning of compassion and gentleness required changes in manners and in substance sometimes expressed as the distance between barbarism and civilization.

For our salvation, it was more symbolically powerful that *He* came down from heaven, than if *She* had come down from heaven. Yet the lessons to be learned from the two sexes come together. They were joined in the image of Mother and Son.

"He was incarnate by the Holy Spirit from the Virgin Mary, and was made Man." Incarnate—assumed body, flesh, knees, knuckles, brows, ears, nose, each to be traced by a mother's hand. As Son of God, he was "begotten, not made," but as Man he was "made" as well as "begotten," made of the body of a woman, Mary, flower of the human race. No human person has ever been her superior. No human person, male or female, has better fulfilled the human vocation. For two thousand years entire cultures have been swept up with love of her, about whom so little is known, yet that little classical in its lines: a sorrowing mother, undeterred by her sorrows, faithful utterly. Her prayer, "Be *it* done to me according to Thy word" is that "yes" said both to God and to suffering that Ivan Karamazov could not utter. It is the simple, classical form of every prayer: "Yes." Whatever *it* is, Lord, even if I do not know what is entailed in it, yes. Complete affirmation of the goodness of God, even if one does not know how a good God can demand what He demands. Her prayer was later to be confirmed by her Son: "Not as I will, Father, but as You will." Yes.

Human beings are not privy to the purposes or ways of God. They must extend a tremendous line of trust. God is God, *whatever.* Human history teaches how terrible that *whatever*—that *it,* which He wills—often turns out to be. History is a butcher's bench.

There is another point to learn from the Virgin. The Creator sees all creation as a seamless garment made real in one act of light and love. He created the sexes and their differences. He created the scheme of human generations. He revealed Himself accordingly. So it is not merely the *utility* of choosing to embody Jesus as a Son that moved Him. There is a sort of necessity involved. For if the Word is to enter history as human, and yet evince divine origin, it was indispensable that the Word be born of a woman and be begotten by God. Initiative and agency must be of God. Human nature must be received from a woman. Here gnosticism simply will not do. To regard sex as irrelevant is to declare the Word less than human or less than divine.

Furthermore, if the Word were to have been simply a *messenger* from God, the Word might have assumed either sex. If the Word is one with God, the begotten one with the begetter, the maleness of Jesus is a symbolic necessity, mirroring in an analogical way the relations of Persons in the Trinity. For in the Trinitarian formula, it was essential to observe (against the Arians) that the Son was *begotten* of God, not created by God, of *one substance* with the Father, not separate from Him. The Creed offers us the revelation of the divine processions in the Trinity that is of a piece with its revelation of the maleness of Jesus. In imagining the whole range of His plan of creation and redemption, the Creator made the image of human generation—and, hence, human sexual difference—central to his purposes. Differences in sex are no mere accident to God's revelation of Himself; they are at the center. They are not merely utilitarian; they are a thread necessary to the whole.

The violent contemporary attack upon the maleness of Jesus—even in its vulgarity naming his male organs as irrelevant—presents itself as an attack upon "sexism." It is actually an attack upon the entire scheme of creation. It is, further, an attack upon the divinity of Jesus and upon his humanity as well. For if maleness is irrelevant, so is human nature. And so also is the divine procession of Son from Father. The notion that the sexes are interchangeable (as in the neuter *person*) alters the very nature of the Trinity. The incarnation of Jesus, begotten of the Father in the Virgin Mary, is an encounter between the absolute necessity of the Trinitarian processions and the natural necessity of human sexual generation. At stake is the very center of Christianity, in the revelation given it both about God and about human life.

For simple Christians down through the centuries the virgin birth said plainly that Jesus is both God and man. Meditation upon this mystery of generation prepared the mind and heart to contemplate the unity in the processions of the Trinity, dark and obscure enough, yet set in such light as we are given by our own human experience of generation.

It is hard to imagine a more concrete attack upon the Christian faith than the declaration that sexual differentiation is irrelevant. That thread being ripped away, the entire vision unravels.

"Then, for our sake, He was crucified under Pontius Pilate: He underwent His passion, and was buried." For Christianity, history is not a morality play. The good do not always win. In the image of the Crucified they very often lose. This does not mean that Pontius Pilate wins. He comes and goes upon the stage of history, in every generation, in every regime. His deeds are their own punishment. Still, awesome is the fact of the power of Pontius Pilate. In every generation he puts the good to death, again and again. It is not pleasant to think about the power of evil in history. One likes to believe that, in the end, the good will win, but the lives of individuals are short, and many do not live to see such victory. Victims continue to die and to be buried. During our lifetime alone, millions have been mutilated, tormented, exterminated, pushed in heaps by bulldozers. Evil continues. In the Christian story, evil is not brought to an end. The Kingdom of Lies is not driven off the stage. Not at all. Until the end of time, it will exact victims.

In our day, the moral style of Pontius Pilate is more than usually pervasive. A great many persons listen to the mad passion of extremists, with whom they agree no more than Pilate agreed with the shouts that he liberate Barabbas. Like Pilate, they do not believe, but neither do they wish to argue. They wash their hands. They allow those who shout their will. They retire to morose reflection.

It is similar with the rising tide of Marxist sentiment. Many do not agree, but neither do they wish to do combat. In every age, all that is required for evil forces to gain is for the good to play Pilate. People fear ridicule. They fear censorship. They fear verbal assault on their persons. They are beaten into silence. The power of evil is always immense, in every generation.

"On the third day, he rose from the dead, as the Scriptures had foretold." The resurrection is central to Christian faith, for it means that Jesus is God. It does not mean that historical events have happy endings. Jesus Arisen met doubt just as He had earlier met doubt. The resurrection was a sign that there is another world, more inclusive than this, in God's sight, in which the passion and the death of this life are grasped in a fuller context. But passion and death are not eliminated by the resurrection.

One by one, each of the apostles would undergo passion and death. That they, like Jesus, will "rise again" does not spare them from suffering in this world. The fact of the resurrection instructs them to hold to realities beyond the veil, hidden, believed but not seen. Our resurrection is no less "real" for not being seen, but it does not alter the power of evil and absurdity in this world. It lifts our minds to another order of reality, which enfolds what we see with our eyes as the regions beyond the atmosphere enfold this planet, as the unknown universe enfolds what humans now know, as the mind of the Creator enfolds far more than this creation. The resurrection does not remove any of us from the stupidities and dangers and lies of this creation. It is not a *deus ex machina*. It does not promise a happy ending for history. It promises that the "Light born from Light" is beyond the bounds of history. History remains a vale of tears and darkness. Only a sliver of light under its door has been allowed to shine through. First, each of us must go through the terrors.

"And He went up into heaven, where He sits at the right hand of the Father." He sits, because He does not intervene, does not promise to make life easier for His followers than it was for Him, does not promise to soften its blows. His promise is only that strength sufficient to our necessities will be given us, pardon for our weaknesses, forgiveness for our sins. He offers no silver linings, false comforts, promises of happy endings. Earth is not heaven. He did not transform earth into a vale of holiness and light, not at all. Evil and good struggle as before. Children cry in the darkness as before. Victims are slaughtered as before. The cry of Job still rises from the earth. This Messiah did not bring, either all at once or even gradually, the kingdom of Peace, Justice, Truth, and Love whose coming He announced. It exists, it has been begun, it has been God's life spread on earth from the beginning, but it is for the most part hidden from view. Occasionally, one catches sight of its beauty, which breaks from sudden insight into the holiness of a life lived under intense suffering, hardly visible to the casual eye. Occasionally, one meets a saint and sees. More often, one encounters the saints in books or hears from others of their extraordinary acts of fidelity and courage. Books by and about the saints are critical in the life of each of us, for from such books we are put in touch with insights

and lessons indispensable to Christian living. The world today needs more emphasis on the brilliance of holy lives. We are drowning in mediocrity and shallowness. The tedium of abundant sensation weighs upon us. We need to be awakened to the depths in which the real human drama occurs, the drama of the soul.

This drama is, for the most part, not visible, not even in the church, not even among the Christians who, looking, are not taught to see much of it even in one another. Yet immense combat roars within us. Turbulent battles rage. All too little of that Kingdom's power flashes outward from us. Even in ourselves, we are more aware of faults, betrayals, and resistance than of grace fully free. Poor material are we, for that Kingdom. Yet its battleground lies within us.

"He will come again in glory to judge the living and the dead." His first coming was not nearly enough. For centuries the earth awaited a Messiah who would transform this vale of tears. He came but He did not, certainly not to the watchful naked eye, transform the world. A new yeast He did place in the resistant dough. But He did not make all things new, except in the sense that He revealed the power of God's love and emboldened our hopes, although not our hopes for history. "He will come again" because once was not enough. For a time yet, the struggle must go on, the confused alarums of darkness and of night, in which ignorant armies clash. Yet even while there are humans still living, in a flash, in a trumpet clash, "He will come again in glory," and among those whom "He will judge" will be some who at that moment will be "living" and many who, having lived, are at that moment among "the dead." In an instant, all will stand under judgment.

We often judge ourselves harshly. At moments, which we speedily shake off, so terrible is the self-accusation, we see all that we ourselves have contributed to the power of lies and deceptions, dishonesties and acts of cowardice, selfishness and infantile ways. It is not so easy to love ourselves. It is not even easy to forgive ourselves. The same Lord who instructed us to "love your neighbor as you love yourself" knew how hard a commandment He thereby laid upon us. Most of us most of the time do not much love ourselves. That is why we so desperately need distraction, seek entertainment, flee from ourselves, disguise dreadful insecurities, and are so easily won over by love or by praise from others. We do not, we cannot love ourselves, knowing what is in us. That is why the news that, despite ourselves, God loves us is so powerful. That He would love the saints is easy to understand. (Yet even saints have their harsh edges, as those who live with them well know.) What is touching is that, knowing everything that is true about us, He nonetheless loves us. What is touching is that sinners are at the heart of His love, that He loves us, not for our virtues, but as we are. He made us. He is not deceived by us. There is nothing to fear from His judgment. All has always been known to Him. His judgment is painful only to our own illusions. *He* will not be surprised in the moment of judging. *His* mind will not be changed. It is only our own self-deceptions that will be shattered.

The sentences above are written as though, in fact, we loved the truth, but we do not. In marriage we soon learn that our spouse does not long share our own illusions about ourselves. Yet we cling to them. Many would far rather detach themselves from their spouses than from their self-love. (Let those who fear truth shun marriage.) "The fear of the Lord is the beginning of wisdom." Every lie in us (and there are seven to every truth) fears God. Every pretense and vanity dreads light. So much that we love about ourselves is false. So much that we cannot bear to face is true. The thicker our defenses, the more tangled the stories by which we clothe our nakedness, the more our flesh trembles, the more the dread in our spirit afflicts even our bodies.

God is truth. In this sense, we have nothing to fear. We love lies. In this sense, we dread Him.

"And His kingdom will never end." In our experience lives and kingdoms do end, all of them without exception. Even history will end, when "He will come again in glory." At last, it will all be over, every chapter completed: Not, it seems, having unrolled to a grand climax, tying up all the loose ends, but simply by interruption, like a string being cut. History is not constructed like a play or a novel, it appears, everything contributing to a final denouement. It seems, rather, like one thing after another. At a certain point, at the appointed hour, the string will be cut. Enough already.

Then the reality will be unmasked. We have all been living within the eternal power and light of God, but we have not, of course, seen beyond the walls of the darkened theater in which the stage of history has been set. On that day, the walls will fall. Light will flood us. We shall see, at last, the entire audience before whom we have been playing. We shall acquire a sense of context. We shall see the larger light within which, like shadows on the wall of a cave, our fitful light has been a dim reflection. We shall see how eternity has always enfolded time, and how the eternal God chose within His longer life a life of communion, to create persons to endure history for a moment in order to create such communion as they could and in fallible liberty be drawn to Him who created them. He will honor those who, without seeing, loved Him in darkness. He will honor the choice of those others who, although it was offered them, refused His love. His is a festival of liberty, an honoring of conscience. No one enters His communion without freely choosing to do so. It will be hell to see, later, what one could have chosen but freely did not. It will be hell to have chosen forever to lie, to have deceived, to have damaged community, to have betrayed one's own best self, to have drawn all things, as if one were a god, to oneself.

It is astonishing, in retrospect, to see what we assert in the Creed about this "one Lord Jesus Christ." He was a man, only a man, born of a woman, during an era that some would regard as backward (that a few others, more clearsighted, however, would judge to have been as highly developed as the human race has attained only three or four times in the cycles of its rise and decline), and yet He is also "God born from God, Light born from Light, True God born from True God." Since "through Him all things were made," He is, quite properly, the one who "will come again in glory to judge."

One thinks of the Lord of Eastern Catholicism shown in the mosaics of Ravenna, the Lord, the Maker of all things. This Jesus whom we sometimes love to see as the gentle carpenter of Nazareth is also, we assert, Lord God Almighty, Creator, Verbum, Judge of the living and the dead. A Judge among his peers, having suffered and died as they do, and yet peerless in Light.

Our emotions toward this Jesus are mixed, emotions toward a man and also God, emotions toward one's Creator and also Judge, emotions towards one's brother and also "Light born from Light." One's emotions toward Him are directed toward the light within one's own conscience, in one's own stirrings toward honesty, and they are also directed toward one's own capacities for choice, decision, and love. For these—one's own light within and one's own willing choices—are, darkly, participations in His own life. "I am in the Father, and you in me, and I in you." Jesus in this sense is not separate from us. He is already within. We already live from his life. Our light, such as it is, springs from "Light born from Light." Our love, such as it is, was not created by us but given us by the Creator, as a participation in His own proper life. Our acts of insight, our daily decisions—those activities that make us persons—draw life from the life of God. The more frequent these acts are in us, the more we act in and through God. The more we inhibit or damage or darken them, the more we absent ourselves from His life. "To live is to live in Christ"—to be active in honesty and love. Such is the God, and His relation to us, the poor words of the Creed bind us to. To say these words with attention is to see ourselves as we often forget to do. It is, therefore, to astonish ourselves anew. Such a God, such a claim, such a perception of our poor selves reduces the soul to silence, causes the heart to bound from within, dries the tongue.

And His kingdom will never end. What can this mean, "never end"? Of sequences without end we have no experience. Yet we experience the birth of our children. We experience the death of our parents. Passing forty, we experience how swiftly the years pass. Looking back, we see how inexperienced we were when our children were born, how callow, how young, although then we thought ourselves adult. In those days, diapers and illnesses and sudden emergencies preoccupied us (the fishhook caught in the cheek, the possibly fatal attack of disease, the all-night hospital vigil over a deathly still child). Later, one parent died, then another. We sensed at the gravesite the bond uniting the generations, the damp earth that has received so many generations now. Compared with our short lives, the ages go on forever: *per omnia saecula saeculorum,* as the Latin phrase of the Mass used to echo again and again, *Amen.*

But even the human race expects its end. In a flash, in fire, or in flood. The end of time. Doomsday.

What does it mean, "never end"? There are moments a young man experiences, playing ball, when the slow afternoon seems to go on forever and the game is intense, concentration acute. When parents call or the game ends, such a young man is astonished at the hour. Where has the time gone? The intensity of concentration made the hours seem like a single moment, all cupped up and held to one's lips for a single sweet sip. Hours seemed like a single instant, a bit of eternity within time. This perception (which occurs often in contemplative work like writing, sewing, reading, praying) introduces us, as it were, to the timelessness of which human consciousness is capable. We seem often to have lived outside of time. At such moments, the clock always keeps ticking relentlessly, but we do not notice it. So consciousness is not identical to consciousness of time. It seems capable of an instantaneousness contrary to its normal ways, a summoning up of powers often hidden from attention. Such moments, reflected on, make human beings aware of belonging *elsewhere,* of play-acting, of being in exile, of living a double life.

And this, according to the Creed, is the case. We *are* living in a double context: within time, to be sure, but also within a framework altogether different, within which time in its sequences is the lesser reality. We try to imagine what it is like for God to see all things, past and present and future within a single glimpse, in a *now,* simultaneous and perfect, even though for those within the sequences of time perspectives are necessarily different. Now, at this moment, God sees all my future days, my death, and all that follows for my children and my children's children, just as He sees—which we do not—all that went before us, for us the past, for Him the present. Eternity is an instant. It is not a long time. It is life complete, understanding full, love entirely ripe. A world "without end" is not a world whose end lies ever ahead; it is a world simultaneous. It is the presence of God from God, Light from Light, true God from true God, in which the only Son of God is eternally begotten, one in being with the Father.

The world view into which the Creed ushers us is not the world view of common sense, although it is at the edge of common sense, on which it makes frequent, often daily, impressions. Things pass. All things pass away. The Lord abides forever. Again and again we experience how important matters pass. Immense griefs, unendurable at the moment, yield to the staccato seconds and then further seconds until, finally, to our surprise, we find one day we have not been conscious of the grief, it has been healed, or covered over. Life goes on. Great moments of exultation similarly pass, and we seem again at the bottom of the bleak valley, in the desert, dry of mouth, faint of hope. The constant, unremitting experience of change teaches us that the things of time, however deeply they impress us, lack full and permanent reality. Something in ourselves abides. (Is it a "something"? Is it "in" ourselves? Mysterious to ourselves is our self, our consciousness, our oddly detached, ever questioning, always questing self.) "Our hearts are restless, Lord," Augustine prayed, "until they rest in Thee." So he, too, dark man of Africa that he was, of bounding heart and aching sensuality, of fiercely hurrying pen and ruminative eye, appeared in flesh upon this earth and passed from it, more centuries before Aquinas than Aquinas is from us. Does Augustine still abide? Immortal, unquenchable yet resting, active, enjoying simultaneity of light, dweller in that City of God larger than and embracing this plodding, slow, play-acting City of Man?

"His kingdom will never end," that kingdom whose reality, He said, is already within. We are already living in it, although we fight against veils, curtains, rushing breezes, never quite enjoying what we have, separated from it and yet drawing sustenance therefrom, in expectation. We are living from a life we scarcely see, of which there are only intimations. We are not what we seem. We see each other, but not truly, for there is more to each of us than any have eyes to see. We are mysterious to each other. The root of our respect and of our awe, the intolerable burden of suspecting grandeur we cannot quite get into focus, is taught us by this Creed.

What the Creed teaches us about ourselves is awesome, for it teaches us that we are not what we seem, bundles of chemicals and passions, entrapped within a drama we are neither masters of nor worthy of. A play within a play, our lives: we waste the days all the while aware that hidden meanings are embodied in our deeds, respectful lest we miss some cues, crashing ahead impatiently, forgetting, maddened by the partial light and the impartial darkness. Our play will have an end. Up will come the lights, without end.

The drama implicit in this Creed exceeds all others, without destroying them. *Redbook* magazine reported once that religious women—to the surprise of secular researchers—enjoyed sex more. Generations of apologetics for the freethinker fell to dust. Sex imagined as eternal drama is more than sex as itch or loneliness. The struggle of the soul —two souls—has turmoil in it playmatehood may lack.

The soul has mystery in it, which the Creed respects.

5. God the Holy Spirit

And I believe in the Holy Spirit, Lord and Life-Giver, who
proceeds from the Father and the Son;
Equally with the Father and the Son he is worshipped and
glorified;
and he has spoken through the prophets.

Least visible in Scripture and in life, the Life-Giver is neither the
Father nor the Son, but the Love in whom they issue: the Holy Spirit,
Paraclete, Fire, Breath, Dove, Presence, Inspiriter, "Love that moves
the sun and all the stars." The Christian God is one. Monotheism is
the proper designation of Christian belief. And yet the Creed distinguishes, as do the Scriptures, as if to teach us that God is not best
imagined as the solitary, lonely *Nous* of Plato, Aristotle, and the
mystics East and West, but rather as a community of Persons: Three-
in-One.

Among Jews a sense of community is rooted in the peoplehood of
Israel, a sense of community reinforced since patriarchal times by
millennia of persecution. Perhaps no people in world history is as
self-conscious and well organized. Even the enemies of Judaism con-
spire to oblige Jews, even those Jews who would rather not be self-
aware, to recall that whatever they may think of themselves their
enemies regard them as Jews. (Seventy percent of the informal efforts
of the United Nations are said to be devoted to assaults on Israel.)
Probably no community of human beings anywhere in the world has
suffered more at the hands of others, even unto the threat of total
annihilation—a threat systematically enacted until about half of all the
living Jews of our time had been brutalized and burned to ash in the
crematoria of Europe. Perhaps no community has been as generous

and solicitous, not only of its own members but of others who are in distress. Even in daily life, one meets few persons of greater internal strength, compassion, and human warmth—tried, as it were, by fire. "See these Jews," one sometimes is tempted to express in the age-old phrase Christians are supposed to emulate, "how they show concern, one for another." The prodigies of Jewish organizing and mutual help defy imagination; one can hardly believe what one encounters. Still today, in many ways, the people most to be imitated by Christians, most properly the instructors of Christians, are the Jewish people whence Christians spring.

In the Jewish testament, there are already foreshadowings of the Holy Spirit, the giver of life, the Spirit of God brooding over the waters. In some ways, indeed, the *Jahweh* of Israel is best imagined under the symbols Christians use for the Holy Spirit: Jahweh is the breath of life, fire, compassion, love, the abiding presence, the light within the law, the light of the mind, the Almighty best approached through study and meditation, the Teacher, the Inspirer.

The rigorous monotheism of Judaism was born in opposition to the polytheism of surrounding peoples. From a Jewish perspective, the thought that Jesus is the Son of God—true God of true God—seems blasphemous, for Jesus is too weak, too unsuccessful in combating evil, and in the course of the history of Christianity too obviously a source of anti-Jewish action. He is "a stumbling block to the Jews" (1 Cor. 1:23), that is, a scandal.

Hence, where Christianity in its faith that Jesus is True God of True God differentiates among the Persons of God, seeing in the very nature of God a community of Persons, Judaism attains an analogous religious consequence through its everyday experience: *to be is to be with people.* To live Judaism is to live a communitarian life. The Christian aim is analogous—how could it be otherwise, since Christianity aims to be a continuation of Jewish conviction, a fulfillment rather than an abrogation of what the Creator had covenanted with his people? For Christians, who do not share the ethnic and cultural homogeneity of the Jewish people, but who are gathered from all peoples, the sense of community cannot spring from the same identical sources as Jewish community. Thus, the symbol of the Trinity is exceedingly important to Christian faith, since it establishes in the Christian conception of the Godhead the same principle: that to be is to be with others. So to speak, that which is most really real in human life gives rise to human notions of the nature of God. For Christians as for Jews, what is most really real—what gives life its meaning, its savor, its fulfillment —is the community of persons. Christians attribute this mode of being to God.

For Jews, both the imperative of monotheism and the rejection of Jesus as God block affirmation of the Trinity. On the face of it, then, and at considerable depth, the Jewish and the Christian conceptions of God diverge. Nonetheless, there are many indications that this divergence is not, after all, so radical as may at first appear. No one sees God. No concept of God is adequate. Christians do not pretend that the vision of God as Trinity, a vision grounded in the revelation of God's nature brought by Jesus, is any other than a mystery, dark and too full for intellect to plumb. To know God is to do his will. In a certain sense, then, the *operational* meaning of believing in God the Father, God the Son, and God the Holy Spirit—Three-in-One—is decisive. For Christians, the operational meaning is to love one another. It is to respect the reality of persons in community. Not everyone who says "Lord, Lord," enters the kingdom of heaven. No one sees God. Therefore, the test people face concerning the accuracy of their faith is whether or not they love their neighbor—not the neighbor whom they do not see, but the neighbor of everyday life; not the abstract "humanity" but the actual persons, with all their deficiencies, encountered in a particular time and place.

The Christian Creed does not instruct Christians in the faith of Judaism; the two faiths are different. Nonetheless, particularly in operation, the two faiths issue in the same practical principle: to be is to be with people; to live is to build community; to honor God is to honor persons. This is the ground of practical alliance between Christians and Jews, even while they each observe faithfully those things that separate them. To speak of God as Christians do is to give offense to Jewish faith. To speak of God as Jews do is to give offense to Christian faith. The two faiths are not identical. For both, the identity of God is shrouded in mystery. For both, God is conceived in terms appropriate to an agent conscious, intelligent, choosing, doing, and loving—God is person. God is not a person as human persons are persons, embodied in time, limited by human flesh. About Him, silence is best. One cannot properly name God as one names other realities of human experience. Yet the human being does, in both traditions, experience God's presence and His love, His unknowable ways and the suffering reserved for those that love Him. In both traditions, the signs of the true servant of God are remarkably similar. How could it be otherwise, among brothers and sisters, creatures of the same Creator, children alike of the covenant of Abraham, Isaac, Jacob, and Moses?

The destinies of Christians and Jews are the closest of all the world's religions. Particularly in the bearing of religious faith upon social, political, economic, and cultural concerns in this world, the vocations of Jews and Christians are remarkably analogous. Both are narrative religions. Both are religions of The Book. Both religions teach respect for this world, for the flesh, for the concrete. Both religions instruct their members in a vocation not merely to escape from this world but to change this world. Both find the historical task of modernization a challenge, yet a challenge to be taken up in faith and in hope. More easily than any other of the major religions both seem to adjust— although not without enormous struggle—to modern urban life. Both have a commitment to intellect in its rational and scientific parts as well as in its mystical, poetic, and intuitive parts.

The Christian Creed articulates the Christian conception of God in a differentiation of Persons rejected by Judaism. Yet so far as practical life goes, and by its own traditions, Judaism seems to attain analogous results.

Thus, to say that the Holy Spirit *proceeds from the Father and the Son* is to suggest, for Christians, a meditation on processions. As fiercely as Jews, Christians are monotheists. There is one God and one God only. Yet the belief that Jesus is true God of true God forces the Christian mind to find some way of articulating its understanding of the unity of God, in a way not forced upon Jews. Christian intellect did not easily find a way to do this. From the beginning and through the controversies of the Middle Eastern period of Christian history, especially in the third and fourth centuries, many false attempts were made. For some it seemed easier to believe that Jesus is not precisely God but some special emissary, illumination, or radiance of God visible in human form. This way of thinking saved the unity of God, but it saved that unity at the expense of the humanity of Jesus. (Saving the unity of God was a greater concern to Arianism than to most forms of gnosticism.) Jesus was an appearance only, a seeming human, a radiant apparition of the Godhead. Or, on the other hand, Jesus was a real man of flesh, a sort of puppet in the hands of God, a creature of God.

The Creed that Christians say in the churches, however, went farther than this. Descended from formulae used in the times of the apostles, from recapitulations used publicly in the generations just after the apostles, and from formulae worked out by and fought for by certain bishops and laity with Athanasius, bishop of Alexandria, this creed insists *both* upon the unity of God *and* upon the differentiation of the Persons of God. Here the orthodox party made use of certain Greek philosophical concepts: *substance, nature,* and *person.* These concepts were newly invented to articulate this particular problem, yet they were drawn into use (and they proved quite useful, indeed).

"What does it matter?" some devout persons might say. "The important thing is to praise God, not to define God correctly. Why enter into metaphysical discussion, around such formidable abstract words?" This problem was compounded by the catechetical practice of the early centuries. In those days, the innermost teachings of the Christian Creed were kept secret, even from many Christians at the beginning of their conversion. Christian life was imagined as "a way," "a journey," and in the first steps of the way it seemed counterproductive to say too much. This was for two reasons.

On the one hand, the most important matter was for the convert to begin living in a new way. Christianity understood itself to be a new way of life, under a new covenant and a new law. Thus, the beginner in Christianity was expected to show signs of living in this new way, practicing new moral skills and virtues, sharing new forms of discernment, giving evidence in behavior of the workings of God's life within. Only slowly were new goals established, new puzzles presented. Early catechists recognized that Christianity is in many ways counterintuitive. It is *not* the ordinary way of the world and the flesh and common sense. It requires a transformation of ordinary values; these are not so much rejected as deepened and surpassed. Insight into the new ways of seeing, thinking, feeling, and acting cannot, in the ordinary case, come all at once. Beginners must walk before they can run. One insight prepares for another. "Do not cast your pearls before swine," early Christian teachers counseled one another. Do not offer more than beginners can absorb. Lead beginners into the mysteries according to their own natural rhythms, accomplishments, and needs. Concentrate on how they *live,* not on the words they repeat. Understanding is shown in living, not in verbal facility. Christianity is a way of *real assents,* not *notional assents,* as Cardinal Newman came to express this point (after long study of the early church fathers) in *A Grammar of Assent.*

The second reason was fear of ridicule by sophisticated unbelievers. The early Christians knew that Christianity had a vision of life at odds with those taught in the most advanced schools of the Mediterranean basin at that time. Yet, paradoxically, Christianity was also *consonant* with many of the best insights of the best thinkers of antiquity; so, at least, early Christian converts in the schools experienced it, as Origen did and later Augustine. But the task of separating what was consonant from what was dissonant required many painstaking hours of reflection, and someone had to undertake the risky task before others could assess results. In the meantime, a simple recital of Christian beliefs would invite such amusement that the bright and the inquiring would be prevented from undertaking the necessary intellectual discipline. Moreover, ridicule often enough led to public condemnation and death. Thus, early Christian teachers proceeded with circumspection. No full Christian Creed was published. The Christian mysteries were closely guarded. Christians appealed to the public first by the manner of their lives. Only then would curiosity be sufficiently piqued that useful disputation could begin.

In those days, world views had a public character. They were argued for and against, in a context suggesting considerable public and even political importance. In general, unitary regimes conveyed not simply political and economic authority but also religious and moral legitimation. To challenge state religions was *prima facie* to challenge the state. There was virtually no private space—at first, not even a church building—that the state did not in principle (and, often enough, in practice) invade. Consider Iran under the Ayatollah Khomeini, with its slaughter of three generations of the leaders of the Baha'i faith in five years, for a modern example of what the unitary regimes of the past were like. We speak today of the "privatization" of religion. By this is meant the social device according to which the civil order no longer commands the religious conscience of the individual. While religious communities are today allowed to function publicly, even with direct public subsidies (as in Europe) or with tax exemptions (as in the United States), religion benefits by an ample social and private realm. Religion is held to be a matter of private conscience, not of state coercion. By contrast, religion was "privatized" in the pre-Constantinian era in the Mediterranean basin by another device. The state already had its religion. Christianity was allowed little or no public space. It was confined within private homes and the privacy of the head. Even its Creed was privately guarded.

Thus, the step taken by the Christian church in the first quarter of the fourth century was a radical and bitterly disputed step. The formulation of a creed that could be committed to memory and recited publicly, containing language in notable measure not canonized by scriptural precedent, seemed to many a great mistake. It would injure sound instruction in the faith among newcomers by encouraging them merely to recite words they might or might not understand. In one sense, *nobody* would understand, since the Creed summarized the mysteries of faith. In addition, misunderstandings might multiply. Some might glibly recite words and *say* they assented, without being able to state clearly or defend adequately what those words signified. Worse, others might assent *notionally,* but without actually changing the way they lived. The habitual use of a Creed as a device for testing orthodoxy might, in both these ways, be self-defeating and falsify the nature of Christianity.

But the opposite danger seemed greater. To refuse to articulate a creed clear about its basic mysteries would have two fatal effects. It would allow the new way of life to relapse into mere sentimentality, in which individuals really believed exactly what they wished, as long as they publicly said they were Christians. Those who believed Jesus simply an appearance of God would be on equal ground with those who believed Him to be true God and true man. Intellectual clarity would fall in importance; sentimental fervor would rise.

Second, if Christianity were to become a form of feeling and inclination, it would soon become compatible with almost anything expressed as an inspiration of "good will." Christianity would lose respect for orthodoxy; nothing would be heresy.

In either case, Christianity would degenerate into pious mush. The blood of martyrs would have been shed in vain. The revelation of Jesus would be subject to the emotional fantasies and public pressures from the spirit of every age. Christian truth could no longer be described as a two-edged sword; it would collapse like a wet noodle into any shape in which it was pushed.

For such reasons, laity in particular in the fourth century, as Cardinal Newman points out, demanded a clarification of the real Christianity. For a lengthy period, many if not most bishops sided with the priest Arius, whose name eventually came to designate the greatest of the early heresies. The views of Arius at that time seemed to grip a majority of those who claimed to be orthodox. Simply put, the teaching of Arius saved the unity of God by viewing Jesus as less than true God. Profoundly embattled, Athanasius and his colleagues succeeded at the Council of Nicaea in both their main objectives: they committed Christianity to intellectual precision and to respect for unambiguous teaching; second, they cast the die that made Christianity a creedal religion. So doing, they won the methodological battle that determined that Christianity would side with intellect over sentiment, and with words of precision, even if such words could not be found directly in Scripture. In an important way, Nicaea made Christianity a religion not of Scripture alone but of theology and philosophy.

This point is worth a moment's reflection. Many Christians cherish the unmediated access to the Word of God that Scripture offers to all who can hear. To be sure, those who cannot read are nourished by hearing the Word of God preached. But, in that case, the Word of God is mediated by the preacher, who may or may not be a profound and discerning interpreter. Therefore, the Council of Nicaea went beyond Scripture alone and licensed two other forms of mediation. First, a council of bishops made a decision about orthodoxy binding upon the community. Second, they did so through the use of philosophical concepts derived from nonscriptural sources.

In one sense this principle of mediation is consistent with the doctrine of incarnation. As Jesus revealed God by assuming human flesh, so the Council of Nicaea revealed God by assuming human philosophical categories. In both cases mediation is tempered to the necessities of the human being, the person embodied in time, in intellectual history, and in the needs of daily life on earth.

In another sense, the principle of mediation is consistent with the way the human mind works. The human being does not understand everything all at once in a single blinding flash of light. Insights normally depend upon prior insights. There is not much use in teaching Aristotle's *Metaphysics* in elementary school, or even in the university, until students have learned how Aristotle uses key words in earlier texts in physics, psychology, ethics, and the rest. Watching the minds of one's own children develop is wondrous, as questions that earlier went over their heads begin to seem vital to them and as books earlier too difficult for them begin to excite their interest.

The human mind proceeds from insight to insight more often by plodding than by leaping. Yet it does leap too. And the pleasure of an insight being born—the pleasure of suddenly, after much effort, getting the point—is a daily experience. In this respect, the life of the intellect is a quest, a journey, a way. Examined more closely, it is a *procession.*

We arrive, then, at the analogy chosen by Nicaea. The Holy Spirit *proceeds from* the Father and the Son. Consider the way in which insight proceeds from an inquiring mind, the way a concept proceeds from an insight, the way love and joy proceed from a verified insight. Suppose you are unhappy about something that happened at work. You are partly angry with yourself but also with others. There was a nasty emotional tangle and you can't sort out what was *really* going on, although you know something unfair happened and you resent being ensnared in it. In the process of talking over your reactions with your spouse, you describe who said what and how you interpreted it. Your spouse asks questions. At first, everything's a muddle. As you talk, you begin to see some motivations in one person that you had been trying not to see. That person does not deliberately set out to harm others, yet that often seems to be what he does. Suddenly, the personality flaw —the immature, unresolved emotional need—comes into focus. Your face brightens. The dynamics of the tangle stand exposed. "That's it," you say. "I hate that side of Peter. He doesn't mean it. But he always does things like that." You now see why you were angry with Peter, and what it was that seemed so unfair. You realize that Peter doesn't intend to be like that; it's like a lameness, a systematic limp. You remember other examples. The pattern is now clear. From now on, you'll watch out for it and meet it more directly.

In some such fashion, the human mind frequently experiences puzzlement, seeks light, and sometimes finds it. This procession from inquiry to insight is remarkable. For one thing, the intellect itself seems stung to action. It is alive, almost beaten raw by experience, eager to go to work. One of the first requirements of understanding is an active intellect. Those who are unconcerned, casual, or lacking in curiosity do not experience the vitality of the mind as often as those who enjoy inquiry and stand always ready to undertake it, even in the most humdrum matters. The active intellect is like a searching light in surrounding darkness. It is restless until it finds what it seeks, until its questioning finds first, answers, and then, answers that satisfy. You see the difference between the former and the latter if your spouse ventures an interpretation of your experience, as in the case above, that you reject, perhaps by saying: "You don't understand Peter. That isn't what he meant at all." The insight or answer your spouse proposed for the muddle won't do. The search continues.

When a satisfying insight emerges, and when, turning it over a few times, the inquiring mind is persuaded that this insight holds up under all relevant objections, the face itself often brightens. The experience of satisfaction is so powerful that it is quite difficult to hide. A click of the fingers is often insuppressible. "That's it. Of course. I should have seen it at once." But what is *it*? Can the insight be put into words? Perhaps not at first. Some persons are good at intuitions, but less good at articulating them. Others are quick to articulate, even without fresh insight. The two skills are not identical. We have often known that we *know,* even when we cannot (or refuse to) put what we know into so many words. This is inadequate knowing to be sure, but it beats the alternative.

Thus, there is a procession from the active intellect to the insight, and another procession from the insight to the word—the exact word, the just word. In both these processions there is joy.

When the object of the inquiry is an intellectual or aesthetic object, the active intellect fired by insight and formed in the shape of the exact word is frequently moved simply to joyous contemplation. One can regard a painting by Tintoretto or Raphael for time that seems timeless, simply absorbed by its unity. The movement of joy that proceeds from the grasp of this unity in this form is experienced as a sort of love for the good, a kind of unity with it, a kind of being drawn into its own intellectual vitality. Such an object seems to give life, to ennoble, and unity with it seems, on the one hand, perfectly appropriate to one's own inquiring intellect and, on the other hand, greater than it. One loves such objects for the appropriate but superior good that is in them. This procession from insight and word to love is often experienced in intellectual and aesthetic life.

When the object of the inquiry is a situation in the world of action and daily life, the active intellect brightened by insight and formed in a diagnosis, tactic, or strategy is frequently moved to act in a more intelligent and (often enough) more healing, helpful way. Ignorant armies do not need to clash by night; sometimes, insight enables human beings to deal with one another more gracefully. The procession from insight and diagnosis to action also issues, frequently enough, in what without sentimentality might be described as love: due respect for the other person in his or her weaknesses as well as in his or her strengths. For the inquiring intellect is often moved to action by the demands of daily life and tries to find a more intelligent and reasonable way of getting through recurring tangles of emotions. One cannot wish the tangles away. One must learn to negotiate them as healthily as possible. Intellect in action is moved by a procession toward realistic love. For to treat human persons intelligently and reasonably, with exact honesty and appropriate compassion for unwitting weakness, is a high form of love.

These are the processions that lie behind the use by the Council of Nicaea of the expression, "who proceeds from the Father and the Son." If we think of the Father as the insight firing the active intellect, the Son as the exact and just Word for this insight, and the Holy Spirit as the love that attends insight and Word, we have an analogy—an analogy only—for the differentiation the Christian Creed discerns in the life of God. (One should note that the *Filioque*, "and the Son," is a medieval Western insertion in the Creed.) The analogy limps, as all analogies do. It is a poor way of summarizing all the main points that Christianity affirms about God: that God is True Light of True Light, the intelligence suffusing all things; that the Word He spoke in one time, at one place, in Jesus of Nazareth is a just and exact expression, in human form, of His very being; and that this God who reveals Himself as Creator and as Redeemer is the God of love—and that all Three are one, in a way distantly mirrored by the way in which the intellect fired by insight, word, and love is one.

This is not an easy concept of God. It does not violate the unknownness of God, the darkness in which God dwells, for it allows no one to see God or to grasp what God in Himself is like. But this concept does borrow from human experience, from experiences all of us often have, to help us to state in a few abstract words what Christianity wishes to say about the community of life of the One God. It is a statement of monotheism. It is also a statement of community. It is, finally, a statement about what human beings ought to *do* in order more to live in God and more to have God live in them. They should, in short, multiply in themselves, as best they can, both in their personal lives and in their professional lives, the frequency of acts of insight, word, and love. "The kingdom of God is within you" (Luke 17:21). The more humans live the life of the spirit—the procession from active intellect to insight, word, and love—the more they lead God's life.

"Equally with the Father and the Son he is worshipped and glorified." The proper name of God is Love. It is in the procession of the Holy Spirit that we come to that proper name. God is not intellect alone, the Divine Watchmaker in the Sky, the austere all-knowing Eye

of so many images from pagan and scientific inquiry. God is not the God of the Enlightenment only. One comes closer to His nature if one grasps the procession in God from Knower to Word to Love: a procession that does not violate God's unity, a procession that is in itself timeless, a procession that in God is simultaneous and all-cupped-up-in-one. In *our* experience, such processions are conditioned by time. Yet even we experience, at least occasionally, the simultaneity of inquiry, insight, word, and love. In the first meeting of the eyes, two human beings seem sometimes to know the whole of each other—not, of course, in literal historical detail, but in a recognition that exceeds all normal knowing. Such is the meeting of Kitty and Levin in the opening pages of *Anna Karenina.* It is an intimation.

In worshipping such a God, no human person demeans human personhood. For what we most cherish in human personhood is, magnified by infinity, what we worship in God: persons in community and, even more exactly, the procession from active, self-determined intellect to insight and word, and the procession of these to choice, action, and love. It would be wrong to say that in worshipping such a God we are worshipping what is best in ourselves. The more exact statement is that in worshipping such a God we are turned in the direction pointed to by what is best in ourselves—our activities of inquiry, insight, choice, and love—and are acknowledging the God in whose image the best of us has been made. Looking for God everywhere else in vain, we discover that He infuses His life within us.

For it is the peculiar characteristic of the active spirit of inquiry and love that human beings who experience activities of insight and love obscurely but invariably perceive, as if out of the corner of the mind's eye, that their powers of insight and loving are participations in something larger, more demanding, more pure than themselves. For persons trying to be honest in inquiry must place every aspect of their own being under judgment, not only their biases and prejudices, and not only their particular angle of vision and location, but also their predilections and loves, their future purposes and past history. The light within us that constitutes what we mean by honesty does not have its source in any part of our own being; for every part of our being stands under its judgment.

It is the same with the power of love. To love is to will the good of the other as other. It is to will neither our own pleasure nor that of the other. It is neither to make the other dependent upon oneself, nor to make oneself dependent upon the other. It is not to love the other as an extension of oneself, nor to love the other as a way of losing oneself in the other. It is to love the other *as other.* More exactly, it is to will the *good* of the other as other—not *my* idea of what is good for the other, nor even, perhaps, the *other's* idea of what is good for herself or himself but, rather, something rather more demanding. It is to will *the* good of the other as other. What this good is may not be easy to discern. It is known exactly and justly solely to God. To seek God's will for oneself is hard enough, but to be bound to seek it for others as well might seem to be impossibly difficult—except that to conceive of life as a journey in which one seeks to do God's will is a condition easily met by taking the first step in that search. To begin to seek the good of another as other, as God wills that good, is already to be fulfilling the goal. In one sense, the beginner in the Christian way is already at the goal. In another sense, of course, each step leads to further demands. Tutored by reality itself, one meets no end to the learning: *world without end.*

"He has spoken through the prophets." The Holy Spirit, the Lord and Life-Giver, the very breath and spirit of life, speaks through all of life, speaks through the very working of our minds and wills—and speaks through the prophets. The God of Christians and Jews has a relation to human history, to human life on planet earth that is vivid and concrete. This God is not wholly "spiritual," speaking to us solely through our inner life. This God became man in Jesus and spoke through the prophets in the Holy Spirit, just as He created all things in the Father. A lover of clay is this God, a God of dirty hands, partial things, and broken things: not remote and clean. He spoke through crusty old men like Isaiah and Jeremiah. The men through whom He spoke sometimes turned away from Him, betrayed Him, fled from Him. The narratives of those through whom He spoke are not altogether pretty. The God of the Christian Creed is a God of earth and place, loving with a peculiar love one place: Israel, and one people: the people of Israel, and the community which ever after knows in that

land and that people its roots. *He has spoken through the prophets.*

I take this sentence also to mean that the Holy Spirit continues to speak to us through those interpreters of the prophets who still make the prophets their study—not only Christians but Jews. The Holy Spirit still speaks to Christians through Jewish voices, in a particularly privileged way. God is always faithful to this people. Although Christians hold to a New Covenant, the Old has not been, cannot be, abrogated by the God who made it. The ways of the human mind are mysterious, and out of simple fidelity to conscience Jews will resist Christianity and remain faithful to the Covenant God made with their fathers. In this way, among others, Christian triumphalism is humbled, since any Christian must note that a conscientious person, looking at the Christian community today or at any time, will not easily detect in it the mastering presence of God. A church of sinners must necessarily seem a stumbling block to those told that Christianity represents humanity redeemed. Who cannot sympathize with the devout Jew who would say: "How are those who are redeemed different from those who are not redeemed?" In the fields of His planting, only God sees all those who are His own, the just, whom He has chosen and who have in turn responded Yes.

The Holy Spirit *has spoken through the prophets*—and does so still. The same Spirit proceeds within us in every inquiry of ours, every insight, every choice, and every love. In such acts, He breathes in us: *Lord, Giver of Life.*

6. *One* Church

I believe in *one*, holy, catholic and apostolic Church.

"I believe in . . . [the] Church." This is, to some, an odd belief. A great many find it easy enough to believe in God, but not in a church. Some despise churches, some are disgusted by them, and some simply believe that they are unnecessary. *Their* belief goes directly to God. Well, so does mine, but I also believe in the church. Just as the God of Israel is present not only directly but also in His people, and just as the God of Christianity is present not only directly but also in His Incarnate Son, so also Christian faith is aimed not only directly at God but also at the church which He gathered together from among the nations. Like Israel, the church is a chosen people. As people must, they organize themselves, they form an institution, they live not only as discrete individuals but as a community of faith, and not only as a mystical community but as a humanly organized historical institution, both together: the Mystical Body of Christ and the organized church.

Organized religion! I remember my friend John Cogley quipping that some persons he had met are tone-deaf regarding religion. They find it hard to believe in a God whom they do not see, so most of those who are tone-deaf, he said, eyes twinkling, join the church. They find the music pleasant, the ceremonies reassuring, the membership and building drives tangible and concrete. They find satisfaction in the worldly activity of church work.

Kierkegaard is very hard on such people. Paganism, he writes, begins just as the choir begins to sing, exactly when the eloquence of the preacher touches the heart, and precisely where flowers and incense please the soul. All this is aesthetics; it is not even on the moral plane, and certainly it is far from true religion.

The faith of Catholics—at least *my* faith—is quite different. I concede to Kierkegaard that aesthetic pleasure is not the criterion of true religion. Indeed, it has sometimes seemed to me that one feels more keenly union with the Crucified when the choir is awful, when the sermon is attic-dry, when the church service is like a suburban sensitivity session with guitars, dancing, and clapping hands, and when the soul cries out in desperate anguish and despair. The "new liturgy" that has followed Vatican II is often a torture to the soul. How ugly and how vulgar it often is. Amateur songs, syrupy renditions of tragic verses from Scripture, clouds of peace, light, love, and joy affect a soft sentimentality far worse than anything we encountered in our childhoods, even at novenas or forty hours, and sicken the healthy aesthetic sense. Compared to the chaste Gregorian chants of our youth, the songs sung in our churches in the 1980s, written by flying nuns and long-haired scholastics (seen on dust jackets, as I once was, in their jeans and turtlenecks), disgust the soul. True religion survives maudlin aesthetics. Believing in the church is often a form of crucifixion. Desolate, the soul cries out for liberation from such abuse. Nevertheless, we pray: "Not my will but thine be done."

For Kierkegaard, the true hero of religion is without support, a lonely knight of faith, noble in his solitariness, who leaps into the darkness in the heroic splendor of isolation. Kierkegaard may not have known how great a relief such faith would be to those who believe that God is to be found in the bored faces in the pews around him, in the dreadful sermons endured without end, in the silly romanticism of secular sentiments paraded as Christian faith. The lonely hero in isolation has it easy.

The scandals of Christianity are three: that God is not only One but One-and-Three, that is, community in the Trinity; that God reveals Himself not in His translucent Godhead but in the man Jesus in an underdeveloped country of a primitive era; and that the God-man calls humans not as existential heroes but as a bumbling and clumsy community of sinners. We believe in the church.

Chesterton believed that the romance of life lies in such a godly strategy. It is not found in the airy spiritual realm. It is found close at hand, in the flesh, indeed in the portly Father Brown. The God of

Christianity delights in practical jokes. His things are never what they seem. That far less than noble parish priest, not very learned, not even very cultivated, by no means a hero and plainly no ascetic, that little fellow carrying his lunch in a brown paper bag: there is Christ. Surprise!

It is possible to be romantic about all this, as Chesterton was. It is also possible to be, from time to time, *depressed* about it. Really, one would like to see a cloud of angels at least once, to glimpse a face transfigured by grace, to witness a miracle or two, to be confronted willy-nilly with an overpowering *mysterium tremendum*. But nothing happens. All one's life, most especially in oneself, one encounters overpowering mediocrity. Flesh seems heavier than mail. The pamphlets in the rack, the dust in the corner, the watermarks on the kneelers, the ragged edges of the dirty hymnals, the quality of *thought* in the preaching, the squirming undisciplined children—everything seems, on gray days, so ineffably tacky. *This* is the Kingdom of God? Someone has to be kidding.

Then there are the insufferable theologians. Surely we theologians set some record for arrogance. "The resurrection," the newly learned student of the latest scriptural exegesis tells us, "is a faith-event." But is it, one wishes to ask, also a *fact*-event? Challenged, the theologian struggles to stifle rage. His barely mastered voice says, "That's not the right sort of question. Modern scholarship shows that such words occur in another paradigm." But, paradigm or no paradigm, did it happen? one persists. Others stir uneasily. One shouldn't be so hard on him. And, in truth, the relation between "taking a look" with one's eyes and the act of faith in divinity is here, as elsewhere, complex.

Still, paradigms! Conscientization! Horizons! Stories! We live in the midst of a new gnosis, secrets revealed only to initiates, special language, elaborate codes, far beyond common sense or touchable fact. "Put your hand in my side and see." As Aquinas puts it, seeing the humanity of Jesus, Thomas the Apostle believed the divinity: simple, yet profound.

We believe in the church, even in the learned ignorance of theologians, whom every church must endure. Sometimes we do good work. Even in us, grace sometimes appears. God can do anything. Indeed, it is part of the pattern of this God that He should accomplish work essential to His Church by such as ourselves.

Vatican II gave unprecedented prominence, indeed, to *periti*, the theological experts who in press conferences "interpreted" the Council. "Theologians 1, Bishops 0." "Progressives trounce conservatives." "Cardinal X gave brilliant speech written by theologian Y."

If during one era of church history we heard all too much of traditional triumphalism—the pope and bishops vanquishing all—recently we have heard our fill of theologians triumphantly reading "the signs of the times" according to their own itches and prejudices, instructing their slower bishops and the rest of us, insinuating that common sense is always wrong in the face of sophisticated scholarship. Occasionally, Scripture is not so much explained as explained away. The magnificent effort of three generations to create a splendid Thomistic revival, bringing back into force majestic centuries of Catholic intellectual realism, systematic, reasoned, voraciously tackling all questions across the whole panorama of intellect and culture, has been dismissed as "scholastic." The new theologian goes directly from the exegesis of Scripture to nuclear warfare, an option for the poor, and revolutionary social democracy. So much we could have gotten from Moscow.

Nonetheless, we believe in the church, the church of and for sinners. The sinner is at the heart of the church. Were we not sinners, aware of being sinners all, the church would be unendurable. It makes us humble. It makes us truthful about ourselves. To others we are as much a scandal as they to us. We each make faith difficult for the others. There is so little of the godly in us. That little can often be seen only by faith, certainly not by immediate inspection. Looking around at one another, we can see without doubt that we are in this together.

That God loves us is a tribute to God. It is miraculous. It is incredibly discerning of Him. I am not sure that we could do it, if He had not first done it.

This is not to say that there is no good in us, that we are totally depraved. Not at all. What is amazing about humans is that sometimes we are honest, compassionate, courageous, even heroic. A father would rush into a burning house to pull out his child; we regard this as natural and altogether normal. The Creator saw His creation and saw that it was good. Yet there are so many times in which each of us knows how we have betrayed the good that is in us. Each of us knows that bitter taste. It is all too frequent. Contrition is daily bread. Not a day passes without it. The church is a community of sinners—more oppressive than that, an institution of sinners. It is poignantly difficult for Roman Catholics, in particular, to be utopian (although the new gnosticism tempts us), for we have centuries of popes to contemplate, not to mention the bloody Crusades, led by popes, monks, and saints. There were false popes and popes in captivity. There were liars and lechers, bastards and the making of bastards. There was greed and power and cruelty. It is an *altogether* human church. Despite this, a full 78 of the 263 popes have been officially recognized as saints. Theologians, alas, have attained a lesser proportion.

"Episcopi inimici Ecclesiae," Augustine once preached: "Bishops are the enemies of the Church." He explained that a bishop is Christ to his flock and none can properly be that. Each defect of the bishop, by that standard, scandalizes some of the faithful. Seeing a bishop, how can anyone believe? If the bishop is pious but not scholarly, his thinness of intellect injures some. If he is scholarly but not pious, why not follow the professors? No one passes the test. Not at first glance.

On second glance, however, one recognizes that the way of grace is normally by humble paths. It is the lowliness of the material that breaks the mind, finally, with awe for the power of God.

And God, in his mercy, judges not as we judge. Péguy writes that St. Louis, the king who gives his cloak to the leper, kissing him on his leprous mouth, is not the measure God mercifully judges us by.[1] St. Louis is a saint. God cherishes that. But God counts Joinville, the king's aide, repulsed by the foolishness of the king and the hideous contagion of the leper, as the normal measure. God is very pleased by the saintly king, but also takes delight in the altogether human response of Joinville, who thinks that only under the pain of sin—not as a spontaneous act of grace—would *he* kiss such a mouth. God calculates the measure of a mortal sin and leprosy, and in Péguy's view has no disdain whatever for Joinville, His ordinary believer. It is quite a thing to kiss a leper. That is no ordinary standard.

God's greatness is shown by his mercy, for only the Almighty, against Whom sin is directed, can forgive sin. No act of God is greater. His mercy is especially shown in His calling together of a church. For most humans are not lonely heroes. Most need the familiarity, even the mediocrity, of institutional life, need company, need peoplehood, need buildings and books and ceremonies, need to engage their bodies and their social instincts as well as their immortal souls.

We believe in the church *because* we believe in God; because it is just like God to have called into being something as plain and humble as the church. The church is of a piece with everything else He has shown Himself to be. It is a work of mercy.

"One Church." This church is *one.* For a Christian, salvation is not every man for himself—it is all sinners together. By intention and aim —*God's* intention and aim—all humans alike are part of His church in a hidden, disguised, and imperfect way. There is an "invisible" extension of the church. For once God decided to work within time in the ways of time, His choice of one people would seem to exclude, but could not really exclude, others. Adapting His workings to the ways of history, God by His grace reveals Himself in every aspect of His creation and to all His creatures. By the light of His law in their minds He calls all to His truth. All who seek Him in justice and light are His. All without exception are called.

Yet each of the world's religions hears God, follows God, in its own way. At their depths, each of these religions honors in humans those participations in God's life that we know as honesty, courage, community, and liberty. Each teaches the disciplines of such activities. These disciplines vary in mode and style. The world's religions are in many ways stunningly different from one another. It would not be judicious to assert that "fundamentally, all say the same thing." Such a brush stroke would be far too broad and thin. We may permit scholars and our own experiences with persons of diverse religions to instruct us, slowly, in what is shared and not shared. We must respect in each other, in our common darkness, our differences as well as our likenesses. In *The Experience of Nothingness* and *Ascent of the Mountain, Flight of the Dove,* I wrestled with some ways of articulating such things for myself.

The Christian Creed, however, sweeps us into a particular vision of God and human destiny, a particular narrative of history, a distinctive story. Through the Creed, we assert that all somehow are children of the same Creator and all, therefore, are somehow involved in the revelation made in Christ, who at a date and in a place suffered, died, was buried, and rose again. All are somehow—not visibly, not obviously —made in the image of this Word. Clearly, all suffer and die and are called with Him to life without end. How? Only through patient study do we discern all the ways in which grace acts in this world, surprising ways, paradoxical ways, seemingly contradictory—even combative— ways, clashing by night.

The scandal of the Christian church is that it is *not* one, although we believe it to be one. This scandal was present from the beginning. Division is a recurrent feature of Christian history, as is sin.

Yet what could one expect of poor humans? Words themselves often divide. Even words uttered innocently are perceived by a loved one in ways the speaker did not intend, and much labor may be required to set understanding right. Words are disturbing symbols. Yet how else can we hear except through words? "The Word came into the world, and the world received it not." The Word even came as a divisive sword, its two edges sharp. If the church is one, it is not one in some simple way. It is one in and through divisions. It is cut, cloven, sheared apart. This is a matter of daily experience.

Yet God is One, although Three. Not even the unity of God is easily comprehended; no more the unity of His church.

We do know, though, we daily experience, the presence of God's life in those with whom we work who do not share in the life of our church. We experience being one with those with whom we are not in all ways one.

To be particular, I have sometimes experienced great unity of spirit with Jews, closer even than with some Christians. In terrible simplicity, I believe there is greater unity of spirit as between Jews and Catholics than between Catholics and Protestants. Is this because, in America, Jews and Catholics tend to experience the history of immigration, as well as a thousand years of experience in central Europe, and even the history of predominantly Protestant institutions, in echoing ways? Is it because we both derive institutionally not only from prophetic but also from priestly traditions, that is, with a learned respect for worldliness, the flesh, priestly casuistry and realistic compromise? Protestants tend to have a more prophetic flair. They seem to be more like pure spirits. Their perfectionist tendencies seem less checked by institutional memories. Catholics and Jews seem to value tradition, ritual, liturgy, and story rather more intimately and comfortably. This business of unity, then, is complex and concretely tangled.

And yet a taste for the spirit is not as powerful among some human beings as among others. We often meet spirits more attuned to ours in communities not our own than in our own local community. Oneness of spirit crosses institutional lines.

Yet we cherish also the diversity of spirits in the church. We are glad to belong to a large church, not a sect, in which nationalities, temperaments, cultures, talents, and gifts wildly diverge. It is a big church, spacious and large. It holds or has held Konrad Adenauer and Emmanuel Mounier, Luigi Sturzo and Sophia Loren, Graham Greene and Eugene McCarthy, Mother Teresa and General Thieu, President Marcos and Bobby Kennedy and George Meany. It could digest Cardinal Spellman and Andrew Greeley, not to mention Phil Donahue and Henry Hyde. There is a lot of room in it. Enough room so as to keep one's distance from many, except at the communion rail.

We are one, even though we are, plainly, not one.

Praise be to God, who can figure it all out.

7. *Holy* Church

We believe in one, *holy,* catholic and apostolic Church.

The church is *holy.* Clearly, as one looks over the assembled parishioners in one's parish church, the holiness of the church does not leap out at the eye. The church is holy because its hidden life is God's life. It is inspirited (although not often visibly) by the Holy Spirit, the Life-Giver. It is holy because it was gathered together from the ends of the earth by His Son. It is holy because, in the fullness of narrative, the Creator invented this world and imagined its history, humbling Himself and making His Will make allowance for human will and human vicissitude. (In the end, even those who turn against God's will, who "receive it not," show the workings of His will, for He also willed their liberty and accepted, with foreknown sadness, their rejection.) The church is holy because God offers all who do His will the vitality of His own light, love, and acting, from which and by which they live. All live in Him as He in them. This is true even where human clay masks inner life.

Thus, the holiness of the church is plain, humble, hidden. It is not revealed as in the splendor of legions of angels. It is hidden in clay. It works like mustard seed. From the outside, one sees the shell and may well cast the seed aside like a pebble or a lump of earth. To touch and sight, the many seeds seem similar. Who is to know which have within them the living plant?

The overpowering characteristic of the Christian God is, therefore, shared by His church. The Christian God seldom, almost never, reveals Himself in glory—to Moses, perhaps, in power that made Moses quake, in Jesus transfigured on the Mount. Mostly, our God hides His divinity. What overpowers the mind is His refusal to overpower it. He calls us to Him in darkness, by our own willingness and determination, by our own faith. He empowers these in us. But we can say no to them, and often do. God does not *force* us by the power of His radiance to be fixed in Him. Like the sun behind the clouds He hides His glory. This humility, this abjectness, this total respect for our liberty (in which we are most in His image) is His most remarkable characteristic. It is characteristic of the Creator, to whom we are only darkly drawn by signs strewn throughout His creation. It is characteristic of the Son, who humbled Himself to being despised and abject, forelorn on the cross. It is characteristic of the Holy Spirit, who so seldom floods our minds and hearts but, typically, solicits and invites us amid many ambiguities. Our God is a humble God.

So is the church humble, not always in its attitudes, which often strike the ear as triumphalist and arrogantly righteous, but in its actual existence. To the testing eye, it is at first an institution like other institutions. Its bishops do not always strike the testing eye as "other Christs"; one strains, indeed, to believe that they are not real estate agents, or lawyers, or professors, or from any typical association of their class. So much is expected of them, and no one of them can be for the observing world all that a bishop ought to be.

Who regarding the history of the Catholic Church does not find much by which to be scandalized? Those of us who are Catholic—I speak for myself—are able to read this history, even its most shocking parts, with "eyes of faith." That is, we see the pathways of grace, the survival of its essential message through the hazards of human greed, venality, weakness, ambition, intransigence, and self-betrayal. Those who read with colder eyes may see an institution quite troubling to them, threatening human liberty and inquiring intellect, implicated in dreadful crimes of persecution and pogrom. We take heart from those critics who, even from afar, marvel at the persistence and vigor of this institution, its remarkable passage through civilizations—critics like Macaulay and Gibbon, for example.[1] And we can well understand how it takes as much faith to believe in the church as to believe in God, perhaps more.

Yet the Christian God is a God who humbled Himself even to calling together a church. He makes holiness manifest in the lowly act of sprinkling water on an infant's head and touching salt to its tongue; in the hearing of boring tales of human sinfulness and mediocrity in the confessional; in distributing the Lord's body and blood as bread and wine; in the laying on of hands; in weddings and at funerals. The holiness of the church lies in pointing to the love of God manifest for us in the daily rounds of ordinary life. The sacraments of the church are as tangible and lowly as a frosted glass of ale—the Catholic Church is physical and down-to-earth in its holiness.

Many of its saints are correspondingly practical men and women, who know the excruciating detail of making decisions about personnel and floor wax, building plans and steam furnaces, fund raising and homilies, feeding the hungry and caring for the outcasts. Mother Teresa and Dorothy Day have been altogether quite human persons, distinctive personalities, each with a temperament angular, in her fashion. So marvelous are such persons that many, seeing them, know that they are in the presence of God. In her saints, too, the church is holy. Yet many are the humble holy persons of daily life in whom grace is not quite so manifest. Who of her sisters in the convent knew how remarkable was the holiness of St. Thérèse of Lisieux, who barely thirty years after her death in 1897 came to be ranked with St. Joan of Arc as the patroness of France? Saints in our midst are often invisible to their closest associates, who know well their angularities and their daily faults. Yet to learn of holiness in the church, there are no sources (outside the Gospel) like books on the lives of the saints, especially their own books.

It is characteristic of the Roman Church to see that the lives of her own holy people are commentaries on the Scripture as important as the learned and discursive commentaries of bishops and theologians. For the narrative of a saintly life is in its own way an exegesis of the narrative of Scripture, a unique living out of the classic story, the "imitation of Christ" being never performed twice in the same way. The lives of the saints help many to understand Scripture. Lives speak louder than words.

So it is that in honoring St. Jane de Chantal and St. Charles Borromeo, St. Clare and St. Benedict, St. Agnes and St. Sebastian, St. Francis de Sales and Mother Seton, St. Elizabeth of Hungary and St.

Louis of France, St. Pius V, the warrior pope of Lepanto, and St. Francis of Assisi, St. Teresa and St. John of the Cross, we condemn ourselves before the holiness to which we are called. We long to let God's grace be more abundant in our lives. We fall down in humility and we aspire.

The holiness of the church is, finally, our own to realize. Grace is given us. The only tragedy for a Christian, as Leon Bloy once wrote, is not to have been a saint.

When we confess that the church is holy, we declare what we ought to be and are not. We feel the claim of the honesty, love, courage, and liberty of God upon us. We feel His life course within us. It wishes to break the bonds we have so far placed upon it. We are saved by grace, to which we must say, though we find so hard to say, yes.

The holiness of the church does not eliminate our wrestling against God. On the contrary, it highlights the struggle within us, our comfort in being who we are rather than who we ought to be. "Be ye perfect as your heavenly Father is perfect." Yet *how* is our heavenly Father perfect? Humbly so, creating this world and not a world more perfect, sending His Son as a poor carpenter, abject and despised, and manifest in St. Peter even as St. Peter denies Him thrice. To be perfect as God is perfect is not to blaze in glory. It is constantly and steadily to begin again, accepting the dynamism of this world as it is, and realigning ourselves with God's life within it, hidden and humble as that life normally is. The most powerful force in the world, Dostoevsky writes, is humble charity. It is God's own life in our midst. To be perfect as the heavenly Father is perfect is to live a life of humble charity.

The word "humble" is, perhaps, a peculiarly Christian word. Its excesses are well known. Its root lies in *humus*, "earth." It suggests down-to-earth, truthful, without pretense, exactly right. It is not humility to feign humility. It is not humility to pretend that one does less well at something than one does. True humility, rather, is learned by the experience of excellence. Those who excel at anything know well, from many failures, how easy it is to misuse one's gifts and also how mysterious gifts are. One's own gifts are greater than oneself; one did not create them nor is one their master. They come from powers one cannot explain. They are given us for our enjoyment and for the good of the human community, which needs them, and as it would be a sin against love not to permit them scope, so it would be a sin against truth to deny them. Humility is radical truthfulness, as close to the root as the *humus*.

Great persons are often surprisingly humble, perhaps because no one becomes great in the eyes of others without taking great risks and being much buffeted by adversity. Greatness is maintained steadily by reading reality as clearly as one can, neither overestimating nor underestimating the difficulties afforded by reality itself, contingent and baffling as it often is. The great have reason to be humble, for they have invariably been humbled often. Their errors and blunders are often more numerous than their successes, but their efforts at fidelity and truthfulness uncannily lead them to learn from experience. Great acts are achieved by doing the right thing at the right time, in the right way, and with the right touch— they utterly depend upon reading reality exactly, seeing through it as one sees through limpid water. They are to an extraordinary extent the fruit of humility, as humility is itself an extraordinary achievement.

Humble charity is, therefore, truthfulness squared, for charity, too, is willing the good of the other *as other*—acting as nearly as one can as God would act, seeing reality plain and honest. It is no true love that fosters illusions. Love that abides is rooted in seeing past illusions to the depth of the other and to the heart of the other's situation.

God is light. God is the light of honesty. God the Creator made the world and its history as it is and in each moment wills the maximal possible burst of His own vitalities in our lives. To discern what these are and to allow His action scope is to be holy as He is, in Him, with Him, and through Him.

The church is holy because truthfulness in deed is what it asks of us, not in its own name, but in His who is its inner life. To see God's life in the church is as difficult as to see it in ourselves. Perhaps this is why we are told to love others as we love ourselves. Even egoism and self-love are, ironically, forms of self-hatred. Invariably, they involve us in pretense. They are the opposite of charity as they are the opposite of humility. The two go together, charity and humility, for both consist in seeing as God sees, acting as God acts; both are achievements beyond our wounded competence, gifts of God to us, grace. To meet a truthful person is to stand in the presence of grace; one feels the radiance. To meet charity in act is to experience the same.

Self-love is, then, badly named. Self-love is to see ourselves, not as God sees us, but according to our own self-deceptions. Turning away from truth about ourselves, we love instead some disguise; we reject our truth, loving our disguise. Self-love, St. Benedict writes, dies fifteen minutes after the soul departs from the body. It is the last of our illusions, the last sin against humble charity. It is the stronghold in us of the Father of Lies, who contests our fate minute by minute.

A writer, for example, is one whose vocation it is to shape words to allow God's light scope; yet betrayal thereof is a writer's daily bread. Flattery diverts the light, and so does hostility. One cannot help knowing one's audience and fearing their judgment. It is extraordinarily difficult to keep one's eye on the ball, to hit the truth exactly, to knock it out of the park, when one worries about what others will say. In a highly ideological era many readers do not seem to care about concrete reality. Many are very quick to notice deviations. Friends nudge one; enemies attack. (St. Sebastian is well chosen as the patron saint of writers.) So much of intellectual life, in a gnostic age, consists in positioning oneself, in keeping one's credentials in order, in flattering the beliefs of one's ideological kin, who clap or boo at each presentation.

Good writing is persuasion. It is tempting to write to what "the traffic will bear." When Pascal judges that there are not three honest men in a century, he did not mean that there are two, or one, but that honesty is exceedingly difficult to maintain even for a day. Mere flattery bends the mind when one believes it; contempt and ridicule bend it when one fears them. One looks constantly for credible evasions.

In this vocation, as in every other, humble charity is hard to find. It is nonetheless precious. It is nonetheless a vocation.

The church is holy because God prompts us to face and to do the truth in every situation in which we find ourselves. The church is *not* holy insofar as we distort, darken, and obscure that light. There are always a thousand reasons to dim that light. Humankind cannot bear too much of it.

The holiness of the church is of God. Its unholiness is our own contribution.

8. *Catholic* Church

We believe in one, holy, *catholic* and apostolic Church.

We believe in one, holy, *Catholic* church. But "Catholic" is a complex concept. It is to be contrasted with the sectarian church, the ethnic church, the exclusive church, and the closed church.

Perhaps we should begin with the temptation of prophets. The Catholic Church is incarnational. It is in the world, although not entirely of it. It is social. It is institutional. It is tempered to the shorn lamb. It is a church for sinners, not solely for saints. It is a priestly church as well as a prophetic church. Indeed, it is led by scores of thousands of priests and by very few prophets in any one century.

Our own age, being an age of mass media with an itch for novelty, suffers more than other ages from the prophet motive. Anybody who can grab a headline may think of himself or herself as a prophet.[1] Many poke fun at the bureaucrats and administrators of the world, the organization men, the plodders who humbly labor at their desks from nine to five, and glorify by contrast those who "hit and run," appearing suddenly in our living rooms on television newscasts for saying something outrageous. An age of news generates thousands of false prophets. News is easily manufactured. All one has to do is shock. "CATHOLIC PRIEST PROMOTES ABORTION." "CATHOLIC NUN SAYS HOMOSEXUALITY OK." Such things are news. But are they really prophecy?

The prophet motive leads to notoriety and power of a sort. Celebrity is now a substitute for fame. The latter is earned by extraordinary achievement. The former is manufactured by freakiness.[2]

An age of news tips the balance of power in the church. Whoever gets on the news becomes a messenger. Such messengers may gain a power over audiences that the messengers sent by Christ seldom possess. Religious persons who are newsmakers may often, then, acquire power greater than that of popes and bishops. Naturally, some would like to legitimate this new power by thinking of themselves—and suggesting that others should think of them—as prophets. This does not make them prophets. Even in biblical times, false prophets outnumbered true prophets by a substantial proportion. Warnings, indeed, were given against listening to false prophets, and even against having ears itchy for "prophecy."

The prophet motive leads easily to the sectarian impulse, which is quite opposite to the Catholic impulse. The sectarian impulse seeks a church of the like-minded, the saved, the saintly, the small homogeneous community. Its normal temptation is to see all others as less than holy and all worldly tasks as somehow corrupt. The sectarian normally sees the outside world as depraved, while trying to nourish a small band of the saved against surrounding darkness.[3]

The fear of nuclear war gives new impetus to sectarianism. It engenders the appropriate apocalyptic mood. It diverts attention from building up economic and political structures. Why bother doing so if the world is coming to an end and if all such institutions are corrupt? The sectarian spirit sees the state, even the democratic state, as an instrument of falsehood and repression. It hardly bothers to distinguish the degree of evil in democracy from that in tyrannies, dictatorships, and totalitarian societies. Buying and selling, producing and distributing are in its eyes vulgar if not vicious acts for which, if it could, it would substitute the love of brother and sister caring for one another. Compared to love, it reasons, political economy belongs to this world and the devil.

For centuries, sectarian preachers have foretold that the world will end in fire. Nuclear weapons have put an end to metaphor. Such weapons *can* end human life in fire and in wind. Sectarian preaching has received empirical support. So nuclear warfare now validates ancient sectarian themes of hellfire and brimstone—awakens, that is, the religious power of fear. Fear of hell is an acceptable, although not the highest, motive for devotion. "The fear of the Lord is the beginning of wisdom." It would be better if humans were moved by love; when they are not, motives of fear have had to do. For the sectarian spirit to deny itself access to the new fear coursing through Western nations, now that the Soviets have taken the nuclear initiative into their own hands, would be a supreme abnegation. The fate of humanity can now be decided by forces hostile to the West; our destiny is no longer in our hands. Millions *are* afraid, and have reason to be. Fear is a paralyzing emotion. It often freezes reason; it induces panic.

The sectarian spirit would try to turn this fear into the energy of conversion, away from this world and its perplexities to Christ and to peace. Since some of the sectarian churches have also been peace churches, the nuclear age unites the classic sectarian themes of apocalyptic fear and peace. The gathered sectarian community will "witness" for peace. Under contemporary conditions, this stance may not be unpopular. It may catch on.

Some, indeed, desire the Catholic Church to become a "peace church." They wish the church to be "prophetic." They wish it to conduct itself like a sect, excommunicating those who do not share its "principles of peace." The logic of these principles may be succinctly stated: it is immoral to *use* nuclear weapons. If it is immoral to use them, then it is also immoral to *possess* them, since even their possession implies an intention to use them. If it is immoral to possess them, then it is also immoral to *manufacture* them. Therefore, no believer can in fidelity to the believing community be involved in any way in any government, military, or defense industry that provides nuclear deterrence. Believers must choose between state and church. If Catholics follow this logic, no Catholic can be president, general, soldier, worker in nuclear weaponry, and so on.[4] The sectarian spirit is in this way absolutist, pure, certain, and righteous. It delights in challenging consciences and in separating them—true believers to this side, dissenters out.

By contrast, we believe in the *Catholic* Church. The first meaning of this commitment is that we are *not sectarian;* we resist the sectarian impulse. The Catholic spirit does not believe that the church is a church of the saved, the saints, the true believers. It is, rather, a gathering of the struggling, the voyaging, the weak, those in whom there remains much unbelief, and sinners. *Lamb of God who takes away the sins of the world, have mercy on us.* Further, the Catholic spirit does not hold that this world or its institutions are depraved. In Greek culture, in Roman law, in Gothic vitalities, in democratic institutions, in economic progress it sees signs of grace. Such things are of this world, surely, and are not the full and proper locus of human salvation. On the other hand, it is the vocation of Catholics to labor in and to build up such institutions, shaping them by degrees ever more closely according to the spirit of the Gospels. For grace normally works not all at once but gradually, as yeast in dough, as a mustard seed buried from sight. The sectarian spirit sees the church as far more pure than does the Catholic spirit and the world as far more depraved. To believe in a Catholic Church is to accept a church of sinners and a world in which grace gradually, not without setback, manifests itself in humble institutions which are never more than sinful and imperfect.

The Catholic spirit contrasts, as well, with the ethnic spirit. To believe in a Catholic Church is to believe in a church composed of all ethnic groups, all peoples, and all nations. Such belief does not deny a proper role to ethnicity but does deny its ultimacy. It does not entail the denial of ethnicity, for Christianity is a religion of incarnation, of flesh and time and place and history. It respects the incarnate nature of human life. The human family is not universalist but particular; human peoples are differentiated by cultures, languages, traditions, customs, and habits.[5] Christianity does not (should not) ride roughshod over these, for to wipe out such things would be to treat humans as though they were angels, rational spirits disembodied from the particularities of history. To be human is to be ethnic. The Catholic spirit, then, is compatible with the ethnic spirit but is not identical to it. The Catholic spirit respects ethnic identity, but opposes ethnocentrism. Jesus the Christ was Jewish in His speech, in His ways of thinking and perceiving, and in His loves and loyalties. He came, He said, not to abrogate but to fulfill the traditions of his people—who were not Hindus, or Ukrainians, or Nigerians, or Aztecs, or Mohawks, but Israelites. Yet He came also for all.

In an analogous way, the Catholic Church is composed of many who received the faith not precisely as individuals but through a social choice, often enough a choice initially made by tribal leaders or kings or councils of elders. In the days of simpler, undifferentiated, and unitary societies, the religion of a realm was vital to the cohesion of everything else within the realm. In varying degrees, individuals within such realms appropriated the Christian faith and passed it on from generation to generation. Religion was incarnated in nations.

Thus, today, being Polish and Catholic is not exactly the same as being British and Catholic, or Spanish and Catholic, or Indian and Catholic, or American and Catholic. Nations and peoples have their own particular vocations within the Catholic fold. To believe in a Catholic Church is to accept these differences. No one of them is ultimately determinative for the others. Yet it cannot be denied, either, that some cultures have been more important than others—Rome, for example, and western Europe—in shaping until now the institutions of the church universal. History itself unfolds as a narrative of shifting foci, changing centers of gravity, and novel sources of spiritual and institutional leadership. This story is still incomplete.

Third, then, to believe in a Catholic Church is to believe in an inclusive church, seeking to discern in all cultures and all particular histories the workings of grace from the beginning. All peoples spring from the Creator, have been made in the image of the Word, and have felt the workings of the Spirit. It remains true that the message of Jesus comes filtered through history, implanted in history at one time and in one place, not everywhere at once. Centuries were required before this message was, in fact, carried to all nations, until now there remain few spots in the world to which the news of Jesus has not been carried. In the nature of things, many distortions have also arisen. As we each year by year come to understand the message more clearly for ourselves, so also the nations are also led to ever fuller understanding.

The British layman Donald Nicholl has written brilliantly of the Catholic spirit in this context as a spirit of *pleroma*, the spirit of fullness.[6] In a sense, the Catholic spirit grows ever larger through its contact with the nations. The Gospels meditated upon and lived out in various circumstances reveal new angles of vision.[7] Buddhism and Hinduism, Tao and Islam, and all the other world religions—above all, Judaism—have spiritual riches to teach. They are not merely to be conceived as passive recipients of the Christian message. On the contrary, in the Christian view, Creator, Word, and Spirit have been active everywhere from the beginning, and it is the task of Christians to learn and to discern as well as to preach. Without in the least denying what is distinctive in the Christian word and historical experience, indeed in giving witness to it as clearly and fairly and wisely as they can, Christians are nonetheless well instructed to recognize that the Catholic spirit has not yet reached its appointed fullness.

The Catholic spirit is, therefore, an open spirit. It is open, not in the empty-headed way of being without content and learned convictions of its own, but in the commonsense way of humble charity. Graced as Christian history has undoubtedly been, daily God's grace is yet more abundant still. The Catholic spirit recognizes the obligation, century by century, generation by generation, culture by culture, of becoming larger than it has been, of expanding to its ultimate vocation. Its aim is to incorporate into itself all signs of God's light, beauty, love, liberty, and communion among the world's peoples. Its aim is not to rest self-enclosed, parochial, shut tight, but to remain alert and docile to the teaching of God in history. God's grace, Georges Bernanos writes, is everywhere. It speaks from the grain of sand, from rocket ships that reach the moon, and from every historical experience of the human race. To be Catholic is to try to include within one's faith all God's actions among His peoples everywhere. The Catholic spirit is a spirit less of limits than of fullness.

The danger here, of course, is sentimentality. There are ways of being "all things to all people" that are fraudulent. A premature and merely enthusiastic syncretism can dilute Christianity to nothing more than vacuous goodwill. The danger of mere eclecticism is great. The danger of gnosticism is still greater.

Thus one may under the abiding power of gnosticism in particular —the single most persistent and potent threat against Christianity— so "spiritualize" Christianity as to deprive it of its actual roots in flesh and history. Christianity is not, cannot be, everything. It denies as well as it affirms. It is falsifiable. Unless it stands for specific interpretations of what is true and false about human experience, it is conceptually empty. The danger of the open spirit is that it may become both intellectually and spiritually otiose. To hold, for example, that the narrative form for human experience embodied in each of the world's religions is equally true is not to honor all but to demean each. Each must be taken seriously in its particular claims. And decisions about each particular truth and particular falsehood must be reached. It is wise to be tentative and respectful. It is not wise to be as open-minded as a sieve. To do so is to abandon every claim to honesty, conscience, and integrity.

Not all faiths, for example, are compatible with the Christian Creed. To hold as part of one's creed a belief in an open church cannot be construed as simply abandoning a creed. That would be absurd.

For it is the lot of humans to proceed to fullness, not as God or angels do, in a glance, all at once. It is to proceed by the ways of embodied spirit, step by painful step, seeking concrete insight and exact verification as one goes, never leaping beyond the evidence, although not hesitating, either, to test new paradigms and new approaches. We proceed in an incarnate way.

Thus, the fourth meaning of Catholic is to love the method of concretion. The Catholic spirit respects the flesh as the Catholic sacraments respect the flesh. Baptism is not solely a spiritual act, although it is that. It is the sensation of cool water flowing on one's brow, a taste of salt upon one's tongue. Receiving the Lord in the Eucharist, one tastes flour and water in a wafer that clings to the roof of one's mouth, melts on one's teeth, and is swallowed, and one tastes wines that differ from occasion to occasion. The Catholic spirit is a spirit of incarnation. Gifts of the spirit seldom come to us apart from the flesh. Faith comes by hearing. Against materialism, the Catholic spirit wishes to say, "Not by bread alone." Against gnosticism, the Catholic spirit wishes to say, "Not by pure spirit alone." The Catholic way is humbly appropriate to our embodied spirits, our slow and plodding ways, our bodies and our flesh.

Chesterton wrote once of an orange-covered pamphlet produced by Dean Inge on the meaning of Protestantism. According to Chesterton, Dean Inge said little positive about Protestantism but a great deal negative about Catholicism. In particular:

The Dean of St. Paul's . . . unveiled to his readers all the horrors of a quotation from Newman; a very shocking and shameful passage in which the degraded apostate says that he is happy in his religion, and in being surrounded by the things of his religion; that he likes to have objects that have been blessed by the holy and beloved, that there is a sense of being protected by prayers, sacramentals and so on; and that happiness of this sort satisfies the soul. The Dean, having given us this one ghastly glimpse of the Cardinal's spiritual condition, drops the curtain with a groan and says it is Paganism.[8]

To the Dean, Newman sounded quite pagan. Chesterton thought otherwise:

Heaven has *descended* into the world of matter. . . . It blesses all the five senses; as the senses of the baby are blessed at a Catholic christening. It blesses even material gifts and keepsakes, as with relics or rosaries. It works through water or oil or bread or wine. Now that sort of mystical materialism may please or displease the Dean, or anybody else. But I cannot for the life of me understand why the Dean, or anybody else, does not *see* that the Incarnation is as much a part of that idea as the Mass; and that the Mass is as much a part of that idea as the Incarnation. . . . Of all human creeds or concepts, in that sense, Christianity is the most utterly profane. But why a man should accept a Creator who was a carpenter, and then worry about holy water . . . why he should accept the first and most stupendous part of the story of Heaven on Earth, and then furiously deny a few small but obvious deductions from it— that is a thing I do not understand; I never could understand; I have come to the conclusion that I shall never understand.[9]

The Catholic view of the faith is quite fleshly. It takes the incarnation so far that it sees grace in everything—even in bureaucrats, even in corporations, even in public officials, even in bishops, and last of all even in theologians.

9. *Apostolic* Church

We believe in one, holy, catholic and *apostolic* Church.

James A. Hickey, current Archbishop of Washington, is my link to the apostles gathered by Jesus ninety-two generations ago. Down the ages, Catholic bishops have followed one another through "the laying on of hands." Through him, too, I go back to Nicaea, largely an Eastern council, to which the pope of Rome sent legates, whose authority was observed. So, in some ways, the Bishop of Rome is more important to my life than the Archbishop of Washington. Were the bishops of the United States—God forbid—ever to be at odds with the Bishop of Rome, instinct would lead me to lean toward the latter.

The papal office distinguishes the Catholic Church among all others. Its existence follows the logic of incarnation. It is not some idealistic, spiritual church that the Catholic Creed embraces, but a particular historical body going back by the physical laying on of hands to the apostles. It is a church of modulated authorities and gifts, each with its concrete historical role. The entire strength and power of the Catholic faith comes from God, of course, but through the particular channels that God chose and made actual from the world of possibilities. As fleshly as the Son of God was, so is each successive leader of this earthly community and its president, Christ's vicar. As God became man, so His church operates in fleshly ways. One looks not only for the Spirit but also for the words of this concrete man, whose historical responsibilities are awesome.

Some, regarding this claim of the papal office, see blasphemy. But so also did the high priests rend their garments at what they took to be the blasphemous claims of Jesus Christ. If these claims are false, either of Christ or of the papacy, or both, then Catholicism is a pretension.

The papacy is often described as a rock. It is so in two senses. It is enduring, and it is a stumbling block to many. Catholics easily understand why so many others are scandalized by the papal office. Sometimes, reviewing the historical record, they themselves are, too. For myself, the central insight of Catholicism is that God works through humble, much despised ways, fleshly ways, tailored to the weakness and sinfulness of all of us. The scene at Bethlehem evokes this insight, as does Golgotha, and so also the sometimes absurd figure of this lonely man, this robe-swathed priest of Rome, this poor pope, frail and particular and sinful like the rest of us. No divine figure he. Yet he is called to an almost impossible task, superhuman in its demands, which of course he cannot always meet. Catholics believe in the Lord's promise that against this rock the gates of hell will not prevail. They well see, however, how mightily the waves of hell can lash against that rock, obscure it, even at times appear to have submerged it.

In believing in the apostolic church, Catholics yield a loyalty of conscience difficult for minds trained to individual liberty of conscience fully to reconcile. As a Catholic, I sometimes feel in extreme tension of conscience with the papacy. Necessarily, the pope speaks as a man of a certain temperament, psychology, culture, and spirit. The particularities of his person are not the same as between one pope and another, nor as between individual popes and all other individual consciences. Even when any pope speaks on the great common matters of the Creed, his voice does not always resonate at the same pitch of intellect as other individual Catholic consciences. Sometimes Catholics are inspired and made proud by what they hear, sometimes disappointed or even outraged. One imagines that listening to Jesus was not totally dissimilar, even though Jesus spoke with a tangible power to which history ever testifies afresh. The pope is not, as Jesus was, God but solely a man called to be vicar of one far greater than he.

The pope and, with him, the college of bishops, successors of the apostles, have a special role in protecting the purity of the Creed. The Creed is like a lifeline to God's formative action among the Jews and in Jesus. The teaching authority of pope and bishops consists in keeping pure the living waters that flow therethrough.

There are in their task immense difficulties. The human intellect and heart are fertile with invention, the human situation is ever changeable, and both human understandings and human words are slippery and unreliable instruments. Understandings come and go, even within the lifetime of one individual. Words change their meanings. So it is by no means easy for an entire community across many centuries and in multiple historical contexts to hold a common creed. The struggle to do so is unrelenting, both in every personal life and in the life of the community.

What disciplines can and should be followed to make the fulfillment of this task more sure of success? Many have been tried. Much depends upon careful education, exact and alert catechetics. It is difficult to be certain that each new believer, in every part of the world, in each new generation, receives a full and exact understanding of the faith. Handing down the faith is, of itself, a superhuman task. Much trust must necessarily be placed in God within each person accomplishing it, yet human vigilance and care are indispensable. Cisterns running sour waters poison faith.

Before Vatican II, there was much legitimately to complain about in the way the teaching authority was functioning. There were many scandals. Good persons doing good work and in a loyal spirit were, nonetheless, being penalized by authorities whose narrowness of mind was patent. Sometimes it seemed that not orthodoxy but partisan passion lay behind authoritative measures. Virtually everyone doing brave and creative work—such distinguished Catholic minds as Henri de Lubac, Yves Congar, Jean Daniélou, Jacques Maritain, John Courtney Murray, and many others—seemed to face ungenerous, unfraternal, and negative attack. The faith of such persons was all the more remarkable for their patient bearing of scandalous adversity.

After Vatican II, the tide seemed to turn in the opposite direction. Theologians grew accustomed at the Council to their role as experts, to lecturing the bishops, and, in some cases, to patronizing them. The bishops came to be treated as students to be taught, as men formed by a defective theological education now held to be out of date. Furthermore, by stressing the need for new bishops of "pastoral" skills, the Council allowed the perception to grow that bishops need not, themselves, be theologians of the first rank or leaders of intellectual acuity but, rather, men of warm hearts. Some theologians encouraged this development. The image of "opening the church"—an image I helped to reinforce—seemed to suggest, with too little qualification, that henceforth anything goes.

Since Vatican II, the balance of power between theologians, on the one hand, and the pope and bishops, on the other, has shifted. The contextual world of theologians is that of the modern university. The strongest psychological pressure they feel is peer pressure from other academics. The modern media of communication give theologians direct access to the public, not simply as in earlier days indirect access through their students. The strong perceptual image of modern communications favors any who protest against an establishment. In any conflict between a theologian and bishop, accordingly, the former is likely to have a favorable press, the latter the role of heavy.

Moreover, the news industry has a natural bias toward the new. Every challenge to traditional authority has news value, not least in matters of sex and politics, including the politics of struggles within the church.

Finally, after Vatican II, theologians who wished to be a kind of avant-garde for the church, usually with the highest of motives, soon learned to make two technical moves quite difficult for bishops to counter. First, they could point out that doctrine is inevitably historical; it develops as understanding grows. This move places on the defensive those who hold to a well-established understanding. Second, theologians could claim to be making "tentative, exploratory" statements and plead that questions remain "open." Reasons could be offered that language is a chameleon, traditions are multiple, pluralism is necessary, creativity requires space, and so forth. Meanwhile, though, each "tentative" step is actually regarded as a wedge for the next step and, cumulatively, each new article or book adds to the weight of a new tradition, precedent, and convention. Through multiple repetition, the shocking can speedily be rendered familiar and, more than familiar, authoritative, by the seal of like-minded peers. The key claim for this process came to be called "dialogue." This word was intended to suggest that bishops and theologians are equal partners in discussion, brothers and sisters speaking in mutual candor and humility. In practice, it meant that bishops yielded authority and theologians gained it. The process hardly ever worked in the other direction. For the theologian always had an ace: he or she could go public. Publicity would invariably favor the theologian. Publicly perceived as an underdog, the theologian could virtually always win public esteem. Publicly perceived as an Inquisitor, the bishop was always the real underdog. In this dialogue, it has been almost impossible for a bishop to prevail with public reputation intact.

Yet this process *could* have worked if theologians had been willing to discipline one another. But the theologian willing to be "more radical than thou" always had the same decisive public edge over his less radical peers that he had over his bishop. For, as it happens, in every sphere covered by the media, the late sixties and the years since have been salad days for radicals. According to myth, dissent requires courage and God's gift of prophecy. In reality, dissent is a cakewalk. Far from listening for God's guidance, one has only to be gifted at shocking others. If, for example, a priest expresses a view that anti-Catholic sentiment has long nourished, news value is assured. Pity the defender of orthodoxy.

This picture is depressingly vulgar. Paul Seabury describes it for the Anglican church in "Trendier Than Thou" in *Harper's,* and Dorothy Rabinowitz profiles the type in *Commentary.* [1] One does not have to be Roman Catholic to recognize the syndrome. Nor is it new. Long ago, Chesterton observed:

We often read nowadays of the valour of audacity with which some rebel attacks a hoary tyranny or an antiquated superstition. There is not really any courage at all in attacking hoary or antiquated things, any more than in offering to fight one's grandmother. The really courageous man is he who defies tyrannies young as the morning and superstitions fresh as the first flowers. The only true free-thinker is he whose intellect is as much free from the future as from the past. [2]

As long ago as 1974, *Time* magazine reported that the Catholic bishops of the United States were tilting toward satisfying the political and religious Left, not the Right. Public reputation means a great deal to any moral leader, perhaps especially a bishop. The powers of this world are arrayed against authority figures; a bishop has little enough margin of safety. Besides, the American way is to give even the crazies a chance. "This, too, shall pass," must have been a daily prayer of many bishops; it certainly was for laymen and laywomen embarrassed by the spectacle.

One theologian has pointed out, meanwhile, that any attempt to bring a new discipline to bear will founder on the social power that the "progressives" have accrued.[3] The latter, like the Arians of old, have gained ascendancy in all major institutions, not only in the Catholic press, but in several national organizations of priests, nuns, and theologians. Contemplating sadly this cycle of events, which saw fellow conservatives like himself tumble from the heights to the depths, from almost unquestioned power to virtual powerlessness, Monsignor George A. Kelly in *The Crisis of Authority*[4] appeals to the U.S. bishops to reassert their responsibilities for orthodoxy. His plea is touching, his task contradictory. For he must first demonstrate how the bishops are responsible for their own present predicament. Then he must cite the failures of the bishops with respect to orthodoxy in order to plead with them to defend orthodoxy. Furthermore, he seems to be pleading for a return to the "closed" church, run with a heavy hand.

I did not imagine twenty years ago, writing articles in praise of dissent, that we theologians would become, as a group, so feckless. Some of our adversaries did. Daniel Callahan rightly pointed out in the early fever of dissent that there was a profounder crisis of faith among the progressives—and a newer and more pervasive form of dishonesty —than many of us wished to admit.[5] What went wrong?

It seems clear that many wish to have Catholicism both ways, like the cleric or nun who never wears collar or habit except in a political demonstration. They want the church to have all its ancient and traditional power. But they also wish to treat it as a voluntary association like any other, in which they dwell part-time and which holds no special claim upon their entire conscience. There are, indeed, many

Catholics of this sort in the world and always have been, "cultural" Catholics or "communal" Catholics. That this is so is no scandal and is even a tribute to Catholicism. But it is not the ideal at which the Creed aims. It is, perhaps, a cultural ideal of modern life: the tolerant, nonconflictual personality style, easygoing and playing life by ear. It is not, in any case, my ideal. I would not like to see the church return to the style of teaching authority known before Vatican II. Nor do I wholly sympathize with the approach of intelligent traditionalist Catholics like Monsignor Kelly and James Hitchcock, or the editors of *The Wanderer.* The church is a community of fraternal correction, and I much appreciate Hitchcock's willingness to argue his case.[6] My own temperament and bent of mind, however, come alive at new challenges and in frontier areas. I am attracted by questions others have not raised, where theological reflection has hardly gone. These characteristics are nourished by American civilization, in its experiment both in democracy and in capitalism. One of my favorite essays in this respect is Friedrich Hayek's "Why I Am Not a Conservative."[7] Hayek points out that the economic and political system he favors is inventive, creative, and regularly concerned with the new. Thus, he can scarcely call himself a conservative. In this respect, true conservatives are anticapitalist and, often, antidemocratic; Tories, in other words. But Hayek is prevented from using the titles "progressive" or "liberal," which truly suit democracy and capitalism, since most persons who use such titles actually use them as protective covers for saying "socialist" or "of the Left." He argues that his own favorite intellectuals are men like Aristotle, Aquinas, Burke, Smith, and de Tocqueville. Reluctantly, and with amusement, he supposes he must call himself a Whig.

Between traditionalists like Monsignor Kelly and the Catholic Left, I wish the liberal Catholic tradition, revised as need be, still stood. My ideal for the teaching authority of the church would be that persons of intellect would follow conscience and reason to the utmost, yet all the while taking responsibility both for bringing the community of faith together and for relating their findings to the great tradition. It is not enough to shock, to divide, to demand change. Great communities do not leap forward overnight and, if they do, their landing place is not likely to be where it ought to be. Great communities, especially in an age of mass communication, can swiftly be misled. Mass hysteria of many kinds has been a frequent enough phenomenon in this century. Moreover, a tremendously rich intellectual and artistic tradition developed through generations of loving labor can be abandoned and lost within a single generation. Our generation, I tremble to write, may in this way have single-handedly squandered the great Catholic renaissance on which three generations before our own had expended massive and brilliant labors. The cheaply radical young graduates of many of our major Catholic universities often know nothing, or almost nothing, of the intellectual heritage of Aquinas and Newman, Bonaventure and Bossuet, Péguy and Mauriac and Maritain and Marcel. We may await severe judgment under God for this betrayal.

We have taken evil too lightly and have not been faithful stewards of traditions entrusted to us. We thought of the church as massive and immovable and did not reckon on its fragility. We disliked the authoritarianism of the traditionalists and were blind to that of the progressives. We were quick to criticize the Right, but slow to criticize the excesses of the Left. We failed to be realists. We failed to be genuinely liberal—self-questioning, generous, saving the past even as we moved into new territory. That liberal ideal, suitably corrected and enlarged, is valid. I hope we may create it afresh.

My good friend Father James V. Schall, S.J., has advised me that I should not use simply the word "liberal" here, for there are too many serious defects in the Anglo-Saxon liberal tradition, in Adam Smith, Jeremy Bentham, John Stuart Mill, and others. He points out that I myself have often written of these defects, from my first book, *A New Generation*, to my latest, *The Spirit of Democratic Capitalism*, and have worked from an intellectual horizon quite different from that of the secular liberal. Father Schall is clearly correct about the difficulties of the title "liberal." Beyond the triad of liberal, traditionalist, and radical (socialist) positions, he believes there is a fourth tradition, perhaps better to be described as "biblical realism" or by some other distinctive name. This fourth tradition includes the authors Hayek cites: Aristotle, Aquinas, Burke, Smith, de Tocqueville, and adds such others as John Henry Newman, G. K. Chesterton, Reinhold Niebuhr, and Jacques Maritain. (I believe that Schall would also add Leo Strauss and Eric Voegelin.) I believe Schall is right.

In reflecting on these matters over several years, I have almost despaired of finding a suitable name. "Whig" does suggest that confluence of liberal and conservative, individual and community, tradition and teleology, and realistic future which I have in mind. And it suggests the mainstream of writers who nourish the perennial wisdom. Yet "Whig" has the faint sense of the attic about it. "Neoliberal" seems more usable, suggesting a revision of the liberal tradition, enlarging it to include conservative ideas like community, tradition, faith, and realism about society and its mediating structures. But no term is fully satisfactory. Perhaps "realist" best captures the Catholic tradition of the philosophy of being and practical wisdom *(phronesis)*, and "biblical" best enlarges it to the Jewish and Christian horizon. Yet "biblical realist" might seem to some premodern. For until the modern era, when the institutions of representative democracy, a market economy, and the pluralistic culture came to be practicable, one could be a "biblical realist" without confronting the institutional questions of modern political economy. It is the practical *liberal* tradition that led the way to institutions of democracy, capitalism, and pluralism. These are great human achievements, reflecting important themes of biblical realism: a sense of sin, providence, liberty of conscience, the communitarian individual, and the like. Such themes could not find institutional expression until the modern era, and still do so only imperfectly.

Although the reality is surely more important than the name, ordinary discourse is much aided by exact and useful naming. On the other hand, the very enterprise of thinking hard about what is really covered by any particular name helps to recreate the horizon necessary for understanding it exactly. Taking a hint from Leszek Kolakowski,[8] I sometimes want to call myself a Liberal-Conservative-Democratic-Market-Communitian-Pluralist-Catholic.

To put it clearly, my intention is to submit to the disciplines of being Catholic and to struggle to keep the integrity of the faith; to advance the tradition of Aristotle, Aquinas, Newman, and Lonergan; and to help bring into the patrimony of Catholic intellect the best wisdom of the Anglo-American experiment in political economy, the best of its empirical temper and practical intellect. (American theology used to be faulted by Europeans for its practical character; lately, they fault it for paying insufficient attention to *praxis*, understood in a Marxian way. Europeans are beginning at last to suffer, as they should, from an inferiority complex vis-à-vis American vitalities.) These aims set me in conflict with those who attack or dismiss Catholic faith; with those who attack or dismiss the philosophy of being and the tradition of practical wisdom; with those who are either antidemocratic or anticapitalist, some for traditionalist and others for socialist reasons; and with still others who make divergent judgments at any of these points. Disputation is the proper habitat of intellect.

Perhaps a concrete example of how this ideal may work is useful here. This example is extreme, but illuminates a boundary. To my knowledge, there is only one point at which, in all conscience, I hold a view at variance with that of the teaching authority of the church: the condemnation of artificial contraceptives. It is possible that I stimulated the first public dissent on this question in English in *Blackfriars* and published the first in America in *Commonweal*. [9] A book I edited on the theme, *The Experience of Marriage*, in which a dozen couples (anonymously) recounted their own experiences, was translated into several European languages. [10] My good friend John Noonan became one of the world's leading experts on the theological history of the question. [11] Alas, receiving the considerations leading up to Pope Paul VI's *Humanae Vitae*, his encyclical reaffirming the traditional viewpoint, the Pope saw fit to reject such arguments as ours. I accept his right to do so, and the fact that he has done so gives me somber pause. Since *Humanae Vitae*, I have written very little publicly about my dissent, not from a spirit of evasion but because I trusted that further experience and inquiry would gradually vindicate my position. One thing is certain. Years after I am gone, the papacy will still be vigorous and Catholic teaching inspiring millions. Many a dissenter in history soon disappears from sight.

On the other hand, study as I may the teaching of the church on this question, I do not find that it applies as it says it applies. There are many complex arguments involved. I cannot give them all space here. Suffice it to make only a few observations. For a good many years I lived as a celibate. I know from experience that sexual love in marriage looks very different from the perspective of a celibate and from that of the married person. Further, it is not difficult to understand why, for centuries, when so many children died in childbirth and life expectancy was, on average, about twenty-five years, each act of conception seemed vital to the continuation of the human race. In the year 1800, the entire population of the world was only 800 million. Today it is 4.4 billion. The upsurge is not because people are making love more often or having more children in each marriage, but because so many of those conceived are born healthy and now live. One can easily understand during most centuries of Christian life, how precious each conception was to human survival. "As food is for the preservation of the body," Augustine wrote, "so is intercourse for the preservation of the race."[12] This analogy is at the heart of Catholic traditions on this subject. It bears careful reflection.

Moreover, it is not difficult to see why the church should be afraid of breaking the tie between lovemaking and conception. One can say that such a tie forces lovers to recall beyond their mutual affection and pleasure the mystery of life. The sacrifice potentially involved ennobles their life together.

Still, it has only been in recent times that the secrets of reproduction have become known. When Pius XI wrote the first modern encyclical on this subject in 1930, it was not then known that, by nature, a woman is infertile during most of her cycle. Based on this new scientific knowledge, Pope Pius XII later approved of "the rhythm method," the natural method of avoiding conception, which limits intercourse to those times of the month when the woman is naturally infertile. Many who practice this method are enthusiastic about it. For them it is reliable and they report pleasure in its naturalness, as opposed to the unpleasantness of the "pill" and its side effects and to the messiness of artificial contraceptives. Critics say the church approves of using *time* to thwart fertility, but disapproves of using *space*. From my point of view, if it is good to respect a woman's infertility as being as natural as her fertility, which the rhythm method does, then artificial spatial aids are also good. There is nothing inherently evil in respecting infertility. God intended it. Temporary infertility is natural. Typically, the church respects the symbolic powers of natural acts. It does not look at them mechanically. Typically, too, it is fairly cynical about individual motivations and self-deceptions. When human beings speak much of mutuality, sensitivity, fulfillment, and the insight that arises from "knowing" another (in the archaic verb for intercourse), the church is inclined to see at least a strain of hedonism and high-blown rationalization. And who can deny it?

On the other hand, in the daily jading and familiarity of married life, sexual love does not quite match up with church documents. Consider the couples who express little or no sexual love. Are they to be honored because, in their marriages, sexual love has gone cold? It is not so easy as clerical literature often suggests to keep sexual love alive. And isn't that a good that *should* be kept alive?

As for having children, let us prescribe that those who are married and who make love *should* have children during their marriage, as the natural fruit of their love. But should they have a child every year? Given what is now known about reproduction, it might be possible for a couple to have children from nearly every act of intercourse. Would *that* be an ideal—so to limit intercourse that perfection would consist in having only as many acts as were necessary for conception? No one suggests that.

Is it the ideal, then, to throw oneself entirely upon the will of God, not even using such knowledge as one possesses, in making judgment about when children ought to come? That does not seem provident.

These seem to be the ideals at which current church teaching seems aimed: either to use the knowledge one has and so to limit the frequency of intercourse to a minimum, or to ignore the knowledge one has and cast oneself upon Providence. These do not seem to me to represent the highest Catholic vision. One can understand that in the days before knowledge about reproduction was available, humans could not act from knowledge; chance ruled. Today it is different. Consider the case of a couple who, having three children, or four, or five, by the end of their twenties, decides to have no more. Is it now to be Catholic morality that they ought to make love never again? This does not seem to me good or wise.

A married Catholic of sound conscience, it seems to me, might well conclude that the true rationale of the Catholic teaching is as follows. First, the married vocation normally calls for having children. The Catholic impulse, indeed, may be to err on the side of generosity in having children, welcoming more than mere worldly prudence would suggest, while still staying within the bounds of proper responsibility. Second, protect mutual love from mere lust or hedonism, rooting sexual love in marital friendship, the highest form of friendship known to the human race: more thorough, more humble, more quotidian, and more complete than any other. Married love is the opposite of utopian. It is nature's own way of teaching realism. It cuts through the illusions of the self with a terrible constant sword. In these ways, personal dignity is respected and also the obligation of one generation to the future of the species.

Now it is clear that authoritative Catholic teaching does not at present go this far. The church worries that "a contraceptive mentality" may sever sexual love from the realities of family life, and that the habit of making love solely for affection and pleasure will give rise to a boundless restlessness. (Indeed, it is in practice true that each spouse is, at some moments, less ready to make love than the other and that marital "demands," however sweetly made, are clearly made by one upon the other.) Recognizing that familiarity often leads to disinterest by one spouse in the other and the search for other objects of affection, the church fears that "the contraceptive mentality" will break familial bonds. Thus infidelity, divorce, and abortion will multiply. These are, alas, sensible concerns. The church knows what is in human beings, having had much and continuing experience with them down the ages. It does not follow, however, that current church teaching can stem the tide of infidelity, divorce, and abortion. The source of these lies in far deeper soil than "the contraceptive mentality"—as abortion clearly shows.

Friendship between husband and wife, and the fidelity of one to the other, are precious human goods, indispensable to any self-governing and realistic society. For it is in such self-governance within familial life that the very model for the self-governance of societies is to be found.[13] If families are incapable of realism, discipline, and friendship, how can mere politics begin to teach the virtues on which free societies utterly depend?

In times gone by, it was not easy to bring healthy children into the world. Even in the time of our grandparents—and the situation was yet more grim in the time of *their* grandparents—many women died in childbirth and even more of their children, often two of four or five, died within the first two years of life. One can visit the tombstones still. Today, by contrast, a single conception is highly likely to result in a living child with an average life expectancy of more than seventy years. Conception has changed its historical character. With that change, the conditions of married life have also changed for mothers and fathers.

I still have hopes that, one day, the church will come to see that frequent acts of sexual love within marriage, even when conception is clearly not wanted, are still much to be desired from a moral and religious point of view. If it is wrong to imagine that every act of lovemaking is an act of friendship, it is also wrong to imagine that each is an act of lust, hedonism, or selfishness.

To believe that lovemaking between friends bound in marriage is holy only when conditions of potential conception are present does not seem correct. That would restrict lovemaking too totally. And to what moral or religious point, which could not be met regardless of the possibility of conception? All the classical and traditional concerns of the church—important and proper as they are—can be met apart from the present restriction.

Some studies show that nearly eighty percent of Catholic married couples in the United States employ contraceptives at some time during their married lives. One may conclude from this that their dissent from the teaching of the Church tells against their virtue or their orthodoxy. But another interpretation may be more correct: they know from experience that the use of contaceptives does not generate in them a "contraceptive mentality." They wish to have children, some of them many children. They delight in their children. They also find it both normal and good to make love frequently, many of them more than once a week throughout their married lives. This they do with mutual consideration, in friendship. They do not understand why lovemaking should be limited solely to those occasions on which they seek pregnancy, or why they ought to be less than provident in seeking pregnancy.

This issue does not lie near the center of the deposit of faith, but it is a matter of daily importance to the married couple. Since Catholic teaching on it rests upon arguments from natural law, the experience of married couples, while not determinative, deserves serious consideration. Their moral reasoning must be articulated. The mere repetition of authority is not sufficient. Those who too swiftly attack dissenters for failing to grasp the argument of natural law teaching in a matter so close to their experience may also be missing something very important. It is not enough to say that the latter are "infected with the prevailing materialism of the age," for that may not be the case. Their knowledge about procreation imposes its own responsibilities upon them. So does marital friendship.

There is one last argument. Some hold that Catholic life is more demanding than ordinary natural life and must demand heroic practice. For myself, I do not see heroism in abstinence under conditions of married life, although I do see it under conditions of celibacy. Many abuses lurk in that direction. Furthermore, a teaching rooted in natural law cannot as a matter of course demand heroism. Married persons, as a general rule, ought *not* to live as celibates. To hold that they should would be to interpret Catholicism as precisely that sort of idealism that is not incarnate, fleshly, and ordinary, and that is opposite symbolically to the ordinary mysteries of the church.

Nonetheless, I recall vividly that birth control is almost the only intellectual position that G. K. Chesterton, in *The Well and the Shallows,* said he held in "contempt."[14] He gave three reasons for "despising" it. (1) The concept deceives, he thought, by meaning the opposite of what it says; its purpose is not "control" but to make "sure that there will never be any birth to control."[15] (2) Birth control is even worse than eugenics, eliminating the mystery from birth and thus treating babies even worse than kittens, since the latter are at least allowed to be born before being rejected. (3) Birth control does not free humans as it claims but confines them within a mechanical process. Much as I respect Chesterton, I do not find these arguments convincing. First, I hold with him to the normal obligation of married couples to "preserve the race" by having children. Generosity in having children is still to be encouraged, even when couples wisely use available knowledge about fertility and infertility. Second, the mystery of birth does not consist of ignorance about fertility or infertility but in the very fact of fertility. To respect that power with foresight is the opposite of showing disrespect for it. The miracle of birth is just as powerful for modern as for ancient families, and fills the heart and mind with awe on each occasion. Some couples who practice birth control have more children than some who do not. Third, through using their knowledge about fertility and infertility, couples do not regard marital love merely as a mechanical process; far from it. In fact, the opposite is sometimes the case: not exercising full human knowledge and will, some women have cried out against seeming to be "baby machines." The entry of human knowledge and will into a decision to have children makes childbirth seem far *less* mechanical, a more fully formed and joyously human act.

In a lyrical passage, Chesterton sums up his vision of childbirth; it is also mine. Indeed, in his emphasis upon freedom, Chesterton seems to concede the central point which I have been trying to make, a point which in his polemic against shallow materialism he uncustomarily misses:

Now a child is the very sign and sacrament of personal freedom. He is a fresh free will added to the wills of the world; he is something that his parents have freely chosen to produce and which they freely agree to protect. They can feel that any amusement he gives (which is often considerable) really comes from them and from him, and from nobody else. He has been born without the intervention of any master or lord. He is a creation and a contribution; he is their own creative contribution to creation. He is also a much more beautiful, wonderful, amusing and astonishing thing than any of the stale stories or jingling jazz tunes turned out by the machines. When men no longer feel that he is so, they have lost their appreciation of primary things, and therefore all sense of proportion about the world.[16]

It would take us too far afield to argue the substance of the moral question further. What I have been trying to highlight is not the substance of the matter but the manner of dealing with a conflict between legitimate authority and conscience. Traditionalists will properly say that a good Catholic ought simply to yield assent, if not upon the merits of the argument (being unable to coerce the mind), then upon reasons of faith in God's chosen instrument of church authority. I recognize the force of this argument. But the traditionalist solution is also flawed. First, the church may in the long run best be served by lively intellect doggedly faithful to itself, respectful, faithful to the light of the mind, receptive, open to argument. This is especially true when the vast majority of the faithful are disregarding church teaching. Sexual love within marriage is a part of ordinary daily life, not some rare and extraordinary moral perplexity. I do not believe that the mass of the Catholic faithful regard the use of contraceptives as they regard fornication, or adultery, or acts of lust or selfishness, or as signs of lack of self-control, and the like. In such matters, lively consciences feel guilt of a sort the use of contraceptives does not engender in them. Why this should be so deserves rational explanation, which I have been trying to offer. I respect the right of the church to pass judgment on such interpretations. My intention is to serve, not to supplant, the authority of the church. The material knowledge about reproduction available to prudent couples is quite different today from what it was when Chesterton wrote. So is the imperative, "As food for the preservation of the body, so intercourse for the preservation of the race." Food serves more purposes than self-preservation; art does not deform it. The preservation of the race no longer requires families as large as once it did, although large families remain a blessing to those who have them. With new knowledge and joyous will, the having of children, although no longer shrouded in ignorance, is still full of mystery and delight. Each couple must decide how many children it is, among other callings, their vocation to nurture. Whatever that number, one or a dozen, sexual love within marriage will remain a normal and lovely sign of their friendship. It is not a sound moral principle that Catholic couples ought to make love as infrequently as necessary in order to have whatever number of children. They should be provident, generous, and free in having children, and loving toward each other.

These, then, are my reflections. I believe that those who hold similar views must continue to make this argument within the church, defending all the traditional values better than the current teaching in fact defends them. If we are correct, church authority will eventually recognize the point. If not, we have tried neither to scandalize others nor to defy authority but to follow where conscience leads. In time, the matter will be decided, not only by authority but by wholesale consent. What we cannot do is to coerce our conscience to accept arguments we do not, in fact, accept. Yet neither can we claim to be speaking with the authority of the church when we do not. Nor can we rest comfortably with the thought that we are out of harmony with the church, as we are. A great incarnate human institution cannot swiftly change ideas that have served it well for centuries, nor should we expect it to. Trusting in the final judgment of God, we make our conscience plain, accept the legitimate role of the authority that holds us to be wrong, do not pretend to be correct, and move forward as best we can.[17] It is painful to be torn between conscience and legitimate authority.

Were we simply to yield to authority, disobeying conscience, we would cut the ground from under any authority rooted in conscience. Were we simply to replace authority with personal conscience, we would absent ourselves from belief in the apostolic church. But it should not surprise us often to find, in a real and vital institution, conflict between one and the other, which time alone can resolve.

As I understand it, this is neither the traditionalist Catholic way nor the way of the new Catholic Left. But it is, I believe, the way of the liberal Catholic tradition. This tradition has its power, its fecundity, and its nobility. It entails willingness to suffer in and with the church.

Moreover, the liberal Catholic tradition, more than any other, makes it necessary to dwell on the interplay between conscience and the apostolic church. Some, within and outside the church, think these must be contradictory, *either* one *or* the other. I do not find it so. The typical Catholic philosophy is never *either/or;* it is typically *both/and;* and so here. Cardinal Newman once wrote in reply to Gladstone (I paraphrase): "If I must propose a toast—which God forbid—I would drink so: First to conscience, then to the pope." Such a toast does not exalt conscience at the expense of God's revelation; on the contrary, it celebrates the precondition of the latter. If humans are incapable of conscience or faithless to it, to what in humans might God address Himself? To accept the proper force of papal authority, one must first nurture, cherish, and uphold conscience. To nothing else does the pope, having no divisions, speak.

On the other hand, to toast conscience first, then the pope is not to place individual conscience *over* the pope. One must be faithful to conscience, come what may. Yet the role of the pope is by no means to scandalize, injure, or trample upon conscience. Far from it. His task is to respect, nurture, and illuminate conscience, to lead it to the fruitful paths marked out by conscience's Maker. There cannot be, in principle, conflict between the Light and a participant in Light, which is what our conscience is: our inner light, offspring of Light. That there are blockages, clouds, confusions, and struggles goes without saying. Yet fidelity to one is always correct in virtue of the authority of the other. Otherwise, not even conscience has any claim over us. Its entire claim is of God.

If God revealed Himself to humankind and called together a historical community to guard this revelation, then the preservation of that revelation is indispensable to succeeding generations. Catholics hold, as Protestants do not, that the papal office has a special grace in this respect, a terrifying and terrible responsibility, utterly appropriate to the human condition. The papacy is human. Its ways are human. Miraculous signs do not accompany its normal workings. Seldom in any one Christian's life do papal interventions bear direct challenge to individual conscience. Yet on heated matters of the hour they sometimes do. Artificial contraception is one such, in my case, as I have tried to show. Let us rise, then, to the general level of theory, concerning a Catholic's responsibility *both* to conscience *and* to the apostolic church. In particular, consider the obligations of a Catholic who is also a philosopher and a theologian.

A Christian who is a philosopher or theologian has three obligations to conscience and the apostolic church. On matters of faith and morals, he or she owes it to the church to understand what it teaches through pope and bishops and to accept these as the authentic teaching of the church for that place and time. (Since challenges to the faith change, as do the meanings of words, this authentic teaching often shifts the front on which it does battle.) Second, the Christian thinker has an obligation to intellect and conscience, precisely as a professional, to think every matter through as clearly as he or she can. This is also an obligation to the church. The church needs the work of independent intellect, even if it ends in dissent. Third, the Christian thinker has an obligation to the historical community of Christians. Truth in history is not merely an abstraction but, for Christians, a life to be lived; truth must be assimilated and related to other truths by an entire community.

For the liberal Catholic tradition, it is crucial to observe that individual truths have a *time value* as well as a truth value. As Cardinal Newman points out, Christian thinkers have an obligation to God's will concerning the ripeness of time. Truths have their own season. Often enough, a thinker is seized by the light of a single idea, even a sound one, but by pressing it too hard and in isolation, prematurely, he or she provokes a rejection, which then injures the reputation of that idea for generations. The community of faith is not, in this respect, like a community of scientists or a community of scholars. The latter do not *live* the ideas that are the objects of their work; for them, ideas once demonstrated even by a single researcher have obligatory force for all. The code of the scientific and scholarly community does not have the same relation to time as does that of a community of faith. The assimilation of notional assents is much more rapid than the assimilation of real assents. Further, it takes place within a limited community of academics. In these respects, the Christian philosopher or theologian may have conflicting responsibilities—one to the community of professional peers, the other to the community of faith. In the long run, over a century, say, the ideals of these two communities may be identical; in the short run, necessarily, there are many conflicts between them.

Finally, the paradigm of the avant-garde may suggest that the community of theologians—professors, mainly, in universities, ecumenical centers, divinity schools, and seminaries—is more "up to date," more "advanced," than the community of faith. Sometimes this may be so. But the paradigm is, in general, illusory. The spirit of the profession of theology has now become rather like that of other intellectual disciplines. Fewer, today, are the theologians who profess to think for and with the church. For many, the primary community of reference consists of their scholarly peers; it is not the community of faith and its canonical authorities. With respect to the authority of the church, some theologians would seem to conduct themselves as free-lancers, bound by the canons of peer review far more than by apostolic authority. This is not altogether bad. This, too, can be an asset to the church. But it does create many difficulties for the daily life of the church. At times, the community of theologians may indeed be breaking new ground for the future life of the church. Yet, often enough, the horizon of an entire generation of theologians, compelling enough during that generation, is rejected by the next generation or the one following that. Far from breaking new paths for the future, many intellectual currents turn out to be swift, dated eddies, historical curiosities deposited quite outside the decisive stream of history. Nothing is more sobering than a rereading of the most respected theologians of preceding generations, from whichever part of the spectrum of opinion. So many of the matters on which they believed their own insights superior are soon regarded as dated.

Conscience has obligations to itself, to its intellectual disciplines, and to the community of faith. No one of these is easy. All three together seem insuperably demanding.

Yet the apostolic church is also a community of mercy. To our daily necessities God's grace is sufficient. It nourishes us at the community's table. Thinking and living for an entire community, not only for oneself, heightens the drama of our lives.

Thus, even reflections poor as these become part of the patrimony of generations, to be assessed, welcomed, or rejected as that community decides. To be Catholic is to live within a historical community far larger than one's own generation, and under an authority which often challenges the dearest prejudices both of the age and of the self. To be Catholic requires fidelity to conscience and, more, to a *community* of conscience. It is, therefore, a calling to intellectual struggle, to inner combat, and to a harsh purgation of the soul. Restful it isn't; there are easier roads to inner satisfaction. One is often tempted by their allures. To be a Catholic is to choose, and choose again.

10. Remission of Sins

I affirm one baptism for the remission of sins.

"One baptism." One of the hints to the distinctively Catholic habit of mind lies in the phrase: one baptism. Were Christianity a gnostic faith, it would scorn water and ritual. What has water to do with the remission of sins? Why should it matter that water is poured on a human head, if the spirit is enlightened? Christianity not only values but insists upon the pouring of water on the matted hair of a suppliant. Christianity is even more physical: it holds to *one* baptism. There is a single prescribed form, one narrow way.

To take part in an actual baptism today is, in fact, to be quite distracted from things of the spirit. Infants squeal, youngsters squirm, godparents are nervous, in-laws are critical, the celebrant tries his best to concentrate—while simultaneously pointing and whispering to inexperienced participants, trying to avoid making too much mess with water, oils, salt, and candlewax, and to intone familiar phrases with feeling. The disconcerting vulgarity of this family event overwhelms "spiritual" meaning. The vulgarity matters.

Since it is through the flesh that a child feels, thinks, decides, lives, so it is also through the flesh that sins are remitted. The restless infant about to be baptized is no angel; having earlier been abundantly fed for the ordeal, she has messed her diaper. Through the flesh she has inherited the faults and flaws peculiar to her immediate family and many others besides. A realistic religion, therefore, wishes to dramatize that it is through this same flesh that the remission of sins is handed down from generation to generation.

All who seek God in their hearts receive the mercy of God, through "baptism by desire" if not through baptism of water. Baptism is not a magic totem. The action in baptism is God's. It is God who taught us this "one baptism." Jesus accepted it from John the Baptist and commissioned His apostles to "baptize all nations." God's instruction is physical, in compassion for the ordinary ways of flesh.

By comparison with gnosticism, and even with certain more spiritual forms of Protestantism, Catholicism proposes a sacramental way of life: it sees God acting through human ministers performing physical acts (at baptism, in penance, in the holy Eucharist, and the rest), rather than purely as Spirit to spirit. Of course, God acts in the latter way, too; nothing sets bounds to His action. Yet more than most major religions, Catholicism sticks close to bodily ways, physical deeds, appointed ministers, prescribed forms. To those of enlightened or purely spiritual temper, such physicality suggests paganism and crude superstition. Nonetheless, humbly enough, Catholicism is faithful to the *embodied* person—"man and woman He made them"—and to the ways of flesh. Catholicism, a religion of the spirit, is not a religion for spiritualists.

That is why one may speak of a distinctively Catholic realism. Because Christianity *is* a religion of the spirit it attracts idealists and leads all to aspire impossibly high. Because it is also a religion of the body and of workaday history, it also teaches prudence and measure, patience and forgiveness. It is an altogether human temptation to wish that we humans were not as limited by our bodies, histories, particularities, and quirks as we are. It is altogether human to demand a "prophetic" church. It is easy to desire that the Catholic people should be idealistic, honest, kind, generous, giving, pure; that they would be a light unto the nations; that the radiance of their spirit would astound the world. Instead, one encounters everywhere a lethargic, fault-ridden, conflicted body of human prejudices, faults, and sins. One sees one's fellow parishioners in sports shirts, observes the sun glinting off Fords in the parking lot, watches the suburban gathering at happytalk prayer, and groans for all that has been lost. The church is priestly, incarnated, and compromised more often than it is prophetic. This is the church that the Lord has called. It is an act of Catholic realism to stress this point. The moment the young begin to dream glowing dreams of sinlessness, it is Catholic realism to temper those dreams—

not to uproot them, for they too are an indispensable part of human life and forward-moving energy—but to insist upon the ways of patience, prudence, and practical result. For the Catholic, there is no escaping into some better world. It is human destiny to work with the stuff of this world as it is.

Catholicism, in this respect, is native soil for artists. Like every form of art, the life of a Catholic is spiritual and fleshly at the same time. The artist struggles with stubborn materials, with discipline and craft, against self-deception in a way paradigmatic for Christians.[1] In the Protestant tradition (a noble, edifying tradition), there is a tendency to link ethics with the world of obligation, law, and duty. In the Catholic tradition, the analogue for ethics is art. Thus, for Aquinas, art is right reason (spirit, including charity) applied to *making* things, and prudence—the form of all the virtues, until supplanted by charity— is right reason (spirit, including charity) applied to *doing* things. No one has written better on this theme than Jacques Maritain.[2] From the days of the catacombs, from the days of the Byzantine basilicas, Catholicism has had a natural affinity for the arts. For in their involvement in flesh and in materials, the arts offer a splendid analogue for the sacraments. Icons, mosaics, frescoes, paintings, music, and incense —all belong to worship. We honor artists not solely for their vision but because they respect material things. They are masterfully sensitive to grain and texture. They learn discipline. Soulcraft, for the artist, is fleshcraft.

This is, no doubt, the point of Chesterton's quip that Catholicism is a thick steak, a good cigar, and a frosted stout. In such things God is. To try to spiritualize the way to God is a fundamental, though understandable, error. Cardinal Newman writes:

No one can really respect religion and insult its forms. Granted that forms are not immediately from God, still long use has made them divine *to us;* for the spirit of religion has so penetrated and quickened them, that to destroy them is, in respect to the multitude of men, to unsettle and dislodge the religious principle itself. In most minds usage has so identified them with the notion of religion, that one cannot be extirpated without the other. Their faith will not bear transplanting. . . . Precious doctrines are strung like jewels upon slender threads.[3]

"One baptism" implies one church, which establishes the rules for ritual and excludes some practices while incorporating others. To insist upon "one" may seem to suggest divine arbitrariness. Could not God, who is infinite, have instead commanded many ways? Of course. It is not Catholic to set limits to God, only to observe limits set by God. Contemplating Catholicism from the outside, one sees a hundred or a thousand signs of arbitrariness. If God is everywhere, why is one place especially holy? If God is spirit, why is it necessary to enter a building? From a spiritualist point of view, employing the scales of the spirit, no concrete particular weighs much. Catholicism, not being a spiritualist religion, plods its way through particulars. It selects from the stuff of daily life, choosing and rejecting for its rites according to the divine intention handed down, as poor humans can best understand it, no doubt erring from time to time, and always in need of reform.

For some, this world view of the Catholic is not easy to grasp: this realism about the flesh that insists that for the remission of sins there is one baptism. Yet once one sees its point, the stumbling block is not so great.

And what is this "remission" of sins? Remission is greater than forgiveness. Forgiveness is an act humans may perform. There is even a way in which Christians may be admirable when they do *not* forgive, as when they say: "To my dying day, I can never forgive him for that." If they are saying that they leave judgment to God, while to the extent of their own knowledge they can find no excuse for the evil some villain has done, this attitude is not without religious merit. The word *remission*, however, goes beyond forgiveness. It suggests the difference between God's action and human action. Humans may forgive sin, but only God can wipe it out and make the sinner new. Christians are in this respect called to a lesser task: "Forgive us our trespasses as we forgive those who have trespassed against us." Christians can, indeed, forgive, no longer hold a grudge, no longer demand recompense. God does more than that. Acting upon the soul of his creatures, He wipes out what the old books called the "stain" of sin; that is, redirects the soul away from its preference for sin and turns it toward love of Himself; brings the soul once again into living contact with "the Love that moves the sun and all the stars." God can suffuse the habits of the self-loving self with the light of His own life. This is more than forgiveness. Negatively, it is a purging of the soul, a cleansing, a remission—in a stronger sense, even, than when a cancer is not only checked, but made to disappear, and healthy life is restored.

It was Aquinas, I think, who first observed that the true nature of God is not revealed in justice, which even humans may approach (though not perfectly), but in mercy. The root of the word in Latin, *miseri-cor*, helped Aquinas at this point: it explicitly evokes the image of the heart *(cor)* going out to the miserable. Yet in Judaism and Christianity, mercy on God's part is more than the flowing forth of a heart warm with compassion. It is also the re-constituting, re-creating action of God in the soul of His creatures. In His mercy, God does not merely forgive us but re-makes us. Only God can do that. His divinity is most visible in His mercy.

In contemporary Catholicism there is a tendency to diminish the ancient emphasis on "original sin," to weaken the stress upon personal sin, and to promote the importance of social sin. Furthermore, social sin has become shorthand for capitalism. To participate in socialist revolution is to have one's sins remitted. This is not Catholic faith. A few words about each type of sin may be useful.

In my own thinking about original sin, I have come to the following understanding. The concept of original sin is the one Catholic teaching endlessly and most clearly verified in history. The sin is called original because it has been part of human history from the beginning. In the story of Eden, Adam and Eve turned away from God's simple mandate: eat not of the one tree. Cain slew Abel. From the beginning, in other words, every human has manifested a restlessness under God's invitations and commands, in such fashion that each has regularly and repeatedly turned away from God and toward the solicitations of desire. All humans since time immemorial share in this tendency. A maxim expresses it: every human sometimes sins. Augustine, reflecting on his own conduct, as each of us may, described the evil tendency of the human heart as a sort of trick knee that sometimes causes the heart to limp. It functions but it often breaks its expected stride and is thus defective in its quest for the good. With great effort, we can for a time compensate enough to evade the limp. Yet sooner or later, under stress, when we are weary or off guard, we fall again. This is true even of great saints. This sad fact does not suggest total depravity, only predictable weakness.

Yet there is another point to the notion of original sin: that it is *inherited.* A commonsense understanding of how this comes about seems clear in childrearing. Personality disorders and emotional conflicts among parents clearly have an effect upon children, not perhaps in exact repetition of the parents' defects. Each family has its own distinctive culture and none is perfect. All sorts of irrationalities, quirks, weaknesses, and inclinations are passed along, as well as moral strengths. Infants are not masters of their early environment, but helpless recipients thereof. By heroic efforts, parents sometimes try to "protect" their children from the inheritance they themselves received. They try to create a new beginning in Eden, apart from the evils of this world. The results are invariably ironic.

One reason why the gnostics of our present age wish to discount the importance of original sin concerns its alleged conservative implications. Belief in original sin does indeed imply that there can be no paradise on earth. But is this a conservative belief? Not necessarily. Some may, indeed, conclude from it, with considerable historical force, that the calculus of good and evil among human beings remains fairly constant under diverse historical regimes. Evil in the human heart is not, they may hold, so much eliminated as displaced from one place to another. Thus, some hold, cultures and generations differ less in the quantity of vice they accumulate than in the particular vices that seize their attention. Now it would be conservative to suggest that, on this basis, social reforms are entirely useless. For it may make a great deal of difference *where* vice is encouraged or freely permitted, and *whether* practical techniques are available for turning some vices to creative social purpose. Those of us of reformist tendency, liberals, argue that it is good for social structures to be arranged so as to achieve standards of moral conduct in certain key social locations, even though we understand that vice as a whole cannot be much diminished in quantity. Thus, only a massive police force (and who would police the policemen?) could prevent individuals from indulging in vice in their private lives. Meanwhile, however, social behavior in which others are affected, often unseen others, can be regulated according to some higher standards of honesty, fairness, due process and law. In a differentiated society of the liberal type, independent systems—political, economic, and moral-cultural—regulate one another. Incentives and disincentives may be wisely designed.

In short, belief in original sin does not diminish the energy available to social reform. In order to believe in the achievement of higher levels of civilization, it is not necessary to believe in a state of future sinlessness. Quite the opposite. In order to invent institutions with a realistic chance of making human life morally better, at least in certain transactions, it is not only useful but necessary to form a just estimate of human weakness. A theory of sin—even original sin—lies behind the modern practice of liberal democracy and democratic capitalism. This is a liberal and progressive, rather than conservative, theory. It does not strengthen the status quo. It anticipates and encourages the narrative progress of the human race.

One important insight embodied in the teaching of original sin may be put this way: trust no one over or under the age of thirty. Every human being sometimes betrays his own best spirit. No one of us is to be trusted. "In God we trust"—that is, in nobody else. The practical corollary of this insight is always to seek a diffusion of powers, checks and balances, institutional protections, social disciplines and lawful procedures, in order to diminish at least by a little the number of betrayals, and to place the interests of one against the interests of the other, so as to heighten the probabilities of keeping both honest. Belief in original sin warns against excesses of idealism, reliance upon innocence, and a romantic misreading of the human heart. Would that that heart were other than it is. Since it is not, we imitate God's mercy by strengthening the probabilities of the good, and checking the probabilities of evil at least by a little and at least in some locations.

Furthermore, since belief in original sin springs from insight into the individual heart, it also inoculates the faithful against belief in sinless structures. Some moderns seem to believe that individuals, left to themselves, are innocent and good and that they are "messed up" only by institutions. Alas, humans live in institutions as fish in water or birds in air. Institutions are the habitat of civilization. They are the race's teachers of virtue and progress. Only with painstaking discipline do individuals overcome their infantile self-centeredness, their capacity to fantasize beautiful and ideal worlds centered upon their own contentment. To learn that others *resist* the illusions of the self—not only do not share them but by no means totally admire them—is to begin to live in an other-centered world. Beginning at birth, the center of each child's universe is its own stomach. Many years pass before that center leaves the stomach, then the psyche, then the self. Some never complete that development, and no one perfectly does. Our cosmos, alas, continues to revolve too narrowly upon our own navels.

In this respect, Reinhold Niebuhr's phrase "moral man and immoral society" should be reversed, since the self-centeredness and barbaric impulses of individuals normally need tutoring by language, by institutions such as the family, church, school, and civil society, and by civilizing traditions. In some senses, one speaks of "moral society and immoral man." But the full truth is that institutional structures, like individuals, always fall short of justice, morality, and reasonableness. Every single structure is "sinful." Nonetheless, the phrase "sinful structures" is unfortunate. It seems to imply that, by comparison with present ("sinful") structures, somewhere up ahead are "sinless" ones. If this implication is incorrect, then "sinful" is redundant. Moreover, the sort of judgment required to make accurate comparisons among historical regimes—to compare one set of "sinful" structures with another set of "sinful" structures—is prudential, complex, and uncertain. Thus is deflated the balloon of "sinful structures." The phrase adds nothing helpful to political philosophy or reason. Its purpose is to smuggle religious passion into arguments about what works, importing an accusatory tone of voice into what ought to be civil discussion, dividing those who disagree into good guys and bad.

In Catholic circles, this unwise emphasis upon "sinful structures" arises in ironic circumstances. Since Vatican II, particularly within certain religious orders, the authority of Rome has virtually collapsed. And it is just at this moment that many, including precisely some in such religious communities, imagine *new* sinless structures of authority under secular powers. Thus, one often hears words of considerable contempt for the pope and ecclesiastical bureaucrats, but warm allegiance to guerrilla leaders and socialist bureaucrats. Collectivist habits die hard.

We come, then, to a peculiar contradiction. In *political* matters, authoritarian and collectivist habits are strengthened; bourgeois individualism is condemned. Meanwhile, in *personal* matters, and with respect to *church* authorities, bourgeois individualism is licensed. This contradiction is common in the secular Left, too. Those who are statist in economic matters are frequently libertarians in private morality, as when they would not censor live sex on the public stage, so long as its participants are paid the minimum wage.

About virtually every theological or moral doctrine, doubts are expressed or, rather, a *state* of doubt is said to obtain. Catholics nowadays pretty much believe as they choose, and theologians pretty much take public positions as they please. Direct public attacks upon the moral and theological teachings of the pope and bishops appear frequently in the newspapers, often signed by some among the clergy, religious, and laity. There is much self-congratulation on the state of openness and uncertainty.

Apostolic authority is being challenged, not in a goading but in a contemptuous way, not in particulars but in its very substance. The substance of the Creed is being challenged, less in particulars than in wholesale "redefinitions," and less through specific contradiction than through diminished general fidelity. The Christian address to life through moral living is being challenged, through insisting that things once called immoral now be called moral and things once called moral now be called immoral. Were the church to yield to these challenges, it would cease to be what it has been. It would not be "renewed." It would have become the community of this age.

Many brave and generous people who work with the poor at home or abroad are deeply moved by the latter's helplessness. Expressing compassion, they may employ conventional political phrases, but their true intent is humane and religious. Blaming "the system," they do not really intend to invoke a theory of political economy; they try to gain a hearing for "the voiceless." (Far from being voiceless, of course, the poor and the unemployed appear daily on television and in the newspapers; few others but celebrities have a more lovingly depicted public image.) For such activists, one feels admiration and comradeship. But there are other activists who do rest their case upon a theory. Religious ends are made to coincide with political ends, as when Christianity is defined as liberation from sinful social structures—that is, a preference for a new regime. One may share the religious commitment of such persons and their will to help the poor. One may also disagree with them about which form of regime better helps the poor.

This example is a step toward a larger point. In proportion as some now boast of their new uncertainty regarding personal good and evil, they have become passionately certain about political good and evil. As some have rejected Catholic authority and structure, they have come to hail the authority and structure of socialist revolution. Some are certain that the multinational corporations are evil forces. They say that the structures of the "international capitalist world order" are sinful. This charge is not, in itself, startling. Political economies, particularly in liberal democracies (which constitute the main body of the developed world), claim neither to be the City of God, nor to represent the fullness of the Gospels. Such aims are not within their competence. Instead, they are designed for sinful humans as they are and as worldly constructs for worldly purposes. At the same time, they respect claims of transcendence, personal conscience, and group life. They leave religious persons and communities free to seek higher purposes. In multiple ways, they assist them to do so. But liberal political economies by no means pretend to offer salvation, to fulfill transcendent hungers, or to take the place of true religion. So one may, indeed, judge them very harshly in the abstract. It is only when, in fairness, one asks: *compared to what?* that the judgment is less harsh.

What is startling, though, is to see the displacement of faith in God, the remission of sins, and everlasting life by faith in political transformation. In Nicaragua, books written and printed (at government expense) by Capuchins and Jesuits carry pictures of "Christian revolutionaries," who wear crosses around their necks and carry a submachine gun in one hand and Molotov cocktail in the other, and reinterpret Christianity in terms of Marxist revolution.[4] Marx, of course, made this easy. He framed Marxist doctrine in terms of the quasi-Christian eschatology of Joachim of Flora. Just the same, it is virtually impossible to understand Marx as less than an atheist and a materialist. Otherwise, much of his analysis involving hatred, the morality of armed revolution, class struggle, and violence makes no sense. For this reason, while briefly noting that to be a Marxist one needn't *necessarily* be an atheist or a materialist, some Catholics avoid a full and clear commitment to Marxism, except to borrow certain "methods of Marxian analysis." That is why I write in Chapter 13 that the new heresy is not exactly an identification with Marx but with something deeper, more sweeping, and more vague: a kind of romantic haze about the transformation of this world through revolutionary politics. This is the sort of haze that Marx himself bitterly condemned in *The Communist Manifesto:*

As the parson has ever gone hand in hand with the landlord, so has *Clerical Socialism* with Feudal Socialism.

Nothing is easier than to give Christian asceticism a Socialist tinge. Has not Christianity declaimed against private property, against marriage, against the State? Has it not preached in the place of these, charity and poverty, celibacy and mortification of the flesh, monastic life and Mother Church? *Christian Socialism is but the holy water with which the priest consecrates the heartburnings of the aristocrat.* [5]

So it is, in any case, that sin is now identified with structures—not with *all* structures, but with the structures of democratic capitalism. The logic of this view, clearer to some than to others, is that the chief incarnation of evil in the world is the United States. The remission of sins at which such a faith aims is the destruction of the institutions— the sinful structures—of the United States. The more resolute bite the last bullet, as has Miguel D'Escoto, the Maryknoll priest become Foreign Minister of Nicaragua, who in North Vietnam and Eastern Europe has proclaimed Nicaragua's alliance with the powers of international socialism led by the Soviet Union. Those who shrink from an analysis of power politics, of course, draw back from moral support for the Soviet Union. They confine their activities to moral and political assault upon the United States, as the source of suffering and evil in the world. For them, the Soviet Union and the United States are *twin* evils, mirror societies.

At this point, the theory of sin employed in such analysis takes an odd twist. One of the sins of developed societies, we are told, is that they "privatize" religion,[6] and one of the virtues of political revolutions of the socialist type is that they once again reinstate "social" life. To be sure, there is a clear sense in which democratic capitalist societies —more exactly, *pluralist* societies—cease to be confessional. No one official of the state speaks for the "public" conscience of all. Issues of conscience are hotly and publicly disputed, nowhere more so than in such societies. Historically unprecedented liberties are given to all sorts of associations of citizens. These can and do speak with a voice at once *social* and *public*. In what sense is the Moral Majority, or the National Council of Churches, or the United States Catholic Conference "privatized"? Only in the sense that none speaks for the state as a whole.

To be the conscience of the state as a whole may be, perhaps, what political revolutionaries are really after. *Maryknoll Magazine* recently printed photos of billboards honoring Jesus Christ, which it said were put up by the Sandinist government of Nicaragua. If this were true, it would show that the revolutionary government had, indeed, given religion a public, social character; had, in effect, established religion. The truth is that the billboards were put up by a private businessman and his sister, a nun, against much governmental opposition, and that two of them were defaced and overturned by Sandinist officials.[7]

It is a category mistake to link the word "private" to individual and "social" to the state. Many private institutions are social, large, and not only quite visible in public but established through public subscription and by public participation, while retaining their independence from the state. In democratic capitalist societies, fewer institutions are owned, managed, and run by the state than in socialist countries. That does not make such free institutions any the less social or public. In order to be social, a human enterprise does not need to be state-owned. In order to be open to, supported by, and run by citizens from the public at large, public social institutions do not require state auspices. In free societies religion is not "privatized"; it is social and public. But it is not statist.

Ironically, it is socialist societies that, in fact, drive citizens into intensely privatized lives. When everything becomes subject to politics under punitive authorities, political speech becomes not only dangerous but hopeless. Without economic liberty, the economy cannot be discussed. Without religious liberty, religion cannot be discussed. How this works in present-day Czechoslovakia was recently described:

Conversations with office workers, hotel employees and taxi drivers and casual chats in public places elicited animation from Czechoslovaks only when travel and vacations, leisuretime pursuits (like chess, soccer or skiing), automobiles or country cabins were mentioned. . . .

Everybody cheats in personal relations because nobody wants to talk about his real beliefs and feelings. . . .[8]

The dream of socialism is that everything will be made social and public. The reality is that private space shrinks and human lives are pressed into ever smaller inner rooms. Those who fear "privatized" religion may experience it today under "socialization," in the new catacombs.

Belief in one baptism from the remission of sins, therefore, does not involve one in believing that the inevitable sins of any and every form of political economy will be wiped away by revolutionary magic. It is not the sins of institutions that are remitted, but those of individuals. And under every conceivable, not to mention realizable, human structure in history, the sins of individuals will be manifest indeed, and the flaws and gross mediocrity of institutions will be entirely visible.

What is immensely striking, however, is the power of religious passion no longer bridled by the realism of the Christian Creed. When it is no longer channeled within the banks of biblical realism, religion often pours over into visionary politics. What believers no longer hope for from God and church, they hope from political revolution. No longer believing in hell after death, they work for the arrival of hell on earth, as though it were heaven itself.

11. Resurrection of the Dead

And I look for the resurrection of the dead and the life of the world to come.

The Latin text reads: *Et expecto resurrectionem mortuorum, et vitam venturi saeculi. I await the resurrection of the dead and the life of ages to come.* Is this not one of the most astonishing claims of Christianity, the resurrection of *the body?* As a Christian, I expect the resurrection of the body, *this* body, this bag of flesh, this hair (what is left of it), this embodied person, this *I.* Christianity is not about the soul, or in any case not the soul alone. It does not regard this body as a prison, a cage, a corruption. It is this body that is also saved, that also rises, this body that, together with its soul, Jesus died for and intends to call unto Himself again.

All through Christian history the Platonist heresy has hovered close by, according to which the human being is a spirit in a machine, a spirit imprisoned, a spirit held back by flesh. This is not the Christian view. It is a view older than Christianity, and quite persistent, which Christianity has steadily opposed. The Creed itself here makes the issue stark.

Stubbornly, without knowing how all this is to happen, I believe that the Creator intends to call back to Himself all his living creatures who have accepted His will, to call them back body and soul, the flesh arisen. Unmistakably, at death the flesh goes inert, stiff, heavy; its decay—and its stench—follow shortly. From dust to dust. Yet the miracle of life is not at an end. As first we were formed from dust, so again we shall be called from dust.

While this expectation is essential to the Creed, I do not regard it as necessary for my own satisfaction. It would be quite enough for me to be taught by God how to live, even if life ended after its appointed few years. It is not the promise of living forever that makes Christianity attractive to me. On the contrary, there is something quite romantic and defiant in the belief that we go into night, gently or not gently. The brevity of life gives it poetic sharpness. Even apart from the promise of life everlasting, Christianity has its own compelling beauty.

Yet it is, in fact, everlasting life that Jesus again and again announced. Augustine is quite clear:

We are not Christians, except on account of a future life. Let no one hope for present blessings, let no one promise himself the happiness of the world, because he is a Christian. When this is present, let him give thanks for the consolation of God; when it is wanting, let him give thanks to the justice of God. Let him always be grateful, never ungrateful; let him be grateful to the Father when He consoles and caresses him, and let him be grateful to the Father when He chastens and scourges and disciplines him; for He always loves, whether he caress or threaten.[1]

The promise of eternal life seems to me like a superabundant gift, unnecessary but very much in the character of the Giver. The promise of eternal life is not so much necessary for the believer, as it is a revelation about the nature of God.

Jesus promises eternal life in connection with the eating of the bread —the bread of the Eucharist, the bread of His own body. Here, too, the claim is physical. Eating this bread is not the same as "relating" to others. It is not so much an act of community as it is a physical, bodily eating. Its "communion" is with God, although of course it is also with all others, throughout history, who sup at this same table. The notion of so many modern theologians that the Eucharist is primarily a symbol of community—as if in some spiritual way—seems to overlook the resurrection of the body, the physical act of eating, the use of actual bread as the sign of eternal life, and its link to the physical death of Jesus and his physical resurrection. It seems wrong to stress the spirit but not the body.

Yet Christian belief constantly scandalizes those who are embarrassed by the body. The ordinary reasonable person might understand a religion that appeals to spirituality and reason, that represents our noblest aspirations, that avoids vulgar miracles and superstitions. The more cultivated and highly intellectual person is likely to find that Unitarianism or Ethical Humanism meet higher standards than Christianity. For Christianity involves at least four very difficult theses about human flesh and blood. First, God is born of a woman. Second, this God become man dies on the cross and then bodily arises again, tangibly, physically, and "ascends into heaven." Third, this God says that plain unleavened bread is actually His body, which his followers should eat (as if in cannibalistic ritual). Fourth, this God promises that the bodies of His followers will rise again on the last day, to enjoy eternal life. Such beliefs seem grotesquely physical, fleshly, and utterly contrary to reasonable expectation. Whoever believes such things could, one supposes, believe anything.

Yet there it is. No one can fairly say that the Christian Creed makes the life of reason easy. No one can fairly argue that the Christian Creed encourages those who like a spiritualized, rational religion. No one can fairly say that Christianity lacks vivid carnal, fleshly, bodily sensibility.

On the other hand, once one begins with the insight that human beings are embodied persons, neither wholly material nor wholly spiritual, the Christian beliefs about Jesus begin to seem overwhelmingly touching. They show God bending exactly to the human condition. God meets humans on the native soil of humans, embodied as they are. The point of birth through the Virgin is that Jesus is truly flesh, yet not only human but divine. The point of crucifixion and resurrection is the bond between divine and human. The point of the Eucharist and of the resurrection of the dead is that the human being is not pure spirit but embodied spirit, and that it is the person-in-flesh that God loves and saves, not spirit and reason alone. God loves us as we are.

I find this way of conceiving of my own reality—*our* reality as human beings—immensely comforting, and fitting, and moving. One experiences so many temptations to loathe one's own body and the limits of one's flesh. The temptation toward gentility, toward rationalism, and toward the spiritual (gnostic) interpretation of life is often immensely strong. Many aesthetic and philosophical traditions encourage it.

Yet Christianity insists that we are what we are, and that God not only loves us so but adapted Himself to our condition. This is why, I think, Christmas has for centuries touched the human heart, why the scene at Bethlehem is still emotionally overwhelming. Serious theologians insist that the feast of the resurrection is much more central to the Christian Creed, and that Easter ought to be far more important than Christmas. Yet the essential point is also made at Christmas. Indeed, the logic of Easter is already present in the crib, as Herod searches fruitlessly to kill the babe at birth, slaughtering innocent infants in a brutal and clumsy attempt to do so. Cruelty is present from the beginning. Blood flows even around the manger.

For millions of human beings, whose flesh is weak, the fact that God saves us *in* our flesh, rather than *from* our flesh, touches us almost to the point of sentimentality. It is almost too much. The rationalist in us is embarrassed; the maudlin in us can scarcely resist expansion. Yet the cold eye meets the bracing air of December in the hills south of Jerusalem, at the beginning of a new era in world history.

The resurrection of the dead is of a piece with the birth of the infant at Bethlehem. It all hangs together, this Creed. And its point, after all, is less to raise humans up, although it does do that, than to honor the God whose ways of giving are so humble.

Were Christianity a religion of rationalists and spiritualizers, the spine of the Creed could be done away with and "reinterpreted" by giving it a more spiritual meaning. But many human beings might well be left behind in the process. For the Creed as it stands speaks directly to the most lowly, the most illiterate, the lost, the weak, the least cultivated, those who have no talent for the abstract or the highly logical. It says that God is of them, like them, with them, for them. Who is so poor that he or she is excluded from Bethlehem, or Golgotha, or the Eucharist, or the Last Day?

The power of the Creed lies in the very scandals it sets before the purest spirits. Those who are rich in spirit may find the Creed vulgar. It is vulgar and intends to be. To enter it one must bow a little, allowing the truth about one's own condition to overpower one's highest aspirations and pretensions. Like the poor, the rich too return to dust. Like the ignorant, the enlightened too are body and soul. Like the simple, the sophisticated too go back to basics. Christianity is a great leveler by speaking clearly and simply about the human condition of all. The large things about human life—the inner struggle *for* humble charity, *against* the world, the flesh, and the devil—affect all equally. No one is so poor or so rich, so powerless or so powerful, of such low status or of such high position, as not to feel at the deepest levels of personality the struggle of the immortal, embodied soul.

This is why so much depends upon the simple integrity of the Creed. It is all of a piece. Serially, every line of the Creed illuminates every other line. Cumulatively, all form a seamless and distinctive vision of human life, continuous with pre-Christian history. Judaism, naturally, judges Jesus quite differently, but in its combination of spirit and flesh, in its way of linking the universal and the particular, in its sacramental and liturgical sense, and in its attachment to concrete history, its vision of human reality is of the same cloth as the Christian vision. Here, at least, if not everywhere, one speaks well in speaking of a "Judeo-Christian vision."

As a Catholic, I see in Protestant Christianity a strong impulse toward a more spiritual interpretation of the Creed. The abiding temptation of Protestant Christianity is to leave flesh and earth behind. In "higher" Protestantism, this temptation, while respecting Catholic forms, veers toward a more rationalist religion. In "lower" Protestantism, the temptation veers toward enthusiasm, rooted in feeling and personal experience. These temptations are felt within Catholicism, too. We have our rationalists to one side and our charismatics to the other. And all of us roil under judgment against the great rocks of the Creed.

At the resurrection of the dead and in the life of the ages to come —that is, beyond the present age, beyond history—all will be united once again. We shall discover brothers and sisters we did not know. What will unite us will be the Creed or, more exactly, the reality to which the Creed has directed our attention. This reality embraces all the ages. It unites the generations. It speaks directly to the human condition in every time and place.

It is in this sense that the Creed is dogma: a universal symbol as true in one generation as in another. Short and simple it is, not elaborate or highly detailed. About it, no new discoveries remain to be made. To be sure, questioning intellects always challenge it afresh, probe it, raise ever new difficulties, and cast up many new standpoints. Like a jeweled light, the Creed turns on its axis toward each new challenge, reflecting ancient but perhaps newly inspected light. In an important sense, the Creed is not at all subject to development. It is what it is. It is a deposit, a trust, a judgment upon us. The proper mode for approaching it is fear, lest we betray it or weaken it or corrupt it, passing on to our children less than we ourselves received.

Contrary to the development of human sciences, understanding of the Creed is far more vulnerable to decline than to progress. Indeed, we are several times warned both by St. John and by St. Paul that, toward the end of time, the forces of corruption—the anti-Christ—will have grown stronger than ever before. To keep the Creed intact is a tremendously difficult task. "Progress" concerning the Creed, therefore, is more like the removing of corruptions that accrue to it than like adding new materials to a received body of knowledge.

In this respect, the science of theology is quite different from other sciences. The progress of most sciences arises in large part from the patient and difficult accumulation of new data, and then from the invention of new hypotheses to explain the new data. In theology, the situation is quite different. The data are summarized in the Creed, not to be added to nor subtracted from. Invention occurs because the surrounding verbal and intellectual world changes, and the same data must be thought through afresh in order to cast illumination upon the new situation. This is no easy task. Historical opportunities are often missed. Resistance is raised at the wrong places, and alliances are wrongly entered into. In the human sciences, the old is habitually overturned for the more comprehensive and better tested new. In theology, the task is to keep the old in trust, discerning within every age what corrupts from what enhances its eternal vitality.

When the dead rise and the life of the age beyond history begins, the theology of each generation will then stand under clear judgment concerning where it went wrong and where it remained faithful to its trust. Sheer repetition of familiar words will not have been enough, any more than it was enough for the servant to bury his talent. The Creed is neither served nor kept alive by the repetition of words, but only by the lived understanding of the way of living it sets forth. To grasp the true meaning of the Creed within the intellectual confusion of each age and to live it faithfully is no small task. To do so is to live in fear of the judgment of God, who has entrusted this treasure to us, not solely for ourselves, but for all who would hear of it. Fear of the Lord, Cardinal Newman says, is both the beginning of wisdom and the proper attitude for approaching the task of fidelity to the Creed. This fear raises a further question.

Two chapters back, I called for a resurgence of a revised and enlarged liberal Catholicism, a biblical realism, yet at the end of these reflections on the Creed it may be significant to emphasize what I do *not* mean. Cardinal Newman several times emphasized that his entire intellectual life could be described as a battle against Liberalism. Since I count Cardinal Newman as the very model of what I mean by the neoliberal Catholic, I must explain how the neoliberal Catholic tradition differs from the liberal tradition.

Meditation on the present item of the Creed establishes the context. Like other Catholics, the neoliberal Catholic expects the resurrection of the dead and the life of the world to come. The neoliberal Catholic vision is a vision beyond history, within which the narrative of human history on earth is prologue. In holding to the resurrection of the body, the neoliberal Catholic does not disvalue history; not at all. Christianity does not see human salvation or the meaning of human life *within* history. When a Sandinist official tells Nicaraguans that a fallen guerrilla priest enjoys "the only resurrection there is, the success of the revolution," that is not the neoliberal Catholic view. Its theological error is to assert that the meaning of the resurrection is exhausted by success within this world. Its political error is to assert that the "revolution" will fulfill liberal ideals of liberty, justice, dignity, and human rights. In joining the two symbols—"neoliberal" and "Catholic"—one intends to join both the theological and the political principle. To apply to this world, all theological utterances have both a theological and a political significance. A theology of incarnation demands both.

The neoliberal Catholic recognizes that no one theory of political economy exhausts the possibilities of human history and that none is identical to the Kingdom of God. To believe in the "life of the world to come" is to refuse to *identify* Christianity with any one form of political economy. The neoliberal Catholic vision of political economy is not a vision of the Kingdom of God. It is, rather, a this-worldly vision of a political economy appropriate to sinners, open to the teachings of Christianity, reformable, and more likely than any known alternative to carry forward the slow working of the gospels in human history.

In *The Spirit of Democratic Capitalism*, I have described the neoliberal vision of political economy by contrast with the socialist vision. The liberal vision is three-in-one; it includes a polity based upon the rights of individuals and democratic procedures, an economy based upon relatively free markets and incentives, and a system of moral and cultural institutions (including churches) that is pluralistic. Such a vision arose in history in the United States, Great Britain, and some parts of northwestern Europe. From the beginning, it appeared as an alternative to the *ancien régime*, in which one set of authorities made all important political, economic, and moral-cultural decisions, usually through an alliance of state and church. In terms of class, it represented the arrival on the stage of history of a new class of homeowners, persons of commerce and industry, and republican intellectuals who challenged the monarchies and landholding estates of the old order. It raised the status of peasants and former serfs to that of free laborers. Some of the latter were then solicited by Marxists and non-Marxist socialists as the *new* vanguard of history, the proletariat. A historical struggle arose, not yet concluded, as to whether neoliberalism or socialism actually better meets the aspirations of labor and the conditions of liberty and prosperity.

Many early liberal thinkers, while organizing opposition to the *ancien régime* and seeing few theological intellects rallying to their arguments, seemed to reject the vision implicit in the Christian Creed. Some were antireligious, some anticlerical; others were resolutely materialist or individualistic; some were atheist not solely in conscience but in social ambition. Still others, especially in Britain and America, were neither antireligious nor anti-Christian, but they did oppose the establishment of the old order represented by the Catholic union of church and state. For such reasons, the church often judged the liberals to be its enemies.

Beginning at the end of the eighteenth century, it was already clear to many that a new order of political economy would soon replace the Holy Roman Empire and the feudal order. Arguments waxed very hot about what this order would be. At least in the Catholic Church, especially in Rome, resistance to liberal thinking ran fairly high. Before 1850, Pius IX seemed rather more open to the liberals than earlier popes.[2] Later and bitter experiences in Italy, not least in the Papal States, turned him resolutely and sweepingly against liberalism, which he roundly condemned in a long series of theses in "The Syllabus of Errors."

From my point of view, this historical conflict was a tragedy of enormous proportions. The later conflict between Marxism and Christianity followed from it. In turning away from traditional Christianity, many in the intellectual elites regarded liberalism not simply as a theory of political economy but as a world view intended explicitly to replace Christianity. A residue of Christian feeling and values naturally remained within liberalism. But it is not difficult to understand how Cardinal Newman, for the fifty years following 1830, thought of the world view of liberalism as his chief opponent on the terrain of religion. It was not the politics of liberalism he opposed, nor its economics, nor even its cultural ideals. (His discussions of the gentleman, liberal learning, and the free life of the mind in *The Idea of the University* make this much plain.) Insofar as liberalism usurped the field of religion, however, he opposed it. In this respect, so does the neo-liberal Catholic.

Newman is quite clear about what he resists:

To one great mischief I have from the first opposed myself. For thirty, forty, fifty years I have resisted to the best of my powers the spirit of Liberalism in religion. Never did Holy Church need champions against it more sorely than now, when, alas! it is an error overspreading, as a snare, the whole earth. . . . Liberalism in religion is the doctrine that there is no positive truth in religion, but that one creed is as good as another. . . . It is inconsistent with any recognition of any religion as *true*. It teaches that all are to be tolerated, for all are matters of opinion. Revealed religion is not a truth, but a sentiment and a taste; and it is the right of each individual to make it say just what strikes his fancy.[3]

Another text, from *An Essay on the Development of Christian Doctrine*, states more exactly what Newman designated as liberal principles:

That truth and falsehood in religion are but matters of opinion; that one doctrine is as good as another; that the Governor of the world does not intend that we should gain the truth; that there is no truth; that we are not more acceptable to God by believing this than by believing that; that no one is answerable for his opinions; that they are a matter of necessity or accident; that it is enough if we sincerely hold what we profess; that our merit lies in seeking, not in possessing; that it is a duty to follow what seems to us true, without a fear lest it should not be true; that it may be a gain to succeed, and can be no harm to fail; that we may take up and lay down opinions at pleasure; that belief belongs to the mere intellect, not to the heart also; that we may safely trust to ourselves in matters of Faith; and need no other guide—this is the principle of philosophies and heresies, which is very weakness.[4]

It is one thing to be in favor of pluralism and toleration, as Newman clearly was, both as Anglican and as Catholic. It is another to base one's theory of pluralism and toleration upon the principle of indifference. To practice pluralism, it is not necessary to hold that one opinion is as good as another. No one's views on religion ought to be enforced by the state. But each person ought to argue clearly and forcefully for those truths that he or she believes to be true and against those that seem false. Otherwise, truth itself is debased and human society becomes anti-intellectual and flaccid. The fact that Newman holds to the Catholic Creed, arguing strenuously against distortions of it, is of high social benefit even to those who do not follow him. So it is with others. A pluralist society can thus be enlivened by clear argument, in which each participant passionately cares about truth and error. The fact that there are many voices testifies to human liberty, to the difficulty of the task, and to the feeble hold any one intellect has upon divine light, but it does not imply that one viewpoint is as good as another. Those who are not Catholic, or even Christian, will no more agree to the Catholic understanding than did opponents of Christianity in the days of Origen or Athanasius; but this will not prevent Catholics—or Protestants, or Jews, or humanists—from making their confession as cogently as they can. Should no one do so, on this or on other competing visions of life, the entire body politic would suffer for lack of intellectual vigor.

Thus, Newman described his own principle, "the dogmatical principle," knowing that most who read him in Great Britain would not agree with him. Political pluralism allowed him the liberty of public presentation. While assuring him of no public acceptance, such pluralism needed for its own invigoration to hear a forthright confession of his faith. Trusting the fairmindedness of the English, Newman posited his principle in direct opposition to the widely accepted "liberal principle." In the field of religion, Newman's "dogmatical principle" holds:

> That there is a truth then; that there is one truth; that religious error is in itself of an immoral nature; that its maintainers, unless involuntarily such, are guilty in maintaining it; that it is to be dreaded; that the search for truth is not the gratification of curiosity; that its attainment has nothing of the excitement of a discovery; that the mind is below truth, not above it, and is bound, not to descant upon it, but to venerate it; that truth and falsehood are set before us for the trial of our hearts; that our choice is an awful giving forth of lots on which salvation or rejection is inscribed; that 'before all things it is necessary to hold the Catholic faith,' that 'he that would be saved must thus think' and not otherwise; that, 'if thou criest after knowledge, and liftest up thy voice for understanding, if thou seekest her as silver, and searchest for her as for hid treasure, then shalt thou understand the fear of the Lord, and find the knowledge of God'—this is the dogmatical principle, which has strength.[5]

To my own ear, these words are too harsh. Hardly anyone who has experienced the crises of belief and unbelief during the awful events of the twentieth century can help feeling compassion for fellow seekers in the darkness. I have not the slightest doubt about my own belief in the Creed, but I have come to it in such bleakness, in such suffering, through such a night, that I do not expect anyone to share it with me, although of course more than a billion Christians do. Atheists, too, have been battered by the times. The times are in great flux, and humility is much in evidence. In Newman's time, religious parties seem to have been more vigorous and to have had harder edges, as did the campaigns of freethinkers and atheists. Today, all seem a bit more subdued.

Still, I think Newman is essentially correct. Truth is one, and it is no matter of indifference. To say less is to license the wholesale murder of millions by ruthless men willing to follow relativism to the extreme ends of the earth. While each of us is weak and partial in our vision, we cannot afford merely to affect metaphysical indifference, in order to shock those of simpler certainties. (Sometimes, I confess, Moonies and others innocent in their certainty make me want to shock them.) It is urgent for our consciences that we hold that truth is one, that contradictory positions cannot simultaneously be true, even if we cannot demonstrate to others that it is *we* who are correct and *they* wrong, and even if in that circumstance we both agree to seek practical ways of living in peace with one another. It is not a matter of indifference that free persons hold contradictory moral positions. Both cannot be right. To tolerate both for civic peace is not the same as to declare both positions equally true out of metaphysical or moral indifference. Doubtless, we shall never convert one another. Equally certain, to be indifferent to differences of conscience opens doors to barbarism. Freedom of conscience in the liberal state is a precious good. To defend it by treating conscience as a matter of indifference is to devalue it.

In an odd sense, then, the dogmatical principle—or something like it—is required to give liberty of conscience value. If conscience is merely the excrescence of opinion, each person's as good as any other's, then one person's terrorism is another's revolution, and soon we shall all be swamped in blood. If liberty of conscience is simply an expression of good manners, since conscience has no purchase on reality, then those antibourgeois forces that assign conscience to winning by revolutions have triumphant power on their side. If it cannot be that might makes right, then somewhere beyond police power stands truth. Difficult to discern it may be. Yet it is in the light of our conviction that it *does* stand there, beyond the manipulations of the history-makers, that civilization finds its painful way out of barbarism.

The neoliberal Catholic does believe, then, that truth is one and that it may be discerned through the disciplines of inquiring conscience, although often only darkly, in doubt, and amid disagreement. Truth may be discerned by conscience, and sins against it are an elemental outrage both to our common humanity and to our individual dignity. Lies, distortions, fakeries, and pretensions are not merely offenses against manners or taste but against the human spirit at its root. From a Christian and Jewish point of view, this is because God is Light—"True Light of True Light"—and because human conscience is made in His image, participates in His being, is of Him, and is returning to Him. No doubt, there is a secular and nonreligious equivalent to this conviction, as in Aristotle and in Socrates. It is, in any case, the root of "the dogmatical principle" and the place at which "the Liberal principle," as Newman defines it, fails in its own self-defense.

There are three other points I should mention, on which the great theoreticians of Anglo-Saxon liberalism—Adam Smith, Jeremy Bentham, and John Stuart Mill—fail to satisfy the Catholic intellect. On these three points, the neoliberal Catholic modifies the secular liberal tradition. First, the Catholic mind adds to the liberal emphasis upon the individual a strong sense of the social structure of human life, not only in the family, in associations, and in cultures, but even in the social structure of the psyche. Thus, something like "the communitarian individual" is a more accurate diagnosis of the reality of the relation of the individual to others than the "atomic individual" typically described in the writings of liberal philosophers.[6]

Second, the Catholic mind tends to value tradition and its tacit ways more than the liberal mind does and tends to have a more tragic sense of progress. In this respect, it is closer to Edmund Burke and is exemplified beautifully in Alexis de Tocqueville and Lord Acton.

Third, the Catholic mind, as compared to the resolutely liberal mind, tends to respect a sense of mystery and to find a merely pragmatical account of social problems much too thin. This quality sometimes makes the Catholic mind too mushy and vague and gives the liberal mind a clearer head for technical detail. But the abuse at the liberal extreme is to think too technocratically and to evade the deeper tragedies of human existence. The difference here is elusive; but a real tendency in one direction or the other does seem to be in evidence. In this context, I have always loved Péguy's maxim that "politics begins in mysticism and mysticism always ends in politics." The religious mind with its sense of mystery needs the secular mind with its concern for problem solving, and vice versa.

In such ways, one may say, neoliberal Catholics maintain something of the medieval heritage and rather more resemble Whigs like de Tocqueville and Burke. To secular liberals, they will often seem conservative, since they respect community, tradition, and mystery. Yet neoliberal Catholics tend also to value markets in economics, democratic governance in politics, and pluralism in culture. In these respects neoliberal Catholics differ from both conservative and socialist Catholics.

In theology, neoliberal Catholics differ from traditionalist Catholics and from radical Catholics. Traditionalists tend to draw up the wagons in a circle; to see all novelty, fresh thinking, experimentation as potential perversions (which they may be); and to hold fast to tried and true formulae. Traditionalist Catholics want strong popes and bishops to seize control and to hold the barque of Peter under firm disciplinary helm. On the other side, radical Catholics tend to be anti-institutional, restless with all historical forms, and open and trusting regarding every new dissent, novelty, or challenge. Radical Catholics would be happy with a Protestant-like church, or even a secularized church, as long as moral passion accrued to their historical projects. Radical Catholics think Vatican II did not go far enough. Traditionalist Catholics liked the church better before Vatican II and would like to see another Counter-Reformation.

Neoliberal Catholics have had to learn some hard lessons about their own intellectual carelessness, for radical Catholics sprang from earlier liberal Catholic premises. When I wrote about "the open church," for example, I did not take sufficient pains to set limits as to *how* open it might be. Neoliberal Catholics see a just role for the authority of pope and bishops, intermediate between the closed-circuit authority of the traditionalists and the "anything goes" anarchy of the radicals. A community of faith entrusted with a Creed to protect must have an authoritative teaching office, whose vocation it is to decide, in concrete circumstances, what protects that Creed and what corrupts it. Such decisions may be faulty in many respects—in tone, in concrete detail, in severity or laxity, in timing, in generosity or narrowness of spirit, and in a hundred other ways. At times, the teaching authority reacts too bitterly, at times too leniently. A teaching authority composed of human beings cannot escape the faults of human beings, even if in essential matters it is guided by the Holy Spirit.

If one dispassionately reviews the conduct of the Catholic teaching authority at Trent, in the early nineteenth century leading up to "The Syllabus of Errors," in the position of the Vatican regarding Christian democracy in Italy early in this century, in the 1930s and 1940s with respect to theologians like Congar and de Lubac, and at the Second Vatican Council and its aftermath, one does not find that it acted always in the same spirit or tone, always hit the mark exactly, or always compelled admiration. One is struck, though, by its effort to be faithful to the essential deposit of faith. After the heat of controversy has faded, one always sees that the teaching authority had a point. Often, indeed, those against whom it directed its discipline also had a point, although usually not as sweeping or as permanent as they claimed. This history is checkered, as anyone expects who knows the human heart and mind.

Yet one must conclude—I, at least, conclude—that the mere existence of the teaching authority and, more than that, its demonstrated desire to protect what has been handed down to it, together play an indispensable role in human history. Would that it might act always with luminosity and in a transparently divine manner, with indisputably perfect acuity, and with perfect fairness toward those whom it opposes. It does not. For those who believe that the Spirit of God watches over it, and guides it, and protects it, as I do, recognition that the Creed survives in a vital community until today suffices. One can second-guess historical actions at will. Having experienced one's own errors in history, one is not inclined to judge too harshly.

I am neither a church historian nor an expert in historical episodes. Yet seeing the difficulties faced by other institutions in the tumult of history, the fading of philosophies, and the disappearance of cultural movements, I believe that the integrity of Catholic loyalty to the Creed down through the ages warrants one's faith that God protects this church, despite its humanity and sins. He does not do so as a *deus ex machina*. Grace does not flow through invisible plumbing. Rather, ordinary dyspeptic men ordained for office struggle through their functions, are tested and sometimes bested, yet somehow manage to be instruments of His will. Seeing how God is present in one's own life, it is not difficult to make the leap of imagination to see how He works in the church. One never sees God, or hears Him, feels Him tug the arm, or coerce the conscience. On the other hand, one does sometimes feel that one is trying to do His will, that His grace suffices, and that, if one does one's best, one can be confident He will in some way have accomplished it. One feels this very strongly at times. Sometimes the results go beyond any advance planning of one's own. One salutes such results as representing God's will, not out of a sense of magic, but out of the sense that Providence wills everything His creatures do in His creation—knows it all, wills it all, forgives it all.

If God so guides the lives of each of us, it is not such a long step to see that He guides His church. This is His New City hidden within the City of Man, His obscure way of redeeming the City of Man. That He allowed His Son to face the hazards of history at a time so long ago is of a piece with His allowing His church to careen through the centuries, beset and afflicted, obstructed and detoured, yet doggedly advancing.

Permit me again to contrast neoliberal Catholics with the radicals and the traditionalists. Neoliberal Catholics, more than radical Catholics, see the teaching office of the church as harmonious with the incarnation of God in flesh, the resurrection of the body, and the one baptism for the remission of sins. In every respect, there would have been a more open, spiritual, and even angelic way for God to have spoken to humankind. In each case, God chose the humbler, more concrete, more particular, more human way. Radical Catholics are more enthusiastic about the raised consciousnesses and fresh ideals of their age. Neoliberal Catholics, while open to new things, are more skeptical. Radical Catholics regard neoliberal Catholics as pallid, afraid, lacking the courage to "let go," and—as a crowning insult—too "conservative." Neoliberal Catholics regard radical Catholics as all heart.

Neoliberal Catholics, more than the traditionalists, try to think ahead for the church, clear the path, assimilate fresh materials, impart the vitalities of the Creed into new human struggles. Neoliberal Catholics are more likely than traditionalists to err by involving the church in things which will go badly. Traditionalists are more likely to err by holding the church back from pressing yeast into new dough. Neoliberal Catholics need intelligent traditionalists as good and true critics. The latter need neoliberals as their daily cross.

On the last day, neoliberals and traditionalists and radicals will rise again, still squabbling in the world to come. What we are most lacking in the present age is the neoliberal Catholic witness. Having helped to injure it, I now try to nurse it back to health, again to do battle, left and right.

Part II

WHAT WENT WRONG?

The best Christians and the most vital are by no means to be found either inevitably or even generally among the wise or the clever, the intelligentsia or the politically-minded, or those of social consequence. And consequently what they say does not make the headlines; what they do does not come to the public eye. Their lives are hidden from the eyes of the world, and if they do come to some degree of notoriety, that is usually late in the day, and exceptional, and always attended by the risk of distortion. Within the Church itself it is, as often as not, only after their deaths that some of them acquire an uncontested reputation. Yet these are responsible, more than anyone else, for ensuring that our earth is not a hell on earth. Most of them never think to ask themselves whether their faith is "adapted" or "effective." It is enough, for them, to live it, as reality itself, and reality at its most actual; and because the fruit of all this is often enough a hidden fruit it is none the less wonderful.

—HENRI DE LUBAC, S.J.,
The Splendour of the Church

12. The Church Today: Progress or Decline?

One of my favorite books some thirty years ago was the pastoral letter of Emmanuel Cardinal Suhard, Archbishop of Paris, *The Church Today: Growth or Decline?*[1] This was a germinal book, which had a significant effect upon Pope John XXIII during his years as roly-poly and at first despised papal nuncio in Paris. I borrow Cardinal Suhard's title now because much depends on how one judges the course of the church since Vatican II.

Vatican II did open up the church; there has been excitement and pride in being Catholic ever since. Moreover, the church discovered, just in time, that it is a church of the underdeveloped nations, whose largest continental population lives in Latin America, whose fastest growing population lives in Africa, and whose majority will shortly dwell in the three underdeveloped continents. Today, the most serious Catholic problems are the world's problems, and the most serious problems of the world are Catholic problems. It is a precious thing for the Catholic people to think of themselves as open, experimental, and creative.

On the other hand, there is a difference between utopian openness and realistic openness. The realist is open in order to learn from experience. The utopian is simply open to experience, without learning from it. The point of "bringing the church up to today"—Pope John XXIII's famous *aggiornamento*—was to make the church speak more directly to souls, to increase its spiritual power, to deepen its sense of sacrifice and dedication. This was the experiment. In its name, meatless Fridays and fasting during Lent were dropped or mitigated, the liturgy was mightily rearranged, ancient practices and customs were fractured. And what were the results? Serious experimenters learn from their experiments. What have we learned?

The Catholic Church is large and spacious, and many clearly do not see the record since Vatican II as I do. Considering the optimism many of us felt in those sweet days at the Council, however, it seems proper to ask what we did wrong. We were then quite hard on our predecessors; our progeny will have every right to judge us just as severely. Let me speak for myself. I point in what follows mainly to negative results in full consciousness that my own earlier work helped to prepare their way. There may be time to correct some most egregious errors and, after twenty years of experimentation, to winnow out the golden grain from abundant and choking chaff. *Ecclesia semper reformanda*, the church is always in need of reform, we used to cry with a sense of triumph. More sadly, we see the same need today.

Does today's liturgy, for example, bring congregations closer to God? I have felt the power of some of today's spontaneous liturgies, power that derives from their informal openness to the Spirit. But I have also felt the slippage in modern liturgies, from dependence upon the regular, reliable grandeur and mystery of the service to dependence upon the on-again-off-again performance of the participants. The most vital, awesome moment of the Mass used to be the silence at the consecration, as God become present under forms of bread and wine was slowly raised above the head of the celebrant for the momentary veneration of the world. Today it is often the gregarious, heart-warming handshake at the "Kiss of Peace." The difficulty with the latter is that all sorts of secular ceremonies—from the Kiwanis Club to the annual convention of sensitivity seminar leaders—employ a similar technique. If the meaning of the Eucharist is human relations rather than the majesty of God's presence within us, one does not need church or priests.

When I was young and brash, we used to poke fun at the saccharine hymns used at Benediction of the Most Blessed Sacrament. Yet those hymns were formal and cold compared to the folk songs sung today, cloying the soul with peace, love, joy, and happiness, sounding hardly a note of tragedy, death, and sin. Pangloss could hardly ask for happier liturgies than many heard now in our midst. The old hymns to Mary used to recall, at least, that she had seven swords through her heart. Country music has more sadness in it than much parish hymnody today.

The journalist Richard Reeves, although not a Catholic, grew up among Catholics in Jersey City and, in retracing the American journey of Alexis de Tocqueville, came upon a scene in a typical Catholic parish in Green Bay in 1981 which will be instantly recognized in suburban churches all over the country. The yellow-brick interior reminded him of a high school gymnasium, in which citizens in sports clothes heard a xylophone and guitars before the opening of the informal service with "a bouncy little number" whose words were "The Spirit is a'movin all over, all over the world." The priest, who smiled a lot, sported a "blond afro, the kind that is shaped in beauty parlors" and wore a bright scarlet robe on which a white dove was stitched. The church bulletin, complete with ads from A&W Root Beer and Budweiser, proclaimed:

Think you've been shortchanged in life? . . . Look at the bright side: you have the Spirit. The Spirit caused a public sensation one day two thousand years ago in Jerusalem. The same Spirit can cause a sensation in your life today. Don't hold yourself back for fear of being different. The world can use all the Spirit-filled people it can get.

Reeves left St. Agnes in Green Bay, he writes, humming—and stunned. The words at Mass had not merely been colloquial but like "the dialogue and conversation of a small college dramatic society." "I woke in the middle of this peppy fun. Let's hear it for the Spirit!" Hardly believing that this was *Roman* Catholic, Reeves sought out another church in Green Bay.

The priest was young, a tall, handsome man in a beard and white robes. "Hey!" he was saying as I walked in. "Hey, I've accepted Christ. . . . The Spirit shows itself through, through what? Through sharing! Through giving yourself to others, through being open. . . ."

Reeves comments:

What I had seen was a reformed church, more American than Roman. It was . . . "nice"; the masses I saw were celebrations and they were, amazingly, celebrations of what researchers and sociologists had been telling me were the "new values." The guitar, rather than the organ, provided suitable backup for these pleasant young men urging parishioners to be different, to be themselves, to be open, to share. "The old values are being destroyed," Barry Bingham had said in Louisville. "They begin by saying, 'do your own thing.' "[2]

He would not die for the Eucharist, a famous priest is reported to have said, unless it had a tremendously secularized meaning.[3] The meaning often seems today to come out that way.

As in liturgy, so in theology: it is difficult to find a secular fashion that is now not imported into the Creed. An editorialist in *Today's Parish* notes that everyone has become for him, when he is honest with himself, a "sex object." But now he has learned to move beyond that to the "person" that is neither male nor female. So why should he not sexually desire males as well as females, since both are "persons"? He goes on:

The law of God, you say? Come on, let's grow up theologically too. We say we don't hold an anthropomorphic God, a kind of great puppeteer, old, male (and heterosexual, may one suppose?), so let's really not hold one. No, God works the wonders of his providence, of his love and his laws, right down inside the concrete, living, individual natures he creates and sustains.[4]

A nun trained in theology writes: "The Scriptures are unredeemably sexist." In other words, the world comes first, Scripture second. She continues: "If the word of God can be so corrupted by the mores of the culture in which it is received and in a matter of such centrality, it is in need of correction."[5]

Another theologian writes, "Then we can say with clear conviction and without fear or guilt that if Jesus was not a feminist, he was not of God."[6] Another scholar values liberal theology for reassuring Christians "that they did not need to sacrifice their intellects to assent to conceptions that are simply silly in our century."[7] Another notes that the problem of Scripture is that it contains "concepts which are often outmoded and meaningless to twentieth-century man" and its "metaphors and analogies are archaic and distasteful to modern sensibilities."[8] According to Santayana's marvelous quip, a modernist is a Catholic whose heart is full of love for everyone but the pope. Thus one theologian joins another against the pope:

This is really what Küng is calling for: that the academy replace the hierarchy as the teaching Magisterium of the Church. This cannot be accomplished by the academy itself. It entails the equivalent of the French Revolution in the Church, the deposing of a monarchical for a democratic constitution of the Church.[9]

In a book called *Towards a Church of the Poor,* the model of liberation held up to the poor is a Soviet collective farm. One of the contributors also explains that, in this new definition of the church, "the concepts of evangelization, salvation, reconciliation, church and so on, as they have been traditionally employed, seem to require redefinition."[10]

Horror stories can be found on all sides, of course. The point is that church windows have now been thrown open to many such. With what result? Is the church closer to twentieth-century men and women? Chesterton wrote in *The Catholic Church and Conversion:* "The Catholic Church is the only thing which saves a man from the degrading slavery of being a child of his own age."[11] Has the Catholic Church become now no more than a child of the age? If so, we must expect it not to attract people in but to propel people out.

That is precisely what seems to have happened since the brave experiment of Vatican II, despite what we experimenters intended. The figures seem indisputable. From 1965, the year the Council ended, until 1974 there was an exodus from Catholicism of an unprecedented sort. Conversions in England and Wales dropped from 15,794 to 5,253, and baptisms from 136,350 to 80,587. In France, 41 percent of Catholics attended Mass weekly in 1964, only 14 percent in 1975. In Holland weekly Mass attendance fell from 64.4 in 1966 to 30 percent by 1975. In France in 1973, 151 new seminarians were enrolled, while 422 departed; in 1974, 191 entered and 205 left. From 1967 to 1975, the number of priests in France declined from 40,994 to 21,820. By 1970, every single Catholic seminary in Holland had closed, and a mere 108 students were studying theology, while deaths and defections of priests numbered on average almost 250 each per year. Between 1970 and 1974, the world total of nuns fell by 25 percent and the U.S. total by 39 percent.[12]

There are many ways of interpreting such figures. But surely the Catholic Church has demanded less discipline since 1965. The liturgy after 1965, supposed to be "more relevant," may have been weakened by that. Perhaps some will argue that the weakest in faith have departed while the more committed have remained; but some have argued the opposite. Some say that the Council raised expectations and did not go far enough. Yet it is hard to imagine any extreme position that has not been taken by Catholics openly and provocatively. If limits are being observed too narrowly, which ones? What may Catholics not believe, preach, write, and do, while calling it authentic Catholic witness? A Jesuit has written in *Commonweal:* "Stated briefly, my judgment is this. Homosexual actions are biologically deficient, but they may be psychologically healthy, the best available exercise of one's interpersonal freedom, and may even be a form of authentic Christian spirituality."[13] One searches in vain for the narrow confines of contemporary Catholicism. The sky's the limit. Everything seems included as authentic spirituality.

If so, nothing is. Catholicism, so understood, has lost all point. Is this not why so many leave? What would be the point of staying?

And why shouldn't vocations dry up? A priest is among all men most in turmoil in the new church. A diminishment in his role has occurred in our lifetime.[14] Once his life was centered upon mystery, and his celibacy was a narrow gate leading up and calling attention thereto. Now he is a community leader, doing what a thousand other counselors are doing. His life, all except his celibacy, has been secularized, and fragments of holy mysteries in which, perforce, he is still engaged have been reinterpreted by theologians to exclude much mystery. Why would a man who would not die for the Eucharist unless it were secularized in meaning wish to live the mystery of celibacy? Secularized, celibacy loses point. Secularized, so does the Eucharist and so the Creed. A next step is to seek God in politics.

In *The Whimsical Christian* Dorothy Sayers presents a more relevant creed for the twentieth century. It cuts through all the metaphors of Scripture that offend twentieth-century sensibilities. It applies better, however, to a period twenty years ago and now needs *aggiornamento*. Today even science—yesterday's myth—has joined the devil. A new generation has put in place of science "authenticity," and in place of progress "the option for the poor." But let it stand:

CREED OF ST. EUTHANASIA
(The Atheneum Creed)

I believe in man, maker of himself and inventor of all science. And in myself, his manifestation, and captain of my psyche; and that I should not suffer anything painful or unpleasant.

And in a vague, evolving deity, the future-begotten child of man; conceived by the spirit of progress, born of emergent variants; who shall kick down the ladder by which he rose and tell history to go to hell.

Who shall some day take off from earth and be jet-propelled into the heavens; and sit exalted above all worlds, man the master almighty.

And I believe in the spirit of progress, who spake by Shaw and the Fabians; and in a modern, administrative, ethical, and social organization; in the isolation of saints, the treatment of complexes, joy through health, and destruction of the body by cremation (with music while it burns), and then i've had it.[15]

That this invention of Miss Sayers is not fanciful may be gleaned from this short creed used at Mass by a midwestern priest:

I believe in man, and in a world in which it is good to live for all mankind; and that it is our task to create such a world.
I believe in equal rights for all men, in love, in justice, brotherhood and peace. I must continually act out these beliefs. . . .
And I believe in the resurrection, whatever it may mean. Amen.[16]

Yet the very openness that some of us hoped for has also provided the means by which the church can purify itself. In *The Open Church* I described the struggle at the Council as a struggle between the traditionalists, partisans of a nonhistorical orthodoxy who seemed to operate with an image of the church as eternal and unchanging, and those progressives who wished to shape a historical orthodoxy. The latter were also orthodox, to be sure, but aware of the hazards, the romance, the mistakes, and the gains of history.[17] There were many results I did not expect from the new orthodoxy: that so many of the progressives, especially among priests and nuns but also among the articulate laity, would abandon their places; so complete a break of discipline; the *hubris* of theologians treating bishops as their pupils (although I did expect direct and frank argument on a daily basis). I did not expect a mandatory Latin Mass to be replaced by a mandatory English Mass; nor the virtual disappearance of Gregorian chant and the classical musical patrimony; nor the collapse of the vital Thomistic revival led by Jacques Maritain and Étienne Gilson, Bernard Lonergan and Karl Rahner, M. D. Chenu and so many others: nor the swift withering away of the great intellectual tradition nourished at so much cost by Jean Daniélou and Henri de Lubac, Hans Urs von Balthasar and Louis Bouyer. I did not expect scriptural studies so to eclipse systematic theological reflection; nor Catholic preaching and practice to become ever more untheological and uncritical, in favor of the experiential and fervent ways of Baptists and Methodists; nor the charismatic style so to replace the style of realism; nor easy prophecy so thoroughly to dominate the tradition of prudence.

Contempt for the curia, for the church bureaucracy, and for traditional structures has much too long persisted. It was one thing to desire a break-through against the massive resistance of entrenched ways; it is another to inflame the desire not for reform but for dissolution.

By no means have I become a traditionalist Catholic. I cherish still the liberal Catholic tradition. By this I mean preserving the traditions of the English-speaking world (the force of the word "liberal"), including openness, candor, a taste for due process and full discussion, a reliance upon practical and inquiring intellect, and an attitude of optimism toward history somewhere between tragic and progressive. This tradition still needs to be brought into the patrimony of the church, as earlier were incarnated in it the metaphysical and cultural skills of the Greeks, the legal skills of the Romans, the intellectual brilliance of the French, and the scholarly thoroughness of the Germans.

On the other side, a liberal Catholic well grasps that the Catholic tradition has much to teach liberalism: a sense of tragedy, an emphasis on community and the communitarian (rather than the lonely) individual, and the role of the polity and the moral-cultural system in tempering the free market. A liberal Catholic, then, is one who tries to marry the best in the liberal and the best in the Catholic traditions, enriching each by the other. I was then, and am now, a liberal Catholic. It would satisfy me much if this book, this confession of faith, were to help rekindle the liberal Catholic tradition (see Chapter 11). One of the worst fruits of the Second Vatican Council, it now seems almost twenty years later, is the decline of liberal Catholicism. The only way by which that liberal Catholic tradition can be revived, however, is by becoming *self*-critical, criticizing aberrations to the left, criticizing Marxism, criticizing liberalism itself. Indeed biblical realism might be a better name for what I mean.

To make my meaning concrete, perhaps it will be well to proceed historically a little. The focus of passional energy in the church seems to have shifted from theological to worldly matters. Many who would not die for the Eucharist would die for political causes. Many who cherish uncertainty and broad-mindedness about any conceivable theological matter have crystal-clear views, held with absolutist conviction, about economics, military policy and social issues. The battleground of orthodoxy is hottest in matters of "peace and justice." That is where tumultuous emotions converge. That is where "redefinition" is keenest.

It cannot be said that this is where most bishops—or theologians— have had their best training. The study of the social sciences, of political philosophy, and of economics is relatively new in theological traditions. This is, therefore, where heretical views can grow most luxuriantly. In part, the social disciplines are exactly those fields of scholarship least affected by Catholic intellectual traditions. Sociology and psychology hardly share at all in the classical language of sin and responsibility, prayer and the interior life, the spiritual forces of evil and the inner struggle of the soul. Thus, *The Catholic Encyclopedia for School and Home* records in its article on capitalism (which stands as its treatment of the modern discipline of economics) the following perception:

The men and the classes that were rising to power and that imposed their system of values on the economic and social order of nations evolving into capitalism were often hostile to the teachings of the Catholic church. *For this reason* the church was critical of the rise of capitalism in its early stages.[18] (Emphasis supplied.)

A reader is startled by that "for this reason" and its clear tone of estrangement. For more than a century, the Catholic Church condemned socialism in all its forms and criticized the abuses associated with capitalism. While the Catholic Church developed a profound tradition of social teaching and produced notable experts in the field, economics cannot be said to be a major part of theological studies.

This point may be clearest in the *Esprit* group of Paris and Brussels, nourished for some twenty years (1930–1950) by Emmanuel Mounier and highly influential in North America through the journal *Cross Currents* and the circle of Pierre Elliott Trudeau in Canada. Much that is admirable and vital for Catholic life came from Mounier. But in politics and economics, the most consistent thread of Mounier's thought was hostility against capitalism, against his own bourgeois class, and against liberal democracy. Mounier and his followers praised the anticapitalist, antiliberal vitality of National Socialism in the 1930s, happily joined the "New Revolution" Vichy government until, attacked by the Catholic Right, Mounier was placed under arrest; they then sided with the French Communist Party rather than the Christian Democrats after the war. Mounier championed a Nietzschean, antibourgeois Christianity for superior elites and seriously altered orthodox notions of sin and historical progress. Above all, he was supremely naive about authoritarian social philosophies, careless about the concrete texture of political and economic reality, and too quick to celebrate an Übermensch Christianity. Sometimes Mounier's followers are known as "liberal Catholics," but in fact, Mounier's greatest hostilities were directed against liberalism. A devout and serious soul, he was a champion of the illiberal Left.[19] Jacques Maritain properly diagnosed this tendency.

Before Vatican II, much of modern politics lay outside the assimilating ken of theological studies. Clear exceptions must be made for studies of church and state, including the pioneering work of John

Courtney Murray on religious liberty and Jacques Maritain on the temporal order, the state, and democracy. In economics, John A. Ryan still stands virtually alone in the United States, like Bishop Ketteler and Heinrich Pesch in Germany.

Great traditions of social thought were, of course, nourished at Louvain and Tübingen and by the Jesuits in Rome and in Latin America. Many social experiments followed, such as the priest-worker movements, rural and industrial cooperatives, Catholic Action, and the Christian Democratic parties. Support for labor unions, especially in the United States, has been a high achievement. Still, these were not the staples of mainstream theological reflection. Their character was practical and pastoral.

In undertaking to address the theme of "The Church in the Modern World," and in laying the groundwork for "peace and justice" ministries in every Catholic diocese, the Second Vatican Council quite changed the terrain. In the United States, priests and nuns took to "the secular city" with enthusiasm. The appeal of the first Catholic president, John F. Kennedy, played a symbolic role equal to that of Pope John XXIII; some spoke of "the Two Johns" as the great symbols of the sixties. The civil rights movement drew many into the march on Selma and, later, the massive civil rights march on Washington. The war on poverty drew others. Urban ministry became vital. Most of all, the antiwar movement involved millions.

From fighting for progress within the church, many Catholic leaders were drawn into fighting against city hall and the White House. An anti-establishment passion grew. It was at first focused on Southern sheriffs, the Congress, the Pentagon, the CIA, the FBI. It soon attacked America more broadly, while of course claiming to speak for the better ideals of America. When political activists acquire religious passion—with aims encompassing not only political reforms but cultural revolution—politics verges into the religious sphere. The reference group of religious activists became others on the Left. My own book, *A Theology of Radical Politics*, grew from such soil. Religious and political idealism fused. Many began to describe this phenomenon less in the political language of party or faction and more in the religious language of "the movement."

The war in Vietnam provided symbolic linkage to "oppressed peoples" in the Third World. The American presence in Vietnam, at first perceived as a mistake, began to be perceived as a classic example of American imperialism. Good people were asked to choose between siding with the oppressors or siding with the oppressed. (Inexcusably too late, one learned that siding with North Vietnam might also be siding with an oppressor, less technically powerful but more politically ruthless, of whom the "boat people" were to be the victims.)

The cultural situation was, therefore, ripe for a major theological shift. To be a good Catholic soon became less to be faithful to the Creed than to opt for the poor and the oppressed. The meaning of this "option for the poor" has been deliberately kept ambivalent. On the one hand, the slogan means to gather up all the strictly religious power of the traditional spirituality of poverty—one of the three classic vows of professed religious. On the other hand, the slogan means to describe political revolution. For some, this means revolutions like the American, complete with the New Deal. For others, it means socialist revolution of some not very clearly defined sort, except that the rich and powerful (like Somoza in Nicaragua) will be overthrown and the lives of the peasants made better, possibly but not necessarily through the abolition of private property. For still others, it means Marxist revolution—alliance with the socialist nations led by the Soviet Union and enmity toward international capitalism as the chief source of oppression.

Indeed, Dom Helder Camara, Archbishop of Olinda-Recife, Brazil, the most distinguished voice of the Catholic Third World, urged Catholic theologians to make Marx the center of a new synthesis, as Aquinas had once used Aristotle.[20] Liberation theologians, led by Latin Americans, began reinterpreting the Scriptures and theological traditions in just this way: salvation means liberation from oppression in this world. Liberation theology speaks in many voices and with many refinements. Certain easy slogans are capable of carrying many meanings and masking different purposes. Both Marxists and non-Marxists often forge a popular front. Liberation is desirable; but how?

In support of Dom Helder Camara, many scholars have long noted that Marxism is not only Christianity's most potent rival, but quite readily siphons away basic Christian energies by transforming Christian symbols. Marxism demands total commitment of the individual to the collective, even unto death. It glories in its martyrs. Karl Löwith writes:

Though perverted into secular prognostication, the *Communist Manifesto* still retains the basic features of a messianic faith: "the assurance of things to be hoped for."

It is therefore not by chance that the "last" antagonism between the two hostile camps of bourgeoisie and proletariat corresponds to the Jewish-Christian belief in a final fight between Christ and Antichrist in the last epoch of history, that the task of the proletariat corresponds to the world-historical mission of the chosen people, that the redemptive and universal function of the most degraded class is conceived on the religious pattern of Cross and Resurrection, that the ultimate transformation of the realm of necessity into a realm of freedom corresponds to the transformation of the *civitas terrena* into a *civitas Dei,* and that the whole process of history as outlined in the *Communist Manifesto* corresponds to the general scheme of the Jewish-Christian interpretation of history as a providential advance toward a final goal which is meaningful. Historical materialism is essentially, though secretly, a history of fulfillment and salvation in terms of social economy. . . . [It is] from the first to the last sentence inspired by an eschatological faith, which, in its turn, "determines" the whole sweep and range of all particular statements. It would have been quite impossible to elaborate the vision of the proletariat's messianic vocation on a purely scientific basis and to inspire millions of followers by a bare statement of facts.[21]

Thus, perhaps unintentionally, Vatican II touched off a massive process of transformation. What if Catholicism and Marxism joined hands? That this is a tempting prospect becomes clear when one looks at the figures. Before Vatican II, one imagined the Catholic Church as essentially a European church, with a sort of adolescent cousin in North America and a host of small missions elsewhere. Today demographics reveal a stunningly different picture.

Catholics now number nearly one in five of all persons on earth— almost 800 million of the earth's estimated 4.4 billion persons. The Creed unites these almost 800 million Catholics in one common narrative. Moreover, probably no other community on earth is both so international in scope and so highly organized. Catholics around the world are organized into 1,854 dioceses, 496 archdioceses, and 252 other jurisdictions, each under one spiritual leader. There are an average of 140 parishes per diocese, each with its assigned pastor. A total of 258,451 priests serve the 201,320 parishes of the world. Another 157,878 men serve as religious priests and 74,792 as brothers. There are 937,600 nuns. The celibacy of these nearly 1.5 million ministers of the church enhances their dedication and full-time commitment. All are united through Rome.[22]

By region, there are 290,260,258 Catholics in Central and South America, 266,361,000 in Europe, 74,259,742 in North America, 58,174,000 in Asia, 54,759,000 in Africa, and 5,616,000 in Oceania. Brazil and Mexico have the largest Catholic populations of all the nations of the world. Italy has the third largest. They are followed by the United States, France, the Philippines, Spain, Poland, West Germany, Colombia, Argentina, Peru, Venezuela, Zaire, Czechoslovakia and Canada.[23]

These figures show that Catholicism is now predominantly a church of the Third World. Well over half its members live outside Europe and North America. In one sense, these numbers may be deceiving. In France, many registered by birth as Catholics are by no means practicing; for decades, France has been regarded as de-Christianized and virtually mission territory. Similarly Latin America. In Cuba, for example, the Catholic population shrunk swiftly after the rise of Castro and is now a shadow of what it once was. One cannot be sure that a great many Catholic populations will not, under easily foreseeable circumstances, melt away. In *The Pope's Divisions,*[24] Peter Nichols argues that Catholic dynamism has now slipped away from Europe for two reasons. The first is that population growth is overwhelmingly in favor of Latin America, and the church in Africa is growing at a far faster rate than anywhere else. This argument seems convincing, until one recalls that Great Britain at the height of its power as an ideal of the cultivated, civilized society had a population only a fraction of that of its empire. Spiritual dynamism is not determined by relative size. The second reason, if true, is devastating. It is that Europe is decadent and is hardly likely to be spiritually renewed. About this, one cannot be certain. But the prognosis, as we shall soon see, is not good.

The temptation for Catholicism will, therefore, be great. The "option for the poor" can become, in its way, a ploy for future power. A poorly led Catholicism might be willing to sell its soul and to redefine itself as a form of this-worldly revolution, joining forces with socialism. Naturally, democrats will insist that Christian socialism must be *democratic* socialism, not in the Soviet mold, and perhaps in some new form of political economy the world has not yet seen. Vagueness about the future is all the more necessary here because existing socialist republics, so many of which have come into being since World War II, not only in Eastern Europe but in Asia, Africa, Cuba and Nicaragua, fall far short of socialist promises. There are not lacking some, however, who praise Cuba as the fulfillment of the Gospels.

The lines of the Catholic fall into left-wing authoritarianism have already been drawn. J. Dennis Willigan, S.J., in *The National Jesuit News* in 1972, introduced a proposal for:

. . . the construction of a revolutionary social strategy for the Society of Jesus which is explicitly neo-Marxist and Maoist. . . . To effect this role authentically, the Society of Jesus must purge itself of its bourgeois consciousness and identify with the proletariat, acknowledging that only the proletariat, as the living negation of advanced monopoly capitalism and as the subject of history, can achieve correct and objective social knowledge—the proletariat simultaneously knows and constitutes society.[25]

In 1981, another American Jesuit, using the pseudonym "Daniel Ellison," defended the decision by Nicaragua's junta not to hold elections, since the people were not yet "ready." He questioned the relevance of "democracy," since communists regard U.S. democracy as fraudulent just as Americans think communist democracy is fraudulent. He also defended the Sandinista censorship of *La Prensa* by analogy with the Jesuit vow of obedience: one gives up "external" freedom in order to achieve "inward" liberty.[26] A very high theory of religious transcendence, it appears, can render distinctions among this-worldly matters of political economy highly relativist. In the name of spirituality, authoritarianism of the Left now seems as attractive to some Catholics as authoritarianism of the Right once seemed to others. The liberal Catholic, the biblical realist, opposing both, finds little social support within the church since Vatican II. Might Catholicism sign a pact with Marxism? Christianity has often before betrayed its own Creed. Even within ten generations after Christ, the creed of Arius replaced the Christian Creed and St. Jerome wrote that, after the Council of Rimini in 359, suddenly the Christian world awakened to find itself Arian.[27] Could a similar betrayal lie in waiting for Catholicism today? What to many has looked like progress may well be the early stages of an ever accelerating decline. The evidence is mixed.

On the one hand, it takes very little independence of mind to attend the sessions on economics and theology at the annual conventions of the American Academy of Religion or the Society for Christian Ethics, while setting forth a democratic socialist vision of reality. Virtually no dissent is heard. On El Salvador, Nicaragua, the nuclear freeze, and many other issues, the Left has become not only the stronger party in such associations; it holds a virtual monopoly on publicly expressed views. The most prestigious religious periodicals, while still allowing some debate, operate overwhelmingly within the horizon of democratic socialism. Hardly a critical voice is raised against the comfortable consensus. Furthermore, the contempt commonly expressed for the military, for U.S. business, for conservative politicians, for American foreign policy, and for American culture (alienated, narcissistic, consumerist, racist, sexist, etc.) might to a neutral observer seem like virulent anti-Americanism, consistent with hostility often expressed by Third World spokesmen, except for one thing: American reality is condemned, but an ideal America—some America that is not now and has never been—is still appealed to. The notion seems to be that America must become democratic socialist if it is to fulfill its promises —or at least to become a nation within which democratic socialists would give reluctant approval. The failures of democratic socialism in actual history are seldom addressed. The spiritual and material successes of democratic capitalism—and its unfulfilled agenda—are considered subjects for voicing which one's reputation will be assaulted. One must *not* praise democratic capitalism. One must—if one is truly moral and truly critical—celebrate democratic socialism. The reasons for this "must" are not empirical.

Yet rather than cite the tacit favoritism toward the Left among academic religious leaders, it may be more revealing to look to one of the most independent, fair-minded, and irenic of thinkers, Professor David Tracy of the University of Chicago. Father Tracy is no flaming leftist; even to imagine him as a partisan forces the lips to part in ironic amusement. In his highly acclaimed *Blessed Rage for Order* and again in *The Analogical Imagination: Christian Theology and the Culture of Pluralism*, Tracy has shown an immense capacity for synthesizing and systematizing fairly all the major options in American theology today.[28] In the latter, Tracy says quite clearly that in theology "any use of ideology-critique should possess a healthy hermeneutic of suspicion upon its own stance."[29] Tracy sets forth the stance of theologies of liberation in his usual irenic way:

In the latter case, for example, one often finds the insistence that only personal involvement in and commitment to the struggle for liberating transformation of some particular societal evil (economic exploitation and dependency, sexism, racism, anti-Semitism, elitism, exploitation of the environment) will free the theologian to see and speak the truth by doing the truth in solidarity with all those in the cause.[30]

At another place, contrasting defenders of democratic capitalism and state socialism, Tracy reveals (characteristically, only in a footnote) his own preference:

For myself, revisionary Marxist theories like those of the Frankfurt School, with their ability to locate the nonidentity of reason and society in both systems, and revisionary American praxis-theories like Richard Bernstein's provide responsible alternatives to both state socialism and late capitalism. What seems most reprehensible, however, is the "selective humanism" of some right-wing and left-wing thinkers. What I hope to show in a future book on practical theology, what most needs recovery, is practical reason with an emancipatory thrust—hence the appeal, to me, of revisionary theorists like Bernstein and Habermas.[31]

In a later crucial chapter on the contemporary situation, Tracy's worldview is remarkably European, non-Anglo-Saxon, non-American.

He cites as the four pillars of the modern world Marx, Freud, Nietzsche, and Heidegger; notably missing are the modern inventors of democracy, capitalism, and—Tracy's main subject—pluralism. Of Jefferson, Madison, Smith, Montesquieu, de Tocqueville, Lincoln, Franklin Delano Roosevelt and others we hear as little as we would from a theologian of France or Germany. One of the greatest books of all time on the notion of the public and on pluralism—Madison and Hamilton's *The Federalist*—might as well not have existed. Many of Tracy's individual sentences about American culture are defensive and guilt-ridden, probably more through following academic convention and citing the views of others than through advertence. One would think from many of these sentences that, as history goes, Americans suffer more from "alienation," "structures of oppression," and lack of liberties for and civilities toward women and persons of nonwhite race than any other people in history. The degree to which Tracy does accept a revisionary Marxist view of ultimate collectivization and the meaning of "liberation" is clear in the ringing conclusion of his penultimate chapter:

Above all, the liberation theologies allow all theologians to hear and see the tradition from a perspective faithful to its ownmost self-understanding: from that perspective privileged to the ancient prophets and Jesus alike—the perspective of the outcast, the powerless, the oppressed, the marginalized, all those whose story the rest of us have presumed to tell them. It is perhaps little wonder that I have not yet found the classic text of liberation theology that I have sought—that work that will explode with power as Barth's commentary on Romans once did in the neoorthodox theologies of proclamation. The search for the classic disclosed through and by these theologies, I have come to believe, will not end in any text. The classic of liberation theologies is the classic not of a text but of an event: the event of a liberating praxis wherein the actions of whole peoples whose disclosive, ignored, forgotten, despised story is at least being narrated and heard in ways which may yet transform us all.[32]

Confronting these liberation theologies, Tracy has much too little to say by way of rejoinder. Three pages earlier he sets forth his method: "The first step for all other theologians to take is to listen."[33]

Sooner or later, however, the critical impulse in Professor Tracy will awaken here, too. That, clearly, is the impulse he celebrated at the beginning of his inquiry. If "revisionary Marxism" of the sort Tracy now supports, or Marxism of quite other sorts, is now, as Raymond Aron puts it, the "vulgate" of Western secular discourse today, genuine dialogue with that particular political culture requires more from Christians than a celebratory *yes.* When and where will we hear the *no?* Marxist "analysis" has always failed of predictive ability. It sadly underestimated the spiritual and moral resources of democratic capitalist societies. It fails to diagnose why Marxist-Leninist societies regularly fall into political tyranny and economic devastation ("If the Sahara were socialized, there would soon be a shortage of sand"). Finally, it fails to predict the sorry outcomes of democratic socialist policies. Tracy finds revisionary Marxist analysis "emancipatory." This is an empirical claim. Where, and where not?

I consider David Tracy a valued friend and colleague. Yet his defense of Marxism, even "revisionary," indicates to me how strongly contemporary currents run in that direction. One cannot say that Tracy is swimming against the tide of academic religion, for the most powerful authorities are with him. One cannot say that he will lack for popular acclaim outside the academy, among the peace and justice activists, whose *praxis* his work supports. Indeed, in dissenting from his vision, one cannot help feeling a little afraid.

13. Against the New Idealism

> I aim to change the friends of God into the friends of man;
> believers into thinkers, worshippers into workers, candidates for
> the other world into students of this world. . . .
> —LUDWIG FEUERBACH, *The Essence of Christianity*

THE CLOUDINESS TACTIC

In every age, the Catholic people are torn by contrasting views of reality. It is not easy to determine, in the midst of flame and smoke, which vision of reality will ultimately stand the tests of truth. Each of us is pulled in many conflicting directions by loves, habits, loyalties, aspirations, ideals, comforts, particular character traits, and commitments. Each is besieged, in a pluralistic society, by competing judgments about reality. Each is also affected by best friends and associates, parties and schools of thought. For anyone to find the voice of conscience—the honest, truth-respecting light—in this maelstrom of attractions is nearly superhuman. One watches, over a lifetime, how rare are truly honest intellects, how powerful are reference groups, fashions, and peer pressures. No wonder most people most of the time seek protective coloring in a group. I have known in my forty-nine years only a handful of intellects whose courage has been proved again and again, under withering attack upon their person even by former friends. Even fewer among them think deeply enough always to be disconcerting their friends, by raising ever further questions.

Not long ago Susan Sontag shocked a left-wing audience by pointing out that her and their deepest passion had been to distance themselves from anticommunists and that this passion had led them to make horrible mistakes about communism itself. She spoke of the act of "bracketing," that is, disregarding, unwanted truths. Ironically, in the very act of speaking Miss Sontag took pains to distance herself from other anticommunists and to bracket further unwanted truths, exemplifying the very vice she was renouncing. I find myself admiring her intention, but being bitterly disappointed in how short she fell.[1] There is probably nothing more difficult for an intellectual of the Left than to risk her credentials by radical criticism of the Left. The punishment is excommunication.

For such reasons, heresy conducts itself exactly like orthodoxy. The notion that only Christians who hold to a written creed are dogmatic is absurd. Indeed, in many ways, clarity about the exact limits of a creed is wonderfully liberating. To inquire without taking a stand is impossible; there is then nothing to test. And to be clear about one's standpoint makes every test sharper, whetting the appetite of the inquiring mind. The knowledge that others like oneself also have their creeds helps one to respect and to clarify differences, to mutual benefit.

Sometimes, of course, vagueness has a method to it. A truly utopian vision entails specifics about the sort of order its proponent would be content to be a conservative in. There is, more commonly, a pseudo-utopian vision that is deliberately antihistorical. The point of such a vision is not that it should be fulfilled imperfectly in history but, instead, that it give evidence of its proponent's superior purity of soul. Pseudo-utopian visions are usually rooted in resentment and hostility. In this case, they are clear about what they hate; about what they desire they are said to be "open and experimental." This might be believed if their proponents supplied procedures of disconfirmation, but this is seldom done. Such "experiments" are not seriously intended. Chesterton, as usual, catches the flavor of these flights from reason:

It is not merely true that a creed unites men. Nay, a difference of creed unites men—so long as it is a clear difference. A boundary unites. . . .

It is exactly the same with politics. Our political vagueness divides men, it does not fuse them. Men will walk along the edge of a chasm in clear weather, but they will edge miles away from it in a fog. So a Tory can walk up to the very edge of Socialism, *if he knows what is Socialism*. But if he is told that Socialism is a spirit, a sublime atmosphere, a noble, indefinable tendency, why, then he keeps out of its way; and quite right, too. One can meet an assertion with argument; but healthy bigotry is the only way in which one can meet a tendency. . . . Against this there is no weapon at all except a rigid and steely sanity, a resolution not to listen to fads, and not to be infected by diseases.[2]

Is there, then, a likely powerful heresy of our age and of the decades to come, and if so, what is it? In my view, there is such a heresy. One can feel its presence everywhere. It is difficult to describe because its edges are not hard, it has not quite crested, and it spreads rather like an odorless, colorless gas than like a multiplying plant. Before attempting to define it, however, it might be wise to illustrate from an actual example how heresy once did capture the Catholic Church, the point being not the substance of the heresy, but the speed with which it can triumph.

THE AGE OF ARIUS

People were not content, once, to *disagree* about religion; some would lie, slander, caricature, and kill for it. Thus, Athanasius of Alexandria was falsely accused of bribery and murder by bishops at the Council of Nicaea in 325; he was vindicated, but later driven from his see in Egypt and sent into exile into distant Germany at Trier. In those days conflicts over religion weren't sweetness and light.

In the year 319, a handsome and articulate young priest named Arius, together with a schoolmate of his, Eusebius, who was shortly to become bishop in the imperial city, put a new (but perennially attractive) faith in the place of Catholicism.[3] Many people at that time found it difficult to believe, as humans always find it difficult to believe, that the man Jesus Christ is in every sense one with God the Creator; they found this formula a formidable barrier. To correct this deficiency, and to further certain political goals, Arius and Eusebius maintained that Jesus was less than God, being neither equal to nor eternal with God. Arius and Eusebius knew that Jesus holds a special place among men, and they were even willing to admit, in some sense, that all creation is mirrored in Him. But they wanted to protect God from confusion with a creature. They sought some more relevant way of presenting the greatness of Jesus. They also sought less abstract and less "unintelligible" ways of speech about God and Jesus, some general formulae that all could agree to while remaining rather vague about learned niceties. Their motives were pastoral, political, even ecumenical—they wished to blur differences on which believers divide.

To this end, they prevailed upon the emperor to summon three hundred and fifty bishops to Nicaea for a council. Alas for them, the assembled bishops heeded the arguments of Athanasius.[4]

Although Arius was condemned by the Council of Nicaea in 325 and briefly exiled, Eusebius soon won him reprieve. The two then conspired to have Catholic bishops replaced by Arian bishops one by one, systematically. Arius himself soon died but Eusebius and others carried on the struggle for decades. They had Athanasius exiled. By 359, they had won most of the sees of Christendom, and four hundred bishops—but not the pope—gave their assent at the Council of Rimini to a loose formula favorable to Arianism. Later still, the barbarians who sacked Carthage—in the region where St. Augustine was born and raised—made a vague version of Arian doctrine prevail in much of the West. The people, however, remained more orthodox than the bishops.[5]

The lesson we must learn is that the church can easily be subverted from within, position by position, see by see, and never more easily than when political turmoil is in the air.

BEYOND MARX: PERFECTIONIST IDEALS RESURGENT

Substitutes for Catholic faith are not new in Catholic history. They are perennial. They afflict every generation. Some early Fathers believed they would get worse as history proceeded. If we were to ask, then, what is the temptation of our own generation, I think we might discover the outlines of an attractive faith similar enough to the Catholic faith to breed confusion and powerful enough, given time, to prevail. Two things would fuse to give this temptation overwhelming power. First would be special contemporary possibilities and vulnerabilities. Second would be powerful historical currents always attached to Christianity. The first originates in the world, the second in a predisposition within Christian faith itself.

In the world at the present time, I see two vulnerabilities. In the developed nations, millions live far above the level of mere subsistence and are vulnerable to a sharp loss of the sense of reality, making them prone to imagine yet more perfect worlds and dreamy visions. In less developed nations, it is naturally intolerable to admit that centuries of poverty and oppression are the outcome of local habits of thought and life. Some naturally blame all ills upon those more successful and cover despair by placing hope in almost magical utopian solutions.

The possibility and vulnerability of the contemporary world, then, is to imagine a worldly organization that will banish "sinful structures" for once and all, the flaw being perceived to lie not in personal living but in the current world order. There is some truth in this vision, otherwise it would attract few. The great urgent desire of many is to find a spiritual engine to effect a "great transformation" from the present corrupt order into a brotherly, just, and peaceful society and to do so as soon as possible, now, in this generation or the next. Marxism promises such a transformation. Its appeal is great. The contemporary world encourages Christians to borrow the Marxist magic. This some (but not all) forms of "liberation theology" clearly affect to do.[6]

The perennial vulnerability of Christianity matches the worldly vulnerability. Because Christianity is a religion of the spirit, it carries within it a strong spiritualizing, perfectionist current. Despite the fact that Christianity is a religion of the flesh—rooted in the incarnation of God in Jesus and the resurrection of the body—devout Christians are consistently drawn to body-denying, perfect, spiritual visions. On the religious Right, this temptation often takes the form of extreme personal asceticism, mortification of the body, disciplining of the individual spirit. It tries to keep religion pure of worldly social action. On the religious Left, this temptation often takes the form of social dreaminess, a denial of the persistence of evil in clumsy this-worldly institutions. It tries to imagine structures pure of individual sinfulness. The Right favors individual perfectionism; the Left favors social perfectionism.

Perhaps through recoiling from the bitter and violent religious wars of the sixteenth century, the West has tried to moderate the fanaticism of religious disagreement. Edicts of toleration tried to disconnect public policy from the sphere of religious conscience. In Iran and Iraq today, a vicious religious war rages in which entire hordes seek martyrdom for promised paradise. In such religious war, one hears echoes of our own sad past. Centuries of tolerance have much softened religious disagreement, but sometimes with the effect that Christian life is based less on precise *doctrine* informing life than on personal sentiment, habit, taste, and preference. Religious faith has been substantially de-intellectualized. For this reason, the heresy of the present and future is less likely to be strictly theological and more likely to occur in the terms of this world.

Leszek Kolakowski, the greatest Marxist theoretician in our time until harsh experience made him Marxism's most penetrating critic, observes that:

Marxism is a doctrine of blind confidence that a paradise of universal satisfaction is awaiting us just round the corner. Almost all the prophecies of Marx and his followers have already proved to be false, but this does not disturb the spiritual certainty of the faithful, any more than it did in the case of chiliastic sects: for it is a certainty not based on any empirical premises or supposed 'historical laws,' but simply on the psychological need for certainty. In this sense Marxism performs the function of a religion, and its efficacy is of a religious character. But it is a caricature and a bogus form of religion, since it presents its temporal eschatology as a scientific system, which religious mythologies do not purport to be.[7]

Yet as a utopian possibility Marxism suffers a grievous flaw; it has been utilized in practice now since 1917 and few within its domains can suppress a smile of mockery at its empty promises. As a gigantic organizing force of tyrannical power, Marxism is still unsurpassed in human history. It builds armies and police forces and systems of control beyond compare. But it inspires love only where it is not yet in effect.

Even Christians who were at first drawn to Marxism as a more muscled faith than traditional Christianity have recently been drawing back.[8] Some do so because Marxism preaches class struggle, violence, and hatred, and their own inclinations are more pacific. Others do so because Marxism is atheistic; others because its materialism leaves spiritual emptiness; and still others because the societies it inspires are, in practice, ugly.

More dangerous, I believe, is the deeper spiritual current whence Marxism originally received (and still receives) its inner power. Negatively, as Kolakowski notes, this is the power of resentment, the delicious solution of blaming one's misfortunes on malevolent others, whose destruction will magically abolish evil.[9] Positively, however, its spiritual power derives from the ancient quest for a perfect society of comradeship and equality. The atheism and materialism of Marxism play a role here. Since Marxism abolishes God, it abolishes as well the personal dimension of sin. To be good is to work for the revolution. To sin is to resist it. There being no soul and no God, there is to life no religious dimension, only social work, economics, and above all politics.

For Westerners who abandon religion the situation is analogous. Without being Marxists, good persons may give the total energies of life to social work, economics, and politics.[10]

Furthermore, those Christians who abhor an ideal of individual perfection are tempted to interpret Christianity itself as fundamentally a vision of "justice and peace." The religious socialists of Great Britain of the nineteenth century—who were often anti-Marxist—could say in this spirit that Christianity is the religion of which socialism is the practice.[11] In this view, one may be a "good Christian" in one's private life, but if one participates in "sinful social structures" without trying to overthrow them, one lives in sin. The hidden theological doctrine in this heresy, which grows stronger day by day even among bishops, is that sin resides chiefly in social structures. Christianity becomes a social theory.

There are, of course, forms of social democracy and democratic socialism that are neither perfectionist nor utopian and that embody a sort of biblical realism that promises only approximations of justice in this world. Such realism holds that no social structures and, surely, no individual humans are sinless. But where religious life atrophies, political passions often become surrogates for religious passion. Worldly visions invested with religious passion become ersatz religion.[12]

If one reflects on the trends within Catholic theology briefly noted in the press, one grasps some of the outlines of the new faith. Consider the growing power of emotions like outrage, the praise heaped upon "prophets" (who seem to be being produced in record numbers), and the certification of rage as the mark of virtuous conscience. One reads in the letter columns of *The National Catholic Reporter,* the chief organ of the Catholic Left, of much heart rending, tears, expostulations, and ripping of garments.[13] Clearly, these are idealists, who feel deeply. The structure of their ideals is interesting.

Current deeply held ideals seem to breed such loathing of reality that those within their grip experience fantasies of self-destruction. (One Jesuit writes that "the deepest mystery of the Christian faith" is to "be killed, murdered, destroyed, annihilated rather than injure another human being.")[14] The world is not worthy of them and, being too weak to change the world, many fantasize throwing themselves gloriously, rebelliously, defiantly beneath its wheels. The appeal of Che Guevara and other dying revolutionaries expresses in politics the exact appeal that C. S. Lewis, Denis de Rougemont, and Ronald Knox have noted in the romances of courtly love, *Romeo and Juliet,* and *Anna Karenina.*[15] Utopian revolution, like romantic love, succeeds best in death. Humdrum reality would dull its glow. Revolutionaries live "happily ever after" only if they lose.

It is biblical to accept ourselves as we are, weak and sinful, embodied in this differentiated clay that is ourselves, dependent and less than invulnerable, neither beasts nor angels. As the biblical stories about angels have lost their hold upon modern minds, some modern persons have begun to imagine themselves in angelic terms. Angels are persons neither male nor female, not bound by time or space or flesh. So some today think they are "persons," neither male nor female. They announce their rebellion against history, time, and flesh. Yet men are men; women are women. Each of us is embodied, sexed, differentiated. No one is a "person." The drive to eliminate sexual reference is, to use the ancient word, gnostic.

There is some of this same passion on the Right. One is tempted to say it comes with all ideological or absolutist thinking. One sees it in some who are struck with horror at abortions and in others who feel inundated by tides of secularism, statism, and humanism. Kevin Phillips identifies with these absolutist feelings in *The Post-Conservative*

Age. He calls himself a "neo-Marxian populist."[16] He seems to loathe most institutions. He fears the coming of a Fascist nihilism swept up by massive impatience. His appeal to Marxian populism illustrates Susan Sontag's point that Communism is a form of Fascism.[17] They meet in their absoluteness, their impatience, their contempt for incarnation.

The resurgent power of this massive impatience awaited the rise of mass media of communication. These media reach individuals over the heads of mediating institutions. The media of communication, so vulnerable to images of escapism, so bound by the solicitation of utopian ideals, are perfect vehicles for impatience. The inner temptation of Everyman is rebellion against reality. As if with a cathode light, the media are suffused with rebellion. In the name of idealism television makes what is worst in us seem best, and its idealism—its appeal to the elimination of all evils—is not biblical.

This contemporary idealism, which has become the medium in which we learn of ourselves, has three parts. It is, first, a spiritualization of the human being, a resentment of and hostility toward the flesh. It revolts against the limits of the flesh, as if in the name of the disembodied "person," and it simultaneously minimizes the restraints of the flesh, "liberating" embodied persons from "guilt" for the violation of sexual "taboos." If the flesh is insignificant, what does it matter what we do with it so long as we are "loving" and "honest"?

The second feature of the new idealism is its theory of knowledge. It does not highly value common sense and common experience or the lessons of tradition and history. It values consciousness raising. It promotes a superior way of looking at things—looking *through* things, seeing hidden realities. It is a way of enlightenment defined by contrast against common sense. This modern idealism is deceptive, because it parallels so closely the perennial human struggle between ignorance and insight. Idealistic consciousness raising, therefore, seems to be perfectly natural. But idealistic enlightenment and genuine enlightenment differ in how they appropriate the humble lessons of the human body, common sense, and tradition.

Idealistic knowledge is an attempt to become superior to the human race. Genuine knowledge is an attempt to gain humble realism. Idealistic knowledge commonly expresses itself as rage. Genuine knowledge commonly expresses itself as reconciliation and quiet determination. To the modern idealist, reconciliation seems like surrender. To the humble seeker after truth, reconciliation is a step along the way of sound and solid progress.

In the old dispensation, reconciliation is not a mere shrug of the shoulders but a determined willingness to take up one's cross and follow the will of the Lord whithersoever it leads, to keep forging ahead in the darkness. Reconciliation teaches delight in the ironies and tragedies of daily life; and while it well knows anger against injustice, it does not descend to rage against the Creator for having made a world of history in which injustice freely wreaks its havoc. It regards history as a time of battle, in which calm faith triumphs even in defeat. Modern idealism finds all this inferior.

Thirdly, the new idealism, proceeding upon the hidden assumption that persons are, if not gods, then at least rather like the angels, carries within it the conviction that evil arises from social structures. It imagines that if we could throw off the historical order, destroy sinful structures, and begin anew, paradise on earth is possible. It therefore much cherishes antihistorical thinking. Since it imagines that persons are good while social structures are the sources of all evil, it regards the free human spirit as the source of virtue and all establishments of wealth, power, and order as oppressive. You and I—free to be ourselves —are okay. Evil is embodied in those who restrain us. In this sense, contemporary idealism is infantile, full of the rage of innocent children against restrictive parents. Contrasting the liberation of the self to the oppression imposed by authorities, modern idealism misses the essential struggle of genuine liberation: the struggle of the self against the self, the combat of the self against the world, the flesh, and the devil already deeply rooted within the self.

Here a distinction is necessary. Some thinkers hold that the mistake of the West, especially since the Enlightenment, is to have generated a false ideal of the solitary individual. In fact, they say, the human being is always social; thus any genuine theory of the self must include an analysis of social institutions. Of course this is true. But this discovery of the social nature of human beings leads in two quite different directions. One direction is that of socialism, the inevitable (as it is said) collectivization of human life, one hopes on a democratic and cooperative basis. The other direction is that of democratic capitalism: a vision of cultural pluralism, economic pluralism, and political pluralism in which individuals are brought up to nourish a very wide range of social skills in tolerant, open, cooperative, and trusting behaviors. It is an analytical mistake to hold that socialism respects the social nature of humans, while democratic capitalist societies are characterized by "possessive individualism." In actual history, exactly the reverse happens. One may test this proposition empirically. In which actual nations do voluntary associations and cooperative habits actually thrive, and in which do they wither?

The analytical mistake occurs as follows. Democratic socialists argue that a society which aims first at collective habits and collective goods will also produce cooperative citizens. Democratic capitalists argue that in order to produce cooperative citizens one must go by a different route: respect first their individuality, their liberty, and their own judgment about what is primary in their lives, and in actual practice you will produce a more socially cohesive, cooperative, and energetic society. Both theories respect the social nature of humans and the primacy (from one point of view) of systems. These theories may be tested in the real world, empirically, and indeed they have been. For various reasons, however, intellectuals nourished in the humanities and social sciences—exactly the ones most likely to influence theologians —are disproportionately in favor of the democratic socialist ideal, despite its actual historical record.

Thus, the most highly organized doctrine of idealism in our day is embodied in Marxism-Leninism. Its most common Western variant appears, at first, to be more deeply rooted in romantic ideals about the innocence and beauty of the solitary individual. Both Western romanticism and Marxism are radically anti-establishment. Compared to Western romantic individualism, however, the superiority of Marxism-Leninism lies in its social realism. It plainly teaches that, to throw off oppressive structures, disciplined organization and even violence will be necessary. It shows that human life is inexorably social and that the solitary individual alone lacks community, collective purpose, and effective political realism. Western idealism is, however, a fertile ground for Marxist-Leninist doctrine. At Harvard, Solzhenitsyn showed how both spring from identical roots. Western idealism establishes the fundamental interior attitudes. For this reason, Western elites often find it difficult to perceive the radical evil of Marxism-Leninism. And they sympathize, cannot help sympathizing, with its "ideals," which they have already embraced in their hearts.

Odd as it seems, biblical enlightenment requires an unremitting struggle against the form of Western idealism that haunts our hearts, the gnostic impulse within us, the part of us that would wish us to become children of light. The war to eliminate hunger, discrimination, war, and every human evil, that illusory war waged by our own idealism and magnified today by our media of communication, is a false war, unhistorical and unreal in its presuppositions. The secret lust of the same media for excitement, violence, auto crashes, flames, and bombs testifies to its hidden origins in the same unreality. We are taught to imagine ourselves as both virtuous and all-powerful, able to eliminate evil from this world. We are taught that we may, with a little more goodwill, ultimately master history and its evil forces. Those who think themselves superior to history commonly harbor fantasies of self-destruction. One may watch for such signs in oneself.

The ancient name for such idealism as now suffuses so many of our elites in Western and non-Western societies is gnosticism. Its power today arises both from the vulnerabilities of our world and from those of Judaism and Christianity, the dominant sources of all modern ideas about history, development, and morality. Let us try now to tighten this analysis.

One of the main carriers of ancient tendencies today are the intellectual leaders of feminism. The recent study of gnosticism by Elaine Pagels makes this point clear. Gnosticism has roots in the ancient Mediterranean world just before the time of Arius and Eusebius, Athanasius and Augustine. No doubt its origins are shrouded in mists, but newly discovered caches of documents from the second century A.D. help us to study it in the early Christian era. There can be no doubt that Christianity then defined itself *against* gnosticism. Professor Pagels describes how certain Catholics pitted themselves against the orthodox bishops.[18] They attacked the organized church both in its structure and in its vision of good and evil. The structure of the church was particular and historical. Its authorities were male. And its vision of this world and the flesh, of sin and limits, and of femaleness and maleness seemed inferior. The gnostics wished to change the structure of the church, its teachings, and its Scriptures—to purify them and raise them to a higher level of enlightenment. Gnostics and orthodox struggled. The latter won. Contemporary feminism picks up the gnostics' case.

In saying this, however, I must make three distinctions. First, by feminism I do not mean the phenomenon, made possible in our time, of millions of women taking up new responsibilities in the world. Women of immense diversity, especially in the industrialized world, are becoming active players in the world of work and politics and culture. This is fact, not ideology. Second, by feminism I mean a set of doctrines about the world, even an ideal of the way the world ought to look when it has been transformed by new principles, by contrast with which existing principles are "sexist." Feminism, then, as a set of doctrines can be seen in the work of such writers as Kate Millett, Shulasmith Firestone, Gloria Steinem, Rosemary Ruether, Mary Daly, and the rest. Some regard this brace of ideologies, for all their differences usually summarized in the singular noun "feminism," as a world-transforming force. Others link feminism to socialism and describe as the enemies of women the insurance companies, the multinationals, and, in general, capitalism, based as they see it on the white-male principle of competition and aggression. This is ideology, not fact.

The third point to keep clear is that there is something deeper than feminism at work within the ideology of feminism, so defined. It is today's common rage against distinctions between people. The distinguished political philosopher Gerhart Niemeyer describes a "rage against reality" as an attitude "common to the Gnostics of old and the modern ideologists."[19]

One of the motives behind this movement is kindly, however. Distinctions between groups have frequently been abused: men have exploited women; whites have oppressed blacks; priests have lorded it over laity. The other motive is less rational. There is in some people a rage against reality, an anger not against the abuse of difference, but at difference itself. They don't want a universe in which there are men and women, young and old.[20]

Thus, the vision of leading feminist intellectuals does not capture the whole of modern idealism. By linking their case to general categories like the revolt against oppression, the building of socialism, and the attack upon "bourgeois" values, such intellectuals have tried to make their vision inclusive and comprehensive. (One notes that such intellectuals seldom praise women as *women*, but only those who hold the proper opinions: not Margaret Thatcher, or Jeane Kirkpatrick, or Phyllis Schlafly.) Since the ideology of feminism, as distinct from the fact of the growing role of women, may well be the most overrated ideology of our time, already heavily revising its original intellectual baggage, one must seek elsewhere the spiritual currents that lie beneath it and around it.

These Eric Voegelin has usefully assayed in *Science, Politics and Gnosticism*, in which he carefully describes six features that give modern idealism continuity with ancient gnosticism.[21] One way in which Christianity differs from gnosticism lies in its willingness to write its Creed down, in cold particular words, to put them to the test. Despite the fact that gnosticism is *a way of seeing* rather than a codified creed, an attitude rather than a set of propositions, the diagnosis by Voegelin is classic and I here adapt it.

(1) As all humans have reason to be dissatisfied—our hearts being restless—so also are gnostics dissatisfied with their situation. But they find this uncommonly shocking.

(2) Gnostics hold that these dissatisfactions are due to the intrinsically poor organization of the world around them. Gnostics do not assume that the order of being is good, and that it is we humans who are inadequate.

(3) Gnostics hold that liberation from the evils of this poor world is desirable and possible.

(4) Whereas Christians hold that the world will largely remain morally as it is, even as worldly progress is made, and that human salvation comes from grace, gnostics hold that world order evolves

historically into a morally better world. Whereas Christians believe in history as narrative, but not in history as salvation, gnostics believe not so much in progress as in total transformation.

(5) Gnostics hold that this historical transformation is to be achieved by human action. In later centuries, the word for this became revolution—not in the sense of turning back *(re-volvere)* to first principles, but in the sense of a wholly new future.

(6) The gnostic key to this great transformation is science, knowledge (gnosis), a formula discerned by true consciousness (as opposed to false), or by raised consciousness (as opposed to common sense), a special knowledge that has the ring and style of the prophetic (as opposed to the priestly, realistic) mode.

For Voegelin, gnosticism is a parasite on Christianity. It hears the message of Christian perfectionism and the Second Coming.[22] It awaits a New Age. It drinks a full draught of the messianic vision. It interprets the present world as evil. It identifies goodness with a new order. Its vision is social, although it springs from a profound reinterpretation of personal life. Since the primary reality of human existence is the joining of soul and body, embodied personhood, gnosticism makes sex a primary focus of consciousness. Here its vision is ambivalent. It identifies flesh with this world and unawakened consciousness, and it primarily values the *gnosis* of the spirit. Thus it is embarrassed by the body and its limits. It wishes all to live as persons, not as women and men. Particularities scandalize it. Saying that the flesh is not important, it at first attempts to live above and beyond the flesh. Psychological pressures and logic, however, soon lead it to hold that, since the flesh *is* unimportant, then whatever one does with it deserves little notice. In the first moment, gnosticism spiritualizes the flesh (what matters is true love between enlightened minds); in the second, it indulges it.

Because gnosticism is polymorphic, defining it is dangerous; one risks including too much or too little. The merit of Voegelin's use of the concept is to have shown how a similar spirit underlies a great many phenomena that seem at first sight to be wildly disparate. Yet Voegelin sometimes applies it to persons like Hobbes, to whom it is applied so tenuously as to be useless if not simply wrong; and sometimes he uses it so broadly that it may explain too much. Similarly, the term "gnosticism" may accurately be applied to the rational idealism and moral sentimentality into which Reinhold Niebuhr shot so many barbs. In practice, however, it is best to define gnosticism not only by general ideas but by examples in several specific areas.

Two practical tests about the meaning of "gnostic" are highly useful. First, in what respect are one's *own* views likely to be gnostic? Second, what would one count as antignostic? On the first point a Catholic archbishop recently afforded an example. The political Right, he opined, is moved by powers and interests, the political Left by ideas and ideals. This locution attributes to the Left a superior sensitivity (gnosis) denied to the Right. The gnostic character of the claim would be the same even if, in his locution, the terms "Right" and "Left" had been reversed. This move is typical of self-serving human behavior, but it becomes gnostic by its appeal to a form of knowing shared by some but not others. The lesson to be learned is that the moral knowledge of one's opponents ought to be held to be of similar standing to one's own. One thus respects one's own concrete limits. One's claim to a "raised consciousness" or greater sensitivity is suspect. This, then, is one's check upon one's own gnostic tendencies.

On the second point, it is antignostic to recognize that human relations are never merely rational and ideal. "I should like Balls infinitely better," says Caroline Bingley in *Pride and Prejudice*, "if they were carried on in a different manner. . . . It would surely be much more rational if conversation instead of dancing were the order of the day." To which her brother replied: "Much more rational, I dare say, but it would not be near so much like a Ball." C. S. Lewis, to whom I owe this citation,[23] was a lifelong foe of gnosticism in everyday Western thought. The ingredients of his own sustained antignostic position came down to five: (1) Be suspicious of claims to higher sensitivity, higher morality, higher rationality. (2) Look to plain, ordinary facts which are likely to be overlooked. (3) Respect the limits of the human body and embodied psyche. (4) Expect tragedy and sin in everything. (5) Negotiate humbly. Lewis found in such imperatives a sound Catholic, sacramental instinct. This, then, is the antignostic program.

In sexual matters, the gnostic spirit forgets the sheer physical clumsiness of love to stress ecstasy, enlightenment, liberty, personhood, transcendence, joy, fulfillment, liberation, and growth. In this respect, the gnostic spirit is a perfect vehicle for haze-wreathed, romantic advertisements about feminine hygiene, sweet breath, bouncing hair, and the joy of liberating (with a shampoo) "the true you within you." Some aspects of feminism are a reaction against this gnostic approach to the female body and "the feminine mystique." That is why so many feminists at first made an antignostic statement by avoiding the conventions of feminine clothing, cosmetics, and manners. Some of the same feminists, however, then went on to spiritualize sexual love, as if it made no difference whether such love were heterosexual or homosexual. Further, sexual equality became, in practice, sexual interchangeability. No doubt in much modern work sex is irrelevant and there is, in effect, much demand for a more or less neuter work force. But it is an odd rationalism—like not dancing at a ball—so to neuter humanity. Indeed, the humane reaction to such neutering is to stress the differences, rather than the likenesses, between the sexes. This, in any case, would be the antignostic impulse. Orthodoxy respects, as gnosticism does not, differences of body, earth, and fact.

In politics, the gnostic spirit manifests itself in seemingly opposite but related modalities. On the one hand, it tends toward faith in rational persuasion, cherishing the belief that others in other cultures have essentially one's own views and aspirations. The gnostic spirit does not wish to cope with real differences of conviction. It thus ignores the inevitable conflicts, ambiguities, and evils of life, and underestimates the commonsense need for institutions and lawful coercions in human societies. The realism of St. Augustine set Christian social thought upon an antignostic course. On the other hand, the gnostic spirit also tends toward the opposite extreme, at which in the name of beautiful ideals it is willing to excuse the extermination of those who resist such ideals. Addressing himself quite adroitly to both these modalities, Lenin himself mocked the sentimentality of his enemies. He knew that they would sell him the rope by which he would hang them. Meanwhile, he could also count upon them to overlook the murders, the imprisonments, the tortures, the exterminations of those who stood in the way of the building of his glorious new order of humanity. Too sentimental to worry about small encroachments of force, they would also be too idealistic to notice the massive elimination of resistance.

The success of Marxism is based upon an exact diagnosis of the gnostic spirit of our era. Marx created a template that applies to any situation. If you suffer, someone else is to blame and his elimination will bring you happiness. Within its own habitat, Marxism has lost its positive power of persuasion. But the original template still works if the United States is made responsible for the evils of imperialism, racism, sexism, and war. Anti-Americanism is, accordingly, the first and fundamental Marxist doctrine today.

This doctrine has been shrewdly chosen. It perfectly matches the gnostic temper of the West, for gnostics are essentially masochistic. No abasement is lower than self-abasement. Yet pleading guilty never brings about the sense of having been forgiven. It only sharpens two prominent contemporary emotions: outrage and rage. One sees such emotions often among educated Westerners today, who seem to relish being made to feel guilty.

In Latin Catholic lands, anticommunism may also function in a gnostic way, particularly where the ideology of the "national security state" is used to license illegal detention, torture, and execution. Here, too, sexual disorder is often prominent. The masculine role is uncertain, especially in domestic everyday exchange with wives and mothers. The cult of the mistress and a preference for high black boots suggest what is awry. One finds an unhistorical idealization of fatherland, flag, faith, and family, in opposition to unclean and perverted communists. Where politics is imagined as a battle of survival between pure ideas, there due process and compromise, liberal values and democratic methods seem weak and faint-hearted. The gnostic thinks to eliminate ideas by eliminating persons.

Catholic Incarnation

Christian history itself reveals so many ambivalences about sexuality that one sees immediately what Voegelin means by describing gnosticism as a historical companion of Christianity.

The implications stressed by Voegelin are political, and it is here that Catholicism is, in fact, much more clearly threatened than on personal morality. The long teaching of the church on family and childbirth, on sex and childrearing, seems much too formidable an obstacle to gnosticism. By contrast, the church for some centuries now has been outside the main currents of realistic political economy. In attempting to defend a "third way," between capitalism and socialism, the church is in the position of being idealistic in a vulnerable way.[24] The helplessness of Mounier's "third way" in the face of Hitler, Vichy, and Stalin is here a sobering lesson. Moreover, in trying to position itself for power as the Third World comes of age, the church may be sorely tempted to surrender to political gnosticism what it withholds to personal gnosticism.

The experience of the United States has never counted for much in the political or economic consciousness of the church universal. The center of gravity of the church in political economy has not been England or the United States, nor even Holland and West Germany. Its center of gravity lies still in the successor states of the Holy Roman Empire. The church is still predominantly Latin. Added together, its Latin communicants (including Latin America, Italy, France, Spain, Portugal, and the Philippines) account for almost seventy percent of all the Catholics of the world.

For various reasons, Latin traditions in polity and economy are especially vulnerable to gnostic politics. It has been difficult for Latin populations to make the compromises and informal adjustments of democracy work; idealists of multiple kinds compete fiercely to tear structures down. Latin nations, including France, have been far more vulnerable to communism than northern European nations. In some ways, of course, communism and socialism are closer in structure to the Holy Roman Empire than to the communitarian individualism and practical compromising of democratic capitalist nations. Authoritarian societies are more susceptible to direct clerical influence than societies that liberate the social individual and voluntary associations. A centrally planned society more closely mirrors the organization of the church. Pius XI's justly praised encyclical *Quadragesimo Anno* (1931) is nonetheless rather embarrassing for the support his concept of "cor-

poratism" gave Mussolini. Corporatism is a view with medieval antece-
dents dear to Catholic cultures, abetted by the work of Mounier and
the Belgian-German architects of "solidarism." It opposes individualism and liberalism in the name of primary social institutions, like
families and professions, arranged in various schemes of state collectiv-
ism. It remains a powerful vein of thought in Latin America.[25]

As I have argued in *The Spirit of Democratic Capitalism*, [26] Latin
Catholic teaching systematically misunderstands Anglo-American life.
It sees individualism, but misses its communitarian, associative character. It sees an untrammeled free market, but misses the constraints
imposed upon markets by democratic polities and moral-cultural institutions. It sees consumerism, but misses the liberty of conscience
implicit in the free choices of those who make free economic decisions
for themselves. It sees permissiveness, but misses the dignity and the
constraints implicit in inner-directed character and attenuated Puritan
conscience (manifested even in the bodily mortification of jogging).
Were Anglo-Americans to pronounce judgment on the moral character of Latin cultures equivalent to those daily passed by ecclesiastics
on American culture, they would be accused of racism.

For more than three centuries, Latin America pursued the traditional Catholic ideal of political economy and ended with oppression
and poverty. The Latin Catholic Church did not lead the way in
teaching humanity democracy. It too little assisted—often opposed—
institutions of science and invention. It did not encourage the practical
wisdom of producing economic and political development. Latin Catholic nations, rich in natural resources, seem still politically volatile,
more mystical than practical.

For such reasons, there is the gravest danger that the church will
succumb to gnostic politics in worldly matters. The "option for the
poor" is a case in point. Obviously, it is a Christian task to diminish
poverty, to produce the food and goods and services required for a
decent life among the multiplying populations of the world. *This task
is practical.* It is a task for realists—dreamers, perhaps, for it is realistic
to dream so long as one is always learning by results. One cannot
merely fantasize destruction now and magical fulfillment later.
Granted that in most of the world social change is needed, it does not

follow that just *any* change will help the poor. History runs backward as well as forward. The way to political and economic development—toward liberty and bread—is strait and narrow, a matter of intense and persistent practical accomplishment. It is easy enough to fantasize. That, indeed, is the danger.

The failure of the church in Latin nations is that it never imagined and taught a practical this-worldly polity. This seems to have been predominantly a *theological* failure on the part of clergy and laity alike. It is all the more sad, since an overwhelming majority of Latin peoples seems urgently to desire a stable order of democracy, material progress, and cultural creativity. The forces for realism are numerous. The recent turn by theologians toward illiberal and authoritarian fantasies, however, promises, instead, another cycle of poverty and oppression. Yet the issue is still in doubt. Sorry experiences such as those in Nicaragua may yet catalyze the dormant center. The democratic, inventive, productive forces are strong in number. Given a realistic vision of political economy, a strong intellectual foundation, and brave leadership, these may yet win the victory. The practical, antignostic side of Catholicism gives hope for such an outcome.

For by contrast with gnosticism, Catholicism is a this-worldly religion of flesh: books and candles, incense, sound, flowers, pageantry, power, corruption, humanity. Native to it are ornate ceilings, colored glass, paint, and the daily institutional habits of prudence. Catholicism is, of course, an otherworldly religion, too. Former Chancellor Helmut Schmidt of West Germany once observed that Catholic countries seem now to show greater belief in God and hope for the future than Protestant countries.[27] He seemed to suggest that those who believe in God have reasons transcending their own lives for which they would be willing to die. Thus, ironically, for persons of faith in eternity, the future of earth is also less bleak. He seemed also to suggest that neutralism is the native tongue of loss of faith. The passional proclamation "Better Red than Dead" offers the grandeur of peace without combat, defense without expenditure, morality purer than reality itself. (In reality, the antignostic cry is *neither* Red *nor* dead.)

The worldliness of Catholicism, rooted in its commitment to otherworldliness, is, therefore, a fact of great importance to the survival of this planet. It is not the world's only path to realism. But an institution that has maintained itself intact through the long night of history has given evidence of realism. Its surrender to gnosticism would be a tragedy of incalculable dimension.

What, then, does Catholic realism lead us to expect? Wars and rumors of war will never be absent from this sinful planet. Poverty is never going to be eliminated. Perfect justice is never going to be done. Much, of course, can be done. Two centuries ago, there were only 800 million persons on this planet and most of them were, in Victor Hugo's phrase, *les misérables.* Today there are still 800 million desperately poor and hungry ones, but there are 3.6 billion others living above subsistence. Much more can and must be done. Still, it must be done in darkness, amid lies, in tornadoes of passion, and under threat, for such is the reality of the human heart. There are no sinless social structures, whose implementation will make the world fresh as newborn spring. There are no revolutions that can revolve time backward toward Edenic innocence. Evil, long ago unleashed, will assault us until the end. Against it, fragile social gain is won by realism.

That is why, as Pope John Paul II writes, the dearest characteristic of the God we love, who first loved us, is mercy, not justice.[28] Were God a just God, He would have long ago destroyed us. He is patient and merciful. He is no liberator of the social order, for no social order will ever be free of our freedom. That is why gnostic lovers of justice so often create systems of coercion; to make the world just is to ask humans to be slaves. As Romano Guardini puts it:

Yet if we accept Scripture as God's holy word, we learn a strange rule about human nature: that when it becomes necessary to invoke justice, that irreproachable value and crystalline motive, almost always something is rotten in Denmark. Too often 'justice' is used as a mask for quite different things.[29]

Free humans are always less than just, even to themselves, even to their own best possibilities. To know oneself is to disbelieve in utopia. To seek realism is to learn mercy.

We see about us, then, a struggle within the Catholic Church for the soul of the Catholic Church. It is a struggle of tremendous implications.

Catholicism is a religion of the incarnation of God and the resurrection of the flesh. It is the exact opposite of gnosticism. Its teaching on sex is differentiating, sobering, and demanding—but just. Its intellectual mode is realism. Its liturgical mode is somber, carnal, and weighty with history. Its political style is practical wisdom. All the more tragic, then, is the failure of Catholic leaders to grasp the harmony between its own strengths and those of democracy and social market economies. It is the Catholic vision of political economy that is today most out of touch with its own Creed. That is why I fear that the next betrayal of the faith will enter through that armorless heel, to the misfortune of the human race.

Here I must make two points plain. By no means do I hold either democracy or democratic capitalism, or both, to be implicit in the Creed. Neither represents the Kingdom of God; both belong to this world of sin and ambiguity. Both are matters of the temporal order, which changes, and not of the transcendent order in which we place our faith. Both are only humble realities, part of our own incarnation in history at this time and place. If they commend themselves at all, it is only to the degree that, better than any known alternative, traditionalist or socialist, they protect the productivity, liberty, creativity, dignity, community, and individuality both of human persons and human societies. This is not enough to make them objects of faith. In a history of tears, it is enough to make them signs of God's blessing.

Second, I reject the loose thinking by which any nonsocialist society is described as "capitalist" simply because markets function in it. Markets are almost as ancient as the human race.[30] Virtually all precapitalist societies, like those of Latin America, have markets. In Latin America there are only three or four functioning democracies. Nearly all the other polities are under military dictatorship of some degree. Nearly all are based upon the power of the military and the economy of quasi-feudal, precapitalist landholders. Most of such commerce and industry as exists is state-controlled, built on favoritism or landed wealth. There are little commercial or industrial invention, only a small proportion of property owners, a growing but still fragile middle class. Such societies are neither democratic in polity, nor capitalist in economy, nor pluralistic in culture. They are traditional societies of an ancient type, struggling toward new shapes. The ideology of "national security," when combined with modern techniques of oppression, makes some of them particularly ruthless. Indeed, the spirit of the Inquisition seems to have been reborn under the ideology of the national security state. Against it, institutions giving pluralism, religious liberty, political liberty, due process, and other human rights their due weight in social reality are weak. The gnostic mind can make ideals of the Right just as bloody as those of the Left.

In a word, I do not mean to confuse my own respect for the imperfect, this-worldly achievements of democracy and democratic capitalism with my confession of Christian faith. On matters of this world, Christians are free to disagree. Many whose Christianity I admire do not accept either democracy or democratic capitalism as the best *available* forms of political economy for the incarnation of Christianity in this poor world. I would not expect them to accept my politics, nor would some of them expect me to accept theirs. The faith, while relevant to politics and all worldly things, is not about politics.

What dismays me, rather, is the weakness of the church in matters of political economy. This weakness is glaring just at the moment when so much religious passion is being focused on issues of political economy. That is why gnostic visions of political economy may make such headway. I am of course dismayed by the innocent capitulation to Marxism that afflicts so many in the churches, at least in those countries that are not yet Marxist. Yet far deeper and more subtle is idealism of the gnostic sort. Many children of light are too innocent of guile, even of cynicism; they hold high ideals but lack judgment about the evil uses of those same ideals. Some consider it a deformation, not plain realism, to be "anti-Soviet." Some give the benefit of every doubt to self-described "revolutionary" regimes, whose practice is as ancient as Herod's, and to any armed guerrillas who do violence for "justice" and for "the people." To existing liberties, they apply perfectionist standards. To regimes without liberties, if only their politics is correct, they carry flowing rivers of exculpation. The Christian faith is then interpreted as a political faith, whose real content is earthly transformation.

On the other hand, David O'Brien has reminded me that idealism, far from being a danger today, is in short supply. As one example, he mentions the despair and inertia he finds today among activists of the Left; as another, the lethargy and numbness he often finds in audiences in schools, parishes, and local communities. O'Brien thinks we need more idealism, not less. Yet what I mean by "the new idealism" is not idealism in itself. The vocation of Christians and Jews is not merely to reflect the world as it is but change it. Changing the world, however, requires prudence, judgment, and a certain way of bending idealism to proximate and realizable tasks. One reason for despair among activists may be false consciousness, an alienation from the ideals of their own society so complete that they fail to measure accurately the small, significant advances that can be made. Desiring too much, or perhaps desiring an alien ideal, they despair, where a more proximate vision might have kept their moral strength intact. One reason for apathy among many ordinary citizens, on the other hand, may be a surfeit of extravagant utopian claims, which in the normal course of events is bound to be frustrated by obdurate reality. I oppose the new idealism because it is frequently mistaken for true Christian faith, which it is not. Just as in personal life one cannot make oneself a saint by a single act of will, but must wrestle daily against one's personal demons and defects, humbled but persistent, so also in matters of political economy one must learn humility and wisdom. Not by dialectics are we saved, Augustine wrote; nor by politics. Even those divided by faith may be bedfellows in politics. Even when you and I are divided in our political agendas, we may be united in faith. The confounding of eternal faith with the new idealism is a classic error, perhaps the worst in our time. Politics infused with the new idealism is driven toward extremism.[31]

To discriminate what seems to be true faith from false, however, is not easy. Each Christian must do so, in great inner struggle. One of us may err; the others, in fraternal correction, will pull him back. In making public my own faith, I mean to attract such correction. For, in the end, we Christians—and all humans—are a community. Speaking to each other the truth as each sees it is the necessary condition of our pilgrimage. God in His own time will winnow out the true from the false in what is said by each of us.

Even in our disagreements, it is the Creed that propels us.

Notes

Introduction: Expelling the Smoke of Satan

1. *L'Osservatore Romano* (English edition), July 10, 1972.
2. John J. Mulloy, "Michael Novak and the Catholic Church," *The Wanderer*, November 4, 1982, pp. 1, 8. Mulloy writes: "If Novak is more of a Catholic than many of his former colleagues who have now gone so far leftward as to be no longer counted as Catholic, it is certainly not apparent in what, precisely, his Catholicity consists. It would seem to be merely some kind of sentimental attachment to some past tradition that he has inherited, but which does not mean anything important to him when the chips are down, and when important decisions are made" (p. 8). On the distinction between "real assent" and "notional assent," see John Henry Cardinal Newman, *A Grammar of Assent* (Garden City, N.Y.: Doubleday, Image Books, 1955), pp. 49–92; see also the introduction to the same volume by Étienne Gilson, p. 12.
3. George Santayana notes "that after three or four centuries of confused struggles, an institution emerged which called itself the Catholic Church. This church, possessed of a recognized hierarchy and a recognized dogma, triumphed, both over the ancient religion which it called Paganism, and over its many collateral rivals, which it called heresies. Why did it triumph?

   ". . . Had the Gnostic or Manichaean heresies been victorious, Christianity would have been reduced to a floating speculation: its hard kernel of positive dogma, of Scripture, and of hieratic tradition would have been dissolved. It would have ceased to represent antiquity or to hand down an ancestral piety: in fine, by its eagerness to express itself as a perfect philosophy, it would have ceased to be a religion" (*Interpretations of Poetry and Religion* [New York: Harper & Row, Torchbooks, 1957], pp. 82, 83).
4. John Henry Cardinal Newman, *Apologia Pro Vita Sua* (Garden City, N.Y.: Doubleday, Image Books, 1956), p. 111.
5. There is much secrecy and uncertainty about the exact number of priests and nuns who have left their vocations since Vatican II. However, the *Catholic Almanac* reports that in 1965, priests numbered 434,989 and in 1981, 416,321, a decline of 18,668. For women religious, the falloff was even greater: from 1,049,060 in 1965 to 937,600 by 1981, a decline of 111,460. See *1966 National Catholic Almanac* (Patterson, N.J.: St. Anthony's Guild, 1966), p. 383; and *1982 Catholic Almanac* (Huntington, Ind.: Our Sunday Visitor, 1981), pp. 403–404. *Time* reported on May

24, 1976, that over 10,000 U.S. priests had abandoned the priesthood and 35,000 nuns had left their convents. A recent study published by the University of Wisconsin at Madison places the total number of American priests who have resigned between 1965 and 1980 at 11,350; see Richard A. Schoenherr and Annemette Sorense, *From the Second Vatican to the Second Millennium: Decline and Change in the U.S. Catholic Church* (Madison, Wis.: Comparative Religious Organization Studies Publications/University of Wisconsin, 1981), pp. 27–28. See also Peter Nichols, *The Pope's Divisions: The Roman Catholic Church Today* (New York: Holt, Rinehart and Winston, 1981), p. 226, which places the number of nuns and sisters in the United States who have left their orders since Vatican II at 50,000. The period 1965–1980 shows a steady increase in the Catholic population.

6. I did foresee the jester's ironic face and wrote on the first page: "Rome sheds the generations of men like so many skins. The silver water continues to flow from the jester's mouth; the ancient cypresses and olives stand calm and untroubled. A man comes, shares their life for a moment, and disappears." On the last page, I returned to these images: "The jesters of the fountains smile and say, 'This, too, shall pass,' but meanwhile an age of creativity has begun" (*The Open Church* [New York: Macmillan, 1964], pp. ix, 362).

7. Ronald Knox, *Enthusiasm: A Chapter in the History of Religion, with Special Reference to the XVII and XVIII Centuries* (New York: Oxford University Press, 1950).

8. *Washington Star*, July 30, 1981, p. 2.

9. Newman, *Apologia*, p. 127.

10. Steve Max, *Commonweal* 90 (June 13, 1969): 369–372.

11. Newman, *Apologia*, p. 98.

12. Published by the Maritain Center, Box 495, Notre Dame, Ind. 46556.

Chapter 1. The Living Creeds

1. *Celebrating the Eucharist*, vol. 14, no. 3, April–June 1982 (Collegeville, Minn.: Liturgical Press, 1982), p. 160.

2. *Missale Romanum* (Libreria Editrice Vaticana, 1975), pp. 389–390.

3. Rev. F. X. Lasance, ed., *The New Missal for Every Day* (New York: Benziger Brothers, 1949), pp. 98, 99.

4. *Layman's Daily Missal, Prayer Book and Ritual* (Baltimore, Maryland: Helicon Press, 1962), pp. 853–855. The text is an English version of that contained in the *Missel quotidien des Fides*, ed. Fr. Jose Feder, S.J., published by Maison Mame of Tours.

5. *Celebrating the Eucharist*, vol. 14, no. 3, p. 6.

Chapter 2. God the Father

1. See John-Paul Sartre, *Nausea*, trans. Lloyd Alexander (New York: New Directions, 1964): " . . . the diversity of things, their individuality, were only an appearance, a veneer. This veneer had melted, leaving soft, monstrous masses, all in disorder— naked, in a frightful, obscene nakedness" (p. 127).

2. See St. John of the Cross, *Dark Night of the Soul*, trans. E. Allison Peers (Garden City, N.Y.: Doubleday, Image Books, 1959); also see my own reflections on St. John

of the Cross in *The Experience of Nothingness* (New York: Harper & Row, 1970).
3. John O'Donnell, S.J., "I Believe in God," *The Month* (May 1981): 155.
4. Robert Hamerton-Kelly remarks: "There are only eleven places in the Old Testament where God is designated as 'father,' and one where he is explicitly invoked as such, while in the Gospels alone God is designated thus no less than one hundred and seventy times by Jesus, and never invoked by any other name in Jesus' prayers. Even if we include the Old Testament passages where God's parenthood is implied, the discrepancy between the Testaments is so great that we can only conclude that Jesus himself chose to give the symbol a special importance. In doing so he expressed his own peculiar experience of God, and this experience is what we are seeking to understand" (*God the Father: Theology and Patriarchy in the Teaching of Jesus* [Philadelphia: Fortress Press, 1979], p. 20).
5. The most extended treatment of *anima* and *animus* occurs in Martin D'Arcy, S.J., *The Mind and Heart of Love* (New York: Meridian Books, 1956), esp. pp. 195–217.
6. See Carol P. Christ, *Diving Deep and Surfacing Women Writers on Spiritual Quest* (Boston: Beacon Press, 1980); see also Carol P. Christ and Judith Plaskow, eds., *Womanspirit Rising: A Feminist Reader in Religion* (New York: Harper & Row, 1979).
7. See "The Dynamo and the Virgin," in Henry Adams, *The Education of Henry Adams: An Autobiography* (Boston and Cambridge: Houghton Mifflin, Century Editions, 1961), pp. 379–90.
8. See Valerie Saiving, "The Human Situation: A Feminine View," in Christ and Plaskow, eds., *Womanspirit Rising*, pp. 25–42. This article originally appeared in *The Journal of Religion* (April 1960). See also Louis Boyer, *Women in the Church*, trans. Marilyn Teichert (San Francisco: Ignatius Press, 1979); Michael Novak, "Man and Woman He Made Them," *Communio 8* (Fall 1981): 229–249; and additional essays on the relationship between the sexes by John T. Noonan, Mary F. Rousseau, David Burrell, and Katharine Rose Hanley in the Fall 1981 issue of *Communio*.
9. Cited by Karol Wojtyla, *Faith According to St. John of the Cross*, trans. Jordan Aumann, O.P. (San Francisco: Ignatius Press, 1981), p. 272 [*Summa theologica*, II–II, q. 8, a. 7].

Chapter 3. God the Son: True God

1. *The Confessions of St. Augustine*, trans. John K. Ryan (Garden City, N.Y.: Doubleday, Image Books, 1960), book 5, chap. 10.
2. Romano Guardini, *The Lord*, trans. Elinor Castendyk Briefs (Chicago: Regnery, 1954), p. 293.
3. See Hannah Arendt, *On Revolution* (New York: Viking Press, 1965).
4. See *The Confessions of St. Augustine*, book 10, chap. 42.
5. Michael Novak, *The Open Church* (New York: Macmillan, 1964), pp. 56–71. I characterized "non-historical orthodoxy" in the following words: "The theology which has been entrenched for the last four hundred years, then, might fairly be described as 'non-historical' or even 'anti-historical.' It favors speculation which is not called to the bar of historical fact, past or present; moreover, it often seems to fear principles which would make it face such a bar. It sometimes discourages

speculation altogether, and confines itself to making commentaries on a theoretical structure once built up, in the late Middle Ages, in the past. It would be fair to name this theology 'anti-historical orthodoxy,' because it defends a system of propositions as orthodox, while refusing to commit itself to the work of investigating that system's historical justification, or making it relevant to the historical realities of the present. It would be fair to call it 'anti-historical orthodoxy,' but a more neutral designation is simply 'non-historical.' For it defends an orthodoxy suspended, as it were, outside of history, in midair" (p. 56).

6. Quoted in E. A. Maycock, *The Man Who Was Orthodox* (London: Dobson, 1963), p. 189.

7. Donald Keefe, S.J., "Liberation and the Catholic Church: The Illusion and the Reality," *Center Journal* 1 (Winter 1981): 45–64.

8. In a section titled "The Total Banning of War, and International Action For Avoiding War" the Council fathers wrote: "It is our clear duty, then, to strain every muscle as we work for the time when all war can be completely outlawed by international consent. This goal undoubtedly requires the establishment of some universal public authority acknowledged as such by all, and endowed with effective power to safeguard, on the behalf of all, security, regard for justice, and respect for rights.

"But before this hoped-for authority can be set up, the highest existing international centers must devote themselves vigorously to the pursuit of better means for obtaining common security. Peace must be born of mutual trust between nations rather than imposed on them through fear of one another's weapons." These lines sound quite utopian, but realism immediately asserted itself in the very next sentence: "Hence everyone must labor to put an end at last to the arms race, and to make a true beginning of disarmament, not indeed a unilateral disarmament, but one proceeding at an equal pace according to agreement, and backed up by authentic and workable safeguards" (Walter M. Abbott, S.J., ed., *The Documents of Vatican II* [New York: America Press, 1966], pp. 295, 296).

9. See Dale Vree, *On Synthesizing Christianity and Marxism* (New York: Wiley, 1976); and Leszek Kolakowski, *Main Currents of Marxism*, trans. P. S. Falla, 3 vols. (Oxford: Oxford University Press, 1978).

10. St. Augustine, *Enarrationes in Psalmos* 51, 14. Quoted in Peter Brown, *Augustine of Hippo* (Berkeley and Los Angeles: University of California Press, 1967), p. 251. Professor Brown cites H. Rondet, "Richesse et pauvreté dans la predication de S. Augustin," *Revue d'ascetisme et mystique* xxx (1954): 193–231.

11. C. S. Lewis, "Priestesses in the Church?" in *God in the Dock: Essays on Theology and Ethics*, ed. Walter Hooper (Grand Rapids, Mich.: Eerdmans, 1970), pp. 237, 238.

12. See Michael Novak, *Ascent of the Mountain, Flight of the Dove*, rev. ed. (New York: Harper & Row, 1978), p. 60.

Chapter 6. *One* Church

1. Based on a passage in Joinville's *History of Saint Louis*, Péguy gives a poetic account of God's judgment on ordinary and heroic love:

When Joinville had rather have committed thirty mortal sins than to be a leper,
And when Saint Louis had rather be a leper than to fall into one single mortal sin,
I do not conclude, says God, that Saint Louis loves me in an ordinary way
And that Joinville loves me thirty times less than the ordinary way.
That Saint Louis loves me according to measure, in just the wanted measure,
And that Joinville loves me thirty times less than the measure.
I reckon, on the contrary, says God, this is how I figure, this is how I conclude.
I conclude, on the contrary, that Joinville loves me in the ordinary way,
Honestly, just as a poor man is capable of loving me,
Must love me;
And that Saint Louis, on the contrary, loves me thirty times above the ordinary,
Thirty times more than honorably;
That Joinville loves me according to measure,
And that Saint Louis loves me thirty times more than according to measure.

Charles Péguy, *God Speaks*, trans. Julian Green (New York: Pantheon Books, 1945), pp. 32, 33.

Chapter 7. *Holy* Church

1. "She [the Roman Catholic Church] may still exist in undiminished vigour when some traveller from New Zealand shall, in the midst of a vast solitude, take his stand on a broken arch of London Bridge to sketch the ruins of St. Paul's." Thomas Babington Macaulay, "On Ranke's History of the Popes," in *Essays, Critical and Miscellaneous* (Philadelphia: Carey and Hart, 1845), p. 401.

Chapter 8. *Catholic* Church

1. See the brilliant discussion of errant claims to prophecy in Laraine Fergenson, "Thoreau, Daniel Berrigan, and the Problem of Transcendental Politics," *Soundings* 65 (Spring 1982): 103–122.
2. Daniel Boorstin, *Image: A Guide to Pseudo-Events in America* (New York: Atheneum, 1962).
3. An admirable statement of this non-Catholic, sectarian version of Christianity is provided by Stanley Hauerwas in *A Community of Character: Toward a Constructive Christian Social Ethic* (Notre Dame, Ind.: University of Notre Dame Press, 1982).
4. Francis X. Winters, S.J., has argued that on the issue of nuclear arms the American bishops have "formulated a position that imposes on Catholic officials of our Government the burden of choosing between their consciences, as illuminated by church teaching, and their professional careers and commitments. . . . Catholics holding any of these offices [in the military chain of command] are now challenged by episcopal authority to 'stand down' " ("The Bow or the Cloud?" *America* [July 25, 1981]: 29).
5. See John Paul II, *On Human Work* (Washington, D.C.: U.S. Catholic Conference, 1981).
6. Donald Nicholl, "The Catholic Spirit and the Body of Christ," *Clergy Review* (December 1981): 422.
7. See Wilfred Desan, *Planetary Man* (New York: Macmillan, 1972).

8. G. K. Chesterton, "The Protestant Superstitions," in *Chesterton's Stories, Essays and Poems* (London: Dent, 1935), p. 234.

9. Ibid., pp. 236, 237.

Chapter 9. *Apostolic* Church

1. Paul Seabury, "Trendier Than Thou," *Harper's* (October 1958): 39–52; Dorothy Rabinowitz, "The Activist Cleric," *Commentary* 50 (September 1970): 81–83.

2. G. K. Chesterton, *What's Wrong with the World* (1912). Quoted in Margaret Canovan, *G.K. Chesterton: Radical Populist* (New York and London: Harcourt Brace Jovanovich, 1977), p. 49.

3. Rosemary Radford Ruether, "Is a New Christian Consensus Possible?" *Journal of Ecumenical Studies* 17 (Winter 1980): 66, 67.

4. Monsignor George A. Kelly, *The Crisis of Authority: John Paul II and the American Bishops* (Chicago: Regnery, Gateway, 1982). See also his earlier book, *The Battle for the American Church* (Garden City, N.Y.: Doubleday, 1979).

5. Daniel J. Callahan, *Honesty in the Church* (New York: Scribner, 1965).

6. James Hitchcock, *The Rise and Fall of Radical Catholicism* (New York: Herder and Herder, 1971).

7. Friedrich A. Hayek, "Why I Am Not a Conservative," in *The Constitution of Liberty* (Chicago: Regnery, 1960), pp. 397–411.

8. See Leszek Kolakowski, "How to Be a Conservative-Liberal Socialist," *Encounter* (October 1978): 46–47; see also William Kristol's perceptive tracing of the intellectual traditions on which I draw in "Defending Democratic Capitalism," *The Public Interest* 68 (Summer 1982): 101–107.

9. See Michael Novak, "Marriage: The Lay Voice," *Commonweal* (February 14, 1964): 587–590. Also see my essay "Toward a Positive Sexual Morality" in William Birmingham, ed., *What Modern Catholics Think About Birth Control* (New York: Signet Books, 1964), pp. 109–128.

10. Michael Novak, ed., *The Experience of Marriage* (New York: Macmillan, 1964).

11. John T. Noonan, *Contraception: A History of Its Treatment by the Catholic Theologians and Canonists* (Cambridge, Mass.: Harvard University Press, 1966).

12. St. Augustine, *De Bono Conjugali*, 16.

13. See Michael Novak, *The Spirit of Democratic Capitalism* (New York: Simon & Schuster/American Enterprise Institute, 1982), chap. 8, "The Family."

14. See "Babies and Distributism," in *The Well and the Shallows* (London, 1938), p. 142.

15. Ibid.

16. Ibid., p. 145.

17. I read Christopher Derrick's *Church Authority and Intellectual Freedom* (San Francisco: Ignatius Press, 1981) after completing this chapter. I much admire it. He is wholly correct in saying that a Catholic theologian who speaks apart from Peter is "Catholic" only in a cultural, not in a theological, sense. Statements of transcendental weight about faith and morals cannot be uttered by such a theologian; they are merely of private, personal weight, like those of everybody else. Yet there is an undertow in Derrick's book that moves toward different shores than I do. He is at once more coldly analytical (his skeptical side is a pleasure to follow) and more

concerned to protect the security of knowing the truth. These are good corrections to my own temperament. His treatment of the debate on contraception is quite revealingly different from mine.

Chapter 10. The Remission of Sins

1. See Karen Laub-Novak, "The Art of Deception," in Diane Apostolas Cappadona, ed., *Art, Creativity and the Sacred: An Anthology in Religion and Art* (New York: Seabury Press, forthcoming).
2. See Jacques Maritain, *Art and Scholasticism*, trans. Joseph W. Evans (New York: Scribner, 1962), chap. 3, "Making and Doing."
3. Quoted in Vincent P. Miceli, S.J., *The Antichrist* (West Hanover, Mass.: Christopher, 1981), p. 196.
4. Conversation with Humberto Belli, former religion editor of the independent newspaper *La Prensa*, and Jose Estaban Gonzalez, founder and former national coordinator of Nicaragua's Human Rights Commission, August 6, 1982. At this meeting I was shown copies of the magazines in question.
5. Karl Marx and Frederick Engels, *The Communist Manifesto* in *Selected Works* (New York: International Publishers, 1968), p. 55 (emphasis added).
6. Bishop Roger Mahony, of Stockton, California, says: "As an American bishop, I deeply respect our nation's tradition of the separation of church and state. I would deplore, however, any attempt to turn this legitimate separation into a separation of church from society or into a privatization of religion that would divorce our faith and hope from public concerns and crucial moral questions that face us all as citizens" ("The Catholic Conscience and Nuclear War," *Commonweal* [March 12, 1982]: 142).
7. Conversation with Humberto Belli and Jose Estaban Gonzalez, August 6, 1982.
8. Henry Kamm, "The Graying of Prague," *New York Times Magazine*, August 19, 1982, p. 52.

Chapter 11. Resurrection of the Dead

1. St. Augustine, *Enarrationes in Psalmos* XCI, 1. Quoted in Erich Przywara, ed., *An Augustine Synthesis* (New York: Harper & Row, Torchbooks, 1958), p. 478.
2. See E. E. Y. Hales, *Pio Nono: A Study in European Politics and Religion in the Nineteenth Century* (Garden City, N.Y.: Doubleday, Image Books, 1962).
3. John Henry Newman, *Newman Against the Liberals: 25 Classic Sermons by John Henry Newman*, ed. Michael Davies (New Rochelle, N.Y.: Arlington House, 1978), pp. 13, 14.
4. John Henry Cardinal Newman, *An Essay on the Development of Christian Doctrine* (Garden City, N.Y.: Doubleday, Image Books, 1960), p. 339.
5. Ibid., pp. 338, 339.
6. See Michael Novak, "The Communitarian Individual in America," *Public Interest* 68 (Summer 1982): 3–200.

Chapter 12. The Church Today: Progress or Decline?

1. Emmanuel Cardinal Suhard, *The Church Today: Growth or Decline?* trans. James J. Corbett (Notre Dame, Ind.: Fides, 1948).

2. Richard Reeves, *American Journey: Traveling with Tocqueville in Search of "Democracy in America"* (New York: Simon & Schuster, 1982), pp. 396, 397.
3. Daniel Berrigan and Robert Coles, *The Geography of Faith* (Boston: Beacon Press, 1971), p. 79.
4. Quoted in Ralph Martin, *A Crisis of Truth: The Attack on Faith, Morality, and Mission in the Catholic Church* (Ann Arbor, Mich.: Servant Books, 1982), p. 22.
5. Ibid., p. 35.
6. Ibid., p. 22.
7. Ibid., p. 34.
8. Ibid.
9. Ibid., p. 20.
10. Julio de Santa Ana, ed., *Towards a Church of the Poor* (Maryknoll, N.Y.: Orbis Books, 1981), p. 72.
11. G. K. Chesterton, *The Catholic Church and Conversion* (New York: Macmillan, 1926), p. 93.
12. The figures are from Vincent P. Miceli, S.J., *The Antichrist* (West Hanover, Mass.: Christopher Publishing House, 1981), pp. 182–184. Although I dislike the tone of Miceli's book, I have not found a better compilation of figures complete with sources.
13. Edward Vacek, S.J., "A Christian Homosexuality?" *Commonweal* (December 5, 1980): 683.
14. See Peter Nichols, *The Pope's Divisions: The Roman Catholic Church Today* (New York: Holt Rinehart and Winston, 1981), pp. 266–268. See also the analysis by Andrew M. Greeley, "Priesthood," in Edward C. Herr, ed., *Tomorrow's Church: What's Ahead for American Catholics* (Chicago: Thomas More Press, 1982), pp. 92–97.
15. Dorothy Sayers, *The Whimsical Christian* (New York: Macmillan, 1978), p. 10.
16. Quoted in Martin, *A Crisis of Truth*, p. 109.
17. Michael Novak, *The Open Church* (New York: Macmillan, 1964), chap. 5.
18. Robert J. McEwen, S.J., "Capitalism," in *The Catholic Encyclopedia for School and Home* (New York: McGraw-Hill, 1965), p. 265.
19. Of Mounier and others in the personalist movement John Hellman writes: "They consistently placed the interests of Christianity ahead of a concern for liberty" (*Emmanuel Mounier and the New Catholic Left 1930–50* [Toronto: University of Toronto Press, 1981], p. 187).
20. See Arthur F. McGovern, *Marxism: An American Christian Perspective* (Maryknoll, N.Y.: Orbis Books, 1980), p. 2.
21. Karl Löwith, *Meaning in History* (Chicago: University of Chicago Press, 1949), pp. 44, 45.
22. See *1982 Catholic Almanac* (Huntington, Ind.: Our Sunday Visitor, 1981), pp. 403, 404.
23. Ibid., pp. 369–402. Exact population figures are as follows:

Brazil	103,970,000	France	45,557,536
Mexico	66,159,863	Philippines	37,980,000
Italy	55,285,000	Spain	36,254,000
United States	50,449,842	Poland	32,807,000

W. Germany	28,484,000	Venezuela	13,413,239
Colombia	25,068,360	Zaire	12,413,239
Argentina	24,591,600	Czechoslovakia	10,926,363
Peru	15,506,600	Canada	10,344,046

24. See note 14, *supra*.
25. See *National Jesuit News*, February 1972, p. 7.
26. *National Jesuit News*, December 1981, pp. 3, 16, 17.
27. For an account of this episode see George T. Dennis, S.J., "Arianism," in *The Catholic Encyclopedia for School and Home* (New York: McGraw-Hill, 1965), pp. 380–384.
28. See David Tracy, *Blessed Rage for Order* (New York: Seabury Press, 1975); and *The Analogical Imagination: Christian Theology and the Culture of Pluralism* (New York: Crossroad, 1981).
29. Tracy, *The Analogical Imagination*, p. 75.
30. Ibid., p. 70.
31. Ibid., pp. 37–38, n. 36.
32. Ibid., p. 398.
33. Ibid., p. 395.

Chapter 13. Against the New Idealism

1. For the text of Sontag's remarks see *The Soho News*, February 16, 1982; see also Richard Grenier, "The Conversion of Susan Sontag," *The New Republic* (April 14, 1982): 15–19. On "bracketing" see Peter Shaw, "The Incident," in *Encounter* (June–July 1982): 38–40; also see Seymour Martin Lipset, "The Background," in the same issue, pp. 40–42.
2. From G. K. Chesterton, *What's Wrong with the World?* cited by Joseph Sobran, "The Fog," *Center Journal* 1 (Summer 1982): 121. Sobran adds that when you are tempted "to apologize for failing to understand the new theological, political or cultural savant, finally it dawns on you that he has been intent on confusing you all along. His vagueness is not an accident, but a strategy."
3. For other brief accounts of Arius and Arianism, see V. C. de Clercq, "Arianism," in *The New Catholic Encyclopedia* 15 vols. (New York: McGraw-Hill/Publisher's Guild, 1967), vol. 1, pp. 791–794; and Wolfgang Marcus, "Arianism," in *Sacramentum Mundi*, ed. Karl Rahner, 6 vols. (New York: Herder and Herder, 1968–1970), vol. 1, pp. 95–97.
4. See my "Newman on Nicaea," *Theological Studies* 21 (September 1960): 444–453, based on John Henry Cardinal Newman, *The Arians of the Fourth Century* (London and New York: Longman's, Green, 1895).
5. Pope Liberius also refused to bow. See George T. Dennis, S.J., "Arianism," in *The New Catholic Encyclopedia for School and Home* (New York: McGraw-Hill, 1965), p. 384. See also Newman's reflections in *The Arians of the Fourth Century*, pp. 319–323.
6. For surveys and assessments of liberation theology, see Arthur F. McGovern, *Marxism: An American Christian Perspective* (Maryknoll, N.Y.: Orbis Books, 1980); James V. Schall, S.J., *Liberation Theology* (San Francisco: Ignatius Press, 1982); Michael Novak, ed., *Liberation South, Liberation North* (Washington, D.C.:

American Enterprise Institute, 1981); Dennis P. McCann, *Christian Realism and Liberation Theology* (Maryknoll, N.Y.: Orbis Books, 1981); and Quentin L. Quade, ed. *The Pope and Revolution: John Paul II Confronts Liberation Theology* (Washington, D.C.: Ethics and Public Policy Center, 1982).

7. Leszek Kolakowski, *Main Currents of Marxism*, trans. P.S. Falla, 3 vols. (Oxford: Clarendon Press, 1978), vol. 3, p. 526.

8. Gregory Baum, "Liberation Theology and the Supernatural," *The Ecumenist* 19 (September–October 1981): 81–87.

9. Kolakowski observes: "Messianic hopes are the counterpart of the sense of despair and impotence that overcomes mankind at the sight of its own failures. The optimistic belief that there is a ready-made, immediate answer to all problems and misfortunes, and that only the malevolence of enemies (defined according to choice) stands in the way of its being instantly applied, is a frequent ingredient in ideological systems passing under the name of Marxism. . . . At present Marxism neither interprets the world nor changes it: it is merely a repertoire of slogans serving to organize various interests . . ." (*Main Currents of Marxism*, vol. 3, p. 530).

10. See "An Unexpected Kinship," in Aleksandr I. Solzhenitsyn, *A World Split Apart: Commencement Address Delivered at Harvard University June 8, 1978* (New York: Harper & Row, 1978), pp. 53–55.

11. For a survey of non-Marxist religious socialism see Bernard Murchland, *The Dream of Christian Socialism: An Essay on Its European Origins* (Washington, D.C.: American Enterprise Institute, 1982).

12. See Eric Voegelin's analysis of "Ersatz religion" in *Science, Politics and Gnosticism* (South Bend, Ind.: Regnery/Gateway, 1968), pp. 83–114.

13. Responding to the draft statement on nuclear arms prepared by a committee of U.S. bishops, one priest said: "I sit here stunned, utterly amazed, dumbfounded, and angry. . . . I stewed in my frustrations. . . . The blood-letting, revenge, rape, and wholesale carnage that makes up human history will only cease when we stand with Christ and are willing to be killed rather than to kill." Another commented that the draft statement's "justified solutions leave sensitive souls sick at heart." Yet another priest charged that the statement bears "the certain mark of the false prophet: compromise" (see Letters to the Editors, *National Catholic Reporter*, July 30, 1982). A nun is reported to have been "nearly unable to sleep for a week" after reading the document, and a Catholic laywoman active in the antinuclear effort is reported to have wept openly (ibid., p. 2).

14. Fr. Jack Morris, S.J., Letter to the Editors, *National Catholic Reporter*, July 30, 1982.

15. See C.S. Lewis, *The Four Loves* (New York: Harcourt Brace and Jovanovich, 1971); Denis de Rougemont, *Love in the Western World*, trans. Montgomery Belgion (London: Faber and Faber, 1940); and Ronald Knox, *Enthusiasm* (New York: Oxford University Press, 1950). See also James Hitchcock, *The New Enthusiasts* (Chicago, Ill.: Thomas More Press, 1982); and John Lyon, "Gardening, Gnosticism, and the Eschaton: Meditations on Thermonuclear War and Pacifism," *Communio* 9 (Summer 1982): 169–175.

16. Kevin Phillips, *The Post-Conservative Age: People, Politics and Ideology* (New York: Random House, 1982).

17. On this point Seymour Martin Lipset writes: "Thus, the evidence of the similarities between Fascism and Communism has been there for a very long time. What has been missing is the willingness to recognize that Western society, including the United States, is more humane, more democratic, more open to progressive social change than any and all of the regimes that call themselves 'communist.' Those who have searched for an ideological justification for opposing Capitalism, in terms of a struggle between absolute good and absolute evil, obviously have great difficulties, emotional and intellectual, in admitting that Western society is better than its major 'leftist' political rival.

"Western society is obviously far from ideal. It is severely inegalitarian; it discriminates against various minorities; its political democracy is flawed. But the politics of moderation, of the possible, of the attainable, continues to strike ideologues as too insignificant, as unworthy. Those who have lost (or never had) a religious faith, a belief in a Kingdom of Heaven, must project an earthly paradise; and they must blind themselves to the earthly realities of that paradise" ("The Background," *Encounter* [June–July 1982]: 41).

18. See Elaine Pagels, *The Gnostic Gospels* (New York: Random House, Vintage Books, 1981), especially the introduction, pp. xi–xxxix. Pagels observes further: "We can see, then, two very different patterns of sexual attitudes emerging in orthodox and gnostic circles. In simplest form, many gnostic Christians correlate their description of God in both masculine and feminine terms with a complementary description of human nature. Most often they refer to the creation account of Genesis 1, which suggests an equal or androgynous human creation. Gnostic Christians often take the principle of equality between men and women into the social and political structures of their communities. The orthodox pattern is strikingly different: it describes God in exclusively masculine terms, and typically refers to Genesis 2 to describe how Eve was created from Adam, and for his fulfillment. Like the gnostic view, this translates into social practice: by the late second century, the orthodox community came to accept the domination of men over women as the divinely ordained order, not only for social and family life, but also for the Christian churches" (p. 79). See also Robert Haavdt, "Gnosticism," in *Sacramentum Mundi*, ed. Karl Rahner, 6 vols. (New York: Herder and Herder, 1968–1970), vol. 2, pp. 379, 380.

19. Gerhart Niemeyer, "A 'Church' Without a Name?" *Center Journal* (Summer 1982): 113. See also Irving Kristol's comments on perfectionism as a Christian temptation in "The Spiritual Roots of Capitalism and Socialism," in Michael Novak, ed., *Capitalism and Socialism: A Theological Inquiry* (Washington, D.C.: American Enterprise Institute, 1979), pp. 1–14. A treatment of the attraction of gnosticism for Jews is also needed, to round out the picture.

20. Niemeyer, "A 'Church' Without a Name?" p. 113.

21. Voegelin, *Science, Politics and Gnosticism*, pp. 86–88.

22. Ibid., pp. 88, 89.

23. See C. S. Lewis, "Priestesses in the Church?" in *God in the Dock: Essays on Theology and Ethics*, ed. Walter Hooper (Grand Rapids, Mich.: Eerdmans, 1970), pp. 234–239. See also C. S. Lewis, *The Four Loves*.

24. The so-called "Third Way," neither capitalism nor socialism, is not now realized

in any instance, nor is it even a fully developed theoretical construct. It seems, at present, more like a wish or a few broad hints. Perhaps it is only a form of evasion. Its utility is to seem to afford an Archimedean point, a sort of Mt. Olympus, outside of history, from which to pass judgment on existing historical realities. This is less than an appeal to transcendent values, and considerably less than a proximate historical vision toward which realists might move. Catholic social thought cannot long inhabit such rarefied heights. They have already abetted the native utopianism of Latin political cultures, ever holding out ideals unreachable amid humble realities. On problems of the "Third Way," see John Coleman, S.J., "Development of Church Social Teaching," *Origins* 11 (June 4, 1981): 37.

25. See Howard J. Wiarda, "Corporatist Theory and Ideology: A Latin American Development Paradigm," *Journal of Church and State* 20 (Winter 1978): 29–56; also see the volume of essays, Howard J. Wiarda, ed., *Politics and Social Change in Latin America*, 2nd rev. ed., (Cambridge, Mass.: University of Massachusetts Press, 1982).

26. Michael Novak, *The Spirit of Democratic Capitalism* (New York: Simon & Schuster/American Enterprise Institute, 1982), chaps. 16–18.

27. See Walter Laqueur, "Hollanditis," *Commentary* (August 1982).

28. John Paul II, *Rich in Mercy (Dives in Misericordia)* (Washington, D.C.: U.S. Catholic Conference, 1981), pp. 13–14.

29. Romano Guardini, *The Lord*, trans. Elinor Castendyk Briefs (Chicago: Regnery, 1954), p. 262.

30. A Soviet official, defending the slowness of progress in the USSR, observed that market economies are 6,000 years old. He did not observe, understandably, that this makes them older than capitalism, too. See Anthony Lewis, "Putting the Economic Squeeze on Soviets," *New York Times*, August 1, 1982, p. 2E.

31. *The New Republic* has clearly diagnosed this flaw, with penetration exemplary for neoliberal Catholic thought: "For many Catholics today, religious feeling has been redefined in political terms, and the very content of moral life has changed: the old preoccupation with scrupulous personal virtue has been replaced by a generalized sense of good intentions and series of impeccably 'virtuous' stances on public issues. Otherworldliness has given way to utopianism; as a result, the spiritual has come to be understood by many as something in opposition not so much to the profane world as a whole as to the established political order. In such a context, the 'religious' approach to politics almost necessarily takes the form of extremism. After all, what makes a political position 'religious,' 'Christian,' or 'Catholic' is precisely its uncompromising purity of intention, its vehemence, its unwillingness to accede to the exigencies of the secular realm" (Patrick Glynn, "Pulpit Politics" [March 14, 1983]: 14). See also Quentin L. Quade, "Magisterium as Temptation: The Bishops and the Bomb," *Catholicism in Crisis* 3 (February 1983): 26–30.

Selected Bibliography

Adam, Karl. *The Spirit of Catholicism*. Translated by Dom Justin McCann. Garden City, N.Y.: Doubleday, Image Books, 1954.

Arendt, Hannah. *On Revolution*. New York: Viking Press, 1965.

Bouyer, Louis. *Women in the Church*. Translated by Marilyn Teichert. San Francisco: Ignatius Press, 1979.

Callahan, Daniel J. *Honesty in the Church*. New York: Scribner, 1965.

The Catholic Encyclopedia for School and Home. S.v. "Arianism," by George T. Dennis, S.J.; and "Capitalism," by Robert J. McEwen, S.J. New York: McGraw-Hill, 1965.

Chesterton, G. K. *The Catholic Church and Conversion*. New York: Macmillan, 1926.

————. *Chesterton's Stories, Essays and Poems*. London: J. M. Dent and Sons, 1935.

————. *Heretics*. New York: Dodd, Mead, 1935.

————. *Orthodoxy*. Garden City, N.Y.: Doubleday, Image Books, 1959.

————. *Selected Essays of G.K. Chesterton*. Selected by Dorothy Collins. London: Methuen and Co., 1949.

Christ, Carol P. *Diving Deep and Surfacing: Women Writers on Spiritual Quest*. Boston: Beacon Press, 1980.

Christ, Carol P., and Plaskow, Judith, eds. *Womanspirit Rising: A Feminist Reader in Religion*. San Francisco: Harper & Row, 1979.

Corrin, Jay P. *G. K. Chesterton and Hilaire Belloc: The Battle Against Modernity*. Athens and London: Ohio University Press, 1981.

Danielou, Jean. *The Advent of Salvation*. Translated by Rosemary Sheed. Glen Rock, N.J.: Paulist Press, Deus Books, 1962.

De Lubac, Henri, S.J. *Catholicism: Christ and the Common Destiny of Man*. Translated by Lancelot C. Sheppard. London: Burns and Oates, 1950.

————. *The Splendor of the Church*. Translated by Michael Mason. Glen Rock, N.J.: Paulist Press, Dens Books, 1963.

Derrick, Christopher. *Church Authority and Intellectual Freedom*. San Francisco: Ignatius Press, 1981.

Dulles, Avery, S.J. *Models of the Church.* New York: Doubleday, 1974.

Guardini, Romano. *The Church and the Catholic and the Spirit of the Liturgy.* Translated by Ada Lane. New York: Shield & Ward, 1953.

———. *The Lord.* Translated by Elinor Castendyk Briefs. Chicago: Regnery, 1954.

Hammerton-Kelly, Robert. *God the Father: Theology and Patriarchy in the Teaching of Jesus.* Philadelphia: Fortress Press, 1979.

Herr, Edward C., ed. *Tomorrow's Church: What's Ahead for American Catholics.* Chicago: Thomas More Press, 1982.

Hitchcock, James. *The Decline and Fall of Radical Catholicism.* New York: Herder and Herder, 1971.

———. *The New Enthusiasts.* Chicago: Thomas More Press, 1982.

Kelly, George A. *The Battle for the American Church.* Garden City, N.Y.: Doubleday, 1979.

Kelly, J. N. D. *The Athanasian Creed.* New York: Harper & Row, 1964.

———. *Early Christian Creeds.* 3d ed. New York: McKay, 1972.

Knox, Ronald. *The Creed in Slow Motion.* New York: Sheed & Ward, 1949.

———. *Enthusiasm: A Chapter in the History of Religion, with Special Reference to the XVII and XVIII Centuries.* New York: Oxford University Press, 1950.

Kolakowski, Leszek. *Main Currents of Marxism.* 3 vols. Translated by P. S. Falla. Oxford: Clarendon Press, 1978.

Löwith, Karl. *Meaning in History.* Chicago: University of Chicago Press, 1949.

MacGregor, Geddes. *Gnosis: A Renaissance in Christian Thought.* Wheaton, Ill.: Theosophical Publishing House, 1979.

McBrien, Richard P. *Catholicism.* Minneapolis: Winston, 1980.

Martin, Ralph. *A Crisis of Truth: The Attack on Faith, Morality, and Mission in the Catholic Church.* Ann Arbor, Mich.: Servant Books, 1982.

Maycock, E. A. *The Man Who Was Orthodox.* London: Dobson, 1963.

The New Catholic Encyclopedia. S.v. "Arianism," by V.C. de Clercq. New York: McGraw Hill/Publisher's Guild, 1967.

Newman, John Henry Cardinal. *The Idea of a University.* Garden City, N.Y.: Doubleday, Image Books, 1959.

———. *An Essay on the Development of Christian Doctrine.* Garden City, N.J.: Doubleday, Image Books, 1960.

———. *Apologia Pro Vita Sua.* Garden City, N.Y.: Doubleday, Image Books, 1956.

———. *The Arians of the Fourth Century.* London & New York: Longman's, Green, 1895.

———. *A Grammar of Assent.* Garden City, N.Y.: Doubleday, Image Books, 1955.

Nichols, Peter. *The Pope's Divisions*. New York: Holt, Rinehart and Winston, 1981.

O'Connor, Flannery. *The Habit of Being*. Edited by Sally Fitzgerald. New York: Farrar, Straus & Giroux, 1979.

Pagels, Elaine. *The Gnostic Gospels*. New York: Random House, Vintage Books, 1979.

Péguy, Charles. *God Speaks*. Translated by Julian Green. New York: Pantehon Books, 1945.

Pieper, Josef, and Raskop, Heinz. *What Catholics Believe*. Translated by Christopher Huntington. New York: Pantheon Books, 1951.

Pozo, Candido, S.J. *The Credo of the People of God*. Translated and edited by Fr. Mark A. Pilon. Chicago: Franciscan Herald Press, 1980.

Rahner, Karl, ed. *Sacramentum Mundi*. S.v. "Arianism," by Wolfgang Marcus. New York: Herder and Herder, 1968–1970.

Santa Ana, Julio de, ed. *Towards a Church of the Poor*. Maryknoll, N.Y.: Orbis Books, 1979.

Santayana, George. *Interpretations of Poetry and Religion* New York: Harper & Row, Torchbooks, 1957.

Sayers, Dorothy. *The Whimsical Christian*. New York: Macmillan, 1978. An earlier edition was published under the title: *Christian Letters to a Post-Christian World*. Grand Rapids, Mich.: Eerdmans, 1969.

Suhard, Emmanuel Cardinal. *The Church Today: Growth or Decline?* Translated by James J. Corbett. Notre Dame, Ind.: Fides, 1948.

Tracy, David. *The Analogical Imagination*. New York: Crossroad, 1981.

Voegelin, Eric. *Science, Politics and Gnosticism*. South Bend, Ind.: Regnery/ Gateway, 1968.

Wingren, Gustaf. *Credo: The Christian View of Faith and Life*. Translated by Edgar M. Carlson. Minneapolis, Minn.: Augsburg, 1981.

Wojtyla, Karol. *Faith According to St. John of the Cross*. Translated by Jordan Aumann, O.P. San Francisco: Ignatius Press, 1981.